THE MARKETING PLAN

Third Edition

THE MARKETING PLAN

THIRD EDITION

HOW TO PREPARE AND IMPLEMENT IT

WILLIAM M. LUTHER

AMACOM
American Management Association
New York • Atlanta • Boston • Chicago • Kansas City • San Francisco • Washington, D. C.
Brussels • Mexico City • Tokyo • Toronto

This publication is designed to provide accurate and authoritative information in regard to the subject matter covered. It is sold with the understanding that the publisher is not engaged in rendering legal, accounting, or other professional service. If legal advice or other expert assistance is required, the services of a competent professional person should be sought.

Library of Congress Cataloging-in-Publication Data

Luther, William M.
      The marketing plan: how to prepare and implement it /
   William M. Luther.—3rd ed.
         p.   cm.
      Includes bibliographical references and index.
      ISBN 0-8144-7101-3
      1. Marketing.   I. Title.
   HF5415.L83   2001
   658.8′02—dc21

                                              2001022859

Printing number

10   9   8   7   6   5   4   3   2   1

To all the budding entrepreneurs in my family:

Kelly

Lauren

James

Brian

Donald

Justin

Brittany

Kevin

Nicole

Briana . . .

plus the ones to follow

Contents

PART THREE
Developing Your Brand Personality

PART FIVE

Feedback—Using Controls and Market Research to Complete the Loop

Appendixes

Preface

The purpose of this book is to assist you in developing a sound and profitable marketing plan by creating a desirable positioning or personality for your business based on your Fact Book, which is an analysis of market economics, competition, customers, and your own business, and then make that personality come alive with the execution of unique-to-your-industry marketing tools.

The first edition of this book was published in 1982 and the second edition in 1992. In this third edition, I have stayed with basically the same planning structure I have previously recommended—your marketing plan needs to be no more than 10 to 15 pages, but supported by your Fact Book, which may number 100 to 200 pages. Many marketing people will try to develop a plan with little knowledge of the market, and consequently their plan is just wishful thinking. Developing a sound Fact Book will guarantee you a sound plan.

However, in this edition, about 95 percent of the copy is new. I have used more recent case history thumbnails to support my recommendations as well as provide examples of how to use the various marketing tools to their best advantage. I have added new insights I picked up from my consulting work and from marketing people that have attended my public seminars. And, I wanted to discuss a new marketing tool—the Internet.

The book begins with what you should know and do before you write your marketing plan, and then goes into how to develop a memorable personality for your business. The rest of the book is devoted to showing you how to use all the various marketing tools to make your business a market leader. That's where the money is. Marketing tools discussed included "what if" sales models, pricing strategy, advertising, direct mail, telemarketing, trade shows, merchandising, coupons, premiums, sampling, sweepstakes, contests, shoppertainment, electronic kiosks, public relations, Internet, sales management, and customer service. The book concludes on how to add accountability and complete your planning loop by the use of measurable objectives and market research.

William M. Luther
Cary, North Carolina
wml@wml-marketing.com

Introduction

The book consists of five parts. They are:

Part One: The Role of Marketing within a Business

Part Two: Decisions to Be Made before Developing Your Marketing Plan

Part Three: Developing Your Brand Personality

Part Four: Developing Your Marketing Plan

Part Five: Feedback—Using Controls and Market Research to Complete the Loop

The reason this book, which is essentially about how to develop a marketing plan, begins with the material contained in Parts One and Two is that so many people begin writing a marketing plan (which is for just one area of a business) without first analyzing their entire operation. Before you make marketing decisions, you should decide which markets, products, and services should be pushed, what your Internet strategy is, who the customer is and what they want, how the competition will react to your strategies, and whether or not you have the right people running your marketing program.

Therefore, Part One discusses where marketing fits in with the other components and plans for a business. Part One consists of Chapter One, and covers what I believe are the seven components of planning and their interaction within a company. They are:

1. Fact Book: analyzing market economics, competition, your business, and customers.

2. Strategic and/or business plan: selecting markets with good profit potential and isolating critical business strengths needed to become competitive.

3. Operational plan: developing business strengths that can deliver a competitive business, products, or services.

4. Positioning statement: determining how you want your business strengths to be perceived by prospective customers.

5. Marketing plan: translating the positioning statement into recognizable and preferred brands.

6. Action plans: detailed execution of strategies.

7. Feedback: using controls and market research to monitor existing and future conditions for inclusion in the Fact Book.

This discussion on the interplay of marketing within a business is continued in Part Two, which consists of Chapters Two through Six.

Chapter Two covers whether you should link your business to the Internet, and, if so, which of five formats is most suitable to your business. Existing Web sites are used as examples. Chapter Three provides help on prioritizing your markets, analyzing competition, and determining which markets should be pushed and how much marketing pressure should be applied. It even includes an exam, where you are asked to select the right strategy for given situations. Chapter Four is about determining who your customers are, and what they want. A five-step customer analysis is included. Thumbnail case histories are used to emphasize the importance of this critique. Chapter Five shows you how to take the information from your customer analysis and aim it at the right target with the right benefit. Chapter Six is on recommended marketing management. It provides various job descriptions and the role of consultants, including advertising agencies. I also give you my recommendations on how I believe marketing should be managed.

The remaining part of the book is devoted to the development of your marketing plan, but before getting into your various marketing tools, the umbrella of your plan—positioning—is discussed. Part Three: Developing Your Brand Personality, is covered in Chapters Seven and Eight. (Businesses, products, and services are sometimes referred to as a brand.) Chapter Seven covers how to be creative in developing your positioning statement or brand personality—one that is unique, memorable, desirable, and believable—and provides thumbnail case histories of companies that have and have not done so. Chapter Eight provides reasons all your strategies should reinforce your positioning, and once again gives examples of companies that have and have not done so.

Part Four: Developing Your Marketing Plan, includes Chapters Nine through Seventeen. In these nine chapters, I use many business examples to both support my recommendations, as well as illustrate how to use marketing tools to their best advantage. Chapter Nine is on the product or service plan, and discusses pricing strategy and the calculation of your marketing budget. It also presents a "what if" revenue model that you can use to set up the objectives for the remaining components of marketing. The remaining chapters in Part Four illustrate the best use of your various marketing tools.

Chapter Ten illustrates how to use advertising to build awareness and explains how to use reach and frequency to be sure you have sufficient advertising weight. The chapter includes a critique of what I believe are ineffective ads as well as ones I believe are on target. Chapter Eleven is on how to use direct marketing to sell or produce leads. It shows you how to establish and compile a database and use it for direct mail and telemarketing. Chapter Twelve concerns using trade shows to demonstrate what you are selling. It includes determining whether you should use trade shows, and, if so, what decisions should be made before the show opens, actions to be taken during the show, and actions to be taken after the show. Chapter Thirteen is on using merchandising and sales promotion for incremental sales. It discusses sampling, coupons, premiums, sweepstakes, contests, kiosks, and shoppertainment (a concept that makes the buying decision more fun by providing entertainment within your store for customers). Also included is an analysis of the five types of customers you should and should not go after. Chapter Fourteen is devoted to using public relations for free ads. It covers how to outline the situation, determine whether research is needed, develop your plan, execute your plan, and perform the evaluation. Some case histories of successful public relations campaigns are displayed.

Chapter Fifteen discusses how to use the Internet for instant distribution. It includes how to develop your Web site, suggestions on how to get listed by search engines, and how to promote your site. Several Web sites are analyzed to illustrate what did and did not work for them. Chapter Sixteen recommends that you only use your sales team to close the sale. It includes a simple financial analysis system that you can use to determine whether you should send a salesperson out to call on certain targets, or handle them in a less expensive manner. Chapter Seventeen discusses how to use customer service to increase repeat sales. It includes reasons so many companies are weak in customer service, and discusses the type of people you should hire to make this part of marketing work.

Part Five: Feedback—Using Controls and Market Research to Complete the Loop, is covered in Chapter Eighteen. It emphasizes why you must have measurable objectives for each component of your marketing plan so that you can monitor them, and then feed back the results into your Fact Book to complete your planning loop. It discusses the various types of market research to use to keep current on market economics, competition, and customers, and how to test the effectiveness of your advertising.

The book contains three appendixes. Appendix A: A Marketing Plan Outline includes a recommended outline for your marketing plan, along with hypothetical objectives and strategies for each component. Appendix B: Thirty-Eight Market Characteristics That Can Influence Profit Potential will help you critique your markets so that you can apply your marketing pressure in the right place. Appendix C: Explanation of What-If Sales Model provides a detailed example of how to use the model discussed in Chapter Nine.

PART ONE

THE ROLE OF MARKETING

WITHIN A BUSINESS

Chapter One

The Role of Marketing within a Business

M ost books and seminars on marketing plans begin with how to develop the marketing plan. I believe this is a mistake. You should not begin thinking about how you are going to market something until you first determine if you have something customers want, you have the ability to develop or service it, it will work the way you say it will, there will be no adverse legal ramifications, and you can sell or offer it at a profit. If you judge marketing effectiveness by the amount of brand awareness it creates, then Coca-Cola's marketing campaign for the New Coke was a success. The problem was their customers didn't want a new Coke and the company lost millions of marketing dollars because consumers decided to stay with the existing brand.

Apple Computer's Newton message pad was something customers wanted and the marketing campaign resulted in initial sales in the millions. Apple even set up a separate division to handle the brand. The problem here was that the product could not live up to all the promises made by the company and soon the brand sank into oblivion. Microsoft has spent millions of marketing dollars on their Pocket PC, but a superior product, The Palm, still retains 70 percent market share. The companies that were selling the Fen-Phen appetite suppressant now wish they had never heard of the diet-pill, due to the adverse legal ramifications. Even Amazon.com, after spending millions of dollars in promotion and receiving an exorbitant amount of free publicity, has yet to have a profitable quarter.

Someone in your company should be sure you have all your ducks in a row before you start your marketing campaign. Considering that this someone could be you, I am beginning my book on marketing with this one chapter in Part One, The Role of Marketing Within a Business. This is followed by Part Two, Decisions to Be Made Before Developing Your Marketing Plan. Let's begin this chapter with the components of planning.

The Fact Book

Figure 1-1 shows what I believe are the seven components of planning. Starting at the top is what I refer to as the *Fact Book*. The Fact Book is a document in which you insert data and your subsequent analysis of the four components of a market—market economics, competition, your own business, and customers—to determine the direction of new planning documents, as well as monitoring existing activity.

The purpose of the market economics section is to determine whether you can make money in a particular market. The economic data include market factors such as size, growth, margins, pricing sensitivity, distribution costs, regulatory exposure, brand and market life cycle, economies of scale, and barriers to entry. An explanation of these factors is in Appendix B.

The purpose of the competition and your business sections is to determine which business strengths are needed to be competitive in the market and how you believe the competition will react to your strategies. Examples of business strength factors are product or service quality, pricing strategy, distribution, performance on the Internet, and the number

Figure 1-1. Components of planning.

Fact Book

Analyzing market economics, competition, your business and customers.

↑↓

Strategic and Business Plans

Selecting markets with good profit potential and isolating critical business strengths needed to become competitive.

↑↓

Operational Plan

Developing business strengths that can deliver a competitive market position.

↑↓

Positioning Statement

Determining how you want your business strengths to be perceived by prospective customers.

↑↓

Marketing Plan

Translating the positioning statement into recognizable and preferred brands.

↑↓

Action Plans

The detailed execution of one or more strategies.

↑↓

Feedback

Using controls and market research to monitor existing and future conditions for inclusion in the Fact Book and subsequent plans.

of new brands. Information you'll need to analyze competition is each competitor's market share, their current strategy, future goals, where they are vulnerable, and what will provoke their retaliation, as well as copies or photographs of all their marketing material, such as brochures, point-of-sale, print ads, TV and radio scripts, and trade show exhibits.

The purpose of the customer analysis section is to determine how you want your business strengths to be perceived by current and prospective customers. This desired perception is detailed in your positioning statement. It's the personality of your company, products, or services, which I refer to as *brands*. The purpose of your marketing program is to translate your positioning statement into recognizable and preferred brand(s), which should result in increased sales or revenues and subsequent profit. This customer section includes a four-step analysis. First, determine your target audience within the market. Second, list the job titles or demographics of the various groups making the buying decisions within this target audience. Third, prioritize this list, putting the most important groups at the top. Fourth, insert next to the name of each group, the hot button, or major benefit, each one is seeking from your brand category, paying special attention to those groups at the top of the list. You then determine whether your business strengths allow you to deliver these key benefits, and, if so, you have the basis for developing your positioning statement and marketing plan. If not, consider whether you should change markets, develop different business strengths, or go after a more appropriate target audience in the market.

If you want to check your current status in a market, use a fifth step, which is to conduct research to determine how you are perceived by the various groups making the buying decisions. If the results are favorable, your marketing plan is on target. If the results are unfavorable, you have to reexamine all the other components of planning. All steps in this customer analysis are discussed in greater detail in Part Three: Developing Your Brand Personality.

The soundness of all your planning documents, as well as any revisions, is based on the soundness of your Fact Book, so please do not overlook this critical first step. The only time-consuming part of planning is the preparation of the Fact Book. However, after the initial setup, keeping it up-to-date is relatively easy. After the completion of a current Fact Book, the actual development of plans will not take more than a week or two.

Your Fact Book will get up to 100-plus pages after a while, so keep it separate from your plans. The reason is that you want to keep your plans short and concise so they can be operational documents. Your best bet is to put the Fact Book data on your computer using spreadsheets, databases, and your word processor. Market information and business financials can go on a spreadsheet. Customer data can go into a database and a word processing document. For the section on competition, you can scan competitors' brochures, ads, etc., and add them to your word processing document. The data on their strategies, goals, etc., as well as information on your business can also be inserted into the word processing document. You can then print copies of your data from the computer and insert them into a three-ring binder for easy review and group meetings. Put the appropriate data behind four dividers labeled economics, competition, my business, and customers.

As you can see from the discussion above, the Fact Book sets up the next five planning components shown in Figure 1-1, and the last component, feedback, measures the performance of these five components and keeps your Fact Book up-to-date. Feedback will be discussed in greater detail in Part Five. Let's switch to Figure 1-2. Nomenclature of Plans, to discuss these five planning components in more detail.

Strategic and Business Plans

The first and most overreaching of your plans is the *strategic plan* and there is a lot of confusion about its purpose. I believe it is deciding "what are the right things to do." By that I mean selecting the right markets to be in, based on the profit potential of a market and whether you have, or can acquire, the business strengths needed to be competi-

Figure 1–2. Nomenclature of plans.

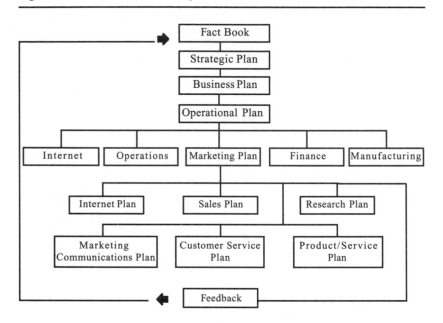

tive. Many companies skip this step and start immediately to plan on what to do with what they have. The problem with this is, what they have may not be right. Two examples are Apple Computer's Newton and Microsoft's Pocket PC. Apple Computer did not have the business strengths to make the Newton do what was promised in marketing and Microsoft's new operating system for the Pocket PC was not embraced either by the trade or consumers.

In your strategic planning, you want to envision the parameters of your markets and field of operations three to ten years into the future, based on the analysis of the data in your Fact Book. Based on this foresight, you develop your strategic plan, stating what you should start doing now to end up where you want to be in the future. It includes subjects such as which markets will be pushed and which ones phased out; what, if any, new technology is needed; do you need more or fewer employees; and what type of new brands should be developed. You should also address your status on the Internet. If you currently have a

Web site, the question is: Is it working? If you don't have a Web site, should you? If so, which type of site is best for you? For example, will you sell off the site or just use it for promotional activity?

The strategic plan is long term, involves all parts of your business, and is the only plan in which you decide "what are the right things to do." All other plans, such as the *business plan*, are concerned with "doing things right." That is, given the direction of the strategic plan, what should you be doing right now, in the short term, to get there?

Your *business plan*, which involves all parts of your business, details what you are going to do during the next couple of years to achieve the long-term objectives of the strategic plan. For example, if your strategic plan calls for a doubling of volume in five years for Brands A and B in Market X, your business plan lays out the specific details of what has to be done during the first two to three years of the five-year plan.

You may think that two long-term plans are a lot for your business. Well, neither has to be fancy. You may want to combine the strategic plan and business plan into one document. If you do combine them, just remember to first decide what are the right things to do before you decide how you are going to do them. If you have a relatively small firm, your plans, except for the measurement of your objectives, don't even have to be in writing unless you are looking for financing. The thought process is what is important in planning. The plan itself is only for communication purposes and if you can get everyone on the same page by oral communication, there is no need to put the plan in writing. This is especially true for start-up companies, where the ability to quickly change direction is more important than a written plan with all the t's crossed.

However, whether you have one employee or 10,000, you have to look ahead to beat the competition. The life of brands is getting shorter. Some survive less than a year. Therefore, you always want to think about tomorrow and you should do it when business is good. The best time to alter your operation is when you are the strongest. Deal from strength. Don't wait until you are weak.

Operational Plan

Just as the strategic plan sets up the business plan, the business plan sets up the *operational plan*. The operational plan runs the business. It covers each area of the company, including finance, Internet, manufacturing, operations, human resources, research and development (R& D), and, of course, marketing. Let's say your business plan calls for $50,000 in revenue for the first year of the five-year plan. Based on this information, you then develop an operational plan, including a marketing plan, to support the $50,000 objective. Notice that the main objectives of the marketing plan are set up by the business plan. If you start your planning process with the marketing plan, you will not know which market to participate in; which brands to feature; how many units operations can produce; what sales objectives to set; and how much to spend on advertising, sales promotion, and so on. Hopefully, you will agree that you can't start your planning with the marketing plan until you first decide the overall direction of your business. Before we discuss the components of the marketing plan, let's talk about the *positioning statement*.

Positioning Statement

If you are positioning a company, the positioning statement is developed in your strategic plan or business plan. If you are positioning individual brands, it belongs in your marketing plan. In either case, the positioning statement has to be compatible with the entire business operation. For example, I believe the positioning statement for Wal-Mart is something like: "Brand names at ridiculously low prices." To obtain and retain this positioning entails the efforts of the entire Wal-Mart operation. However, it is the responsibility of marketing to convey this personality to all potential customers. For companies that are positioning individual brands, like Crest toothpaste, positioning development becomes the responsibility of marketing, although the support, like the ingredient for tartar control, involves the entire operation. Part Three discusses developing your brand personality.

Marketing Plan

The purpose of the *marketing plan* is to translate the positioning statement into recognized and preferred brands. To do so, I recommend that the marketing plan consist of six areas of marketing, although how you group them is up to you. As shown in Figure 1-2, they are as follows.

1. The product or service plan, which sets up the objectives of the various marketing components through the use of a "what if" revenue model. It also addresses such items as pricing strategy, depth of line (number of sizes, shapes, models, policies, etc.), packaging, distribution, and your marketing budget.

2. The marketing communications plan, which includes advertising, sales promotion, direct mail, merchandising, and public relations.

3. The sales plan, which covers the sales team, whether they are your own employees, distributors, commission representatives, or manufacturers' agents. It includes sales goals, sales training, and sales literature.

4. The customer service plan, which includes the activities of all employees who interact with the customer, directly or indirectly, and are not covered in the sales plan. Examples are technical support, telephone operators, nurses, busboys, waiters, and flight attendants.

5. The research plan, which includes market research to keep your Fact Book current, marketing communications research, and the marketing team's liaison with R&D.

6. The Internet plan, which includes the marketing of your Web site.

When people in some companies talk about their marketing plans, they are referring to just the marketing communications plan. In these cases the sales personnel do not converse with marketing communications people and vice versa; marketing managers usually just concentrate on technical issues; research people are tied up analyzing surveys; and customer service personnel are not even considering marketing people. This situation doesn't make much sense, considering that all groups have a common denominator and that is to translate the positioning statement consistently and effectively in order to sell more of something.

A company will never excel in marketing until it gets all five groups—and now the Internet makes six—talking together, working together, and promoting the brand together. A shining example of a company that does is Nordstrom department stores. Their sales clerks and customer service personnel know more about promoting a brand than individuals in most advertising departments. What you want to try to do is to out-Nordstrom Nordstrom. Part Four discusses the six marketing components and Appendix A contains an outline for a marketing plan.

Every plan you develop should contain objectives, strategies, and tactics. An objective is the what, the strategy the how, and the tactic the execution. Objectives state what you want to accomplish. They should be measurable so you know whether or not you achieve them by the end of the plan year. Therefore, each objective should have a goal, a control, and a completion date. An example for a direct mail objective could be: To deliver 200 qualified leads at a cost of $3,000, by 12/31/xx. In this case, the goal is the 200 qualified leads, the control is the expenditure of $3,000, and the completion date is 12/31/xx. The reason for the control is that anyone can accomplish a goal with unlimited expenditures. Without the control, a person may accomplish the goal while bankrupting the business. A consultant may be able to obtain 200 qualified leads for you at the cost of $5,000, but if the value of 200 qualified leads is only $4,000, it's a bad buy.

A strategy states how you are going to achieve the objective. For example, it could relate to an objective pertaining to exhibiting at a particular trade show, developing a dynamic personality for the business, or introducing a new service. A tactic is the execution of the strategy. If a strategy calls for exhibiting at a trade show, the tactic provides the details, such as who will book the space and who will build the exhibit.

Each section of a plan should have one to three objectives (what you want to accomplish). That's all. If you have more than that you are not focused. For each objective you need one to two strategies (how you are going to accomplish the what). For every strategy you need one to five tactics (how you are going to execute the how).

For example, suppose you had a high-resistance housing you wanted to display at a trade show. Sections of your sales promotion plan could look like this:

I. OBJECTIVE: Demonstrate with an expenditure of $5,000 high-impact resistance of new housing on energy monitors to 300 design engineers by December 31.

    A. *Strategy:* Exhibit at July WESPLEX trade show. Offer prize to anyone checking housing with a sledgehammer.

        1. *Tactic:* Bill Johnson to order show space by March 31 to obtain good location.

        2. *Tactic:* Lewis to contact Dynamic Displays, Inc., by April 30 to request initial exhibit design.

        3. *Etc.*

Action Plans

Tactics should just be summarized in the marketing plan. After the complete marketing plan is approved, *action plans* should be written to provide the details of your tactics. If you include all the details of executing a strategy in the marketing plan, you may be confronted with three possible problems:

1. You end up with a 50- to 200-page document that no one will read and the plan just gathers dust on the shelf.

2. If the plan is not approved, you have wasted time developing all the details.

3. Using a separate action plan to detail your tactics lets the people who will actually execute the plan decide for themselves how they should do it.

An action plan contains the detailed execution of one or more strategies and should include at least three factors:

1. Each necessary step or task

2. Who will be responsible for accomplishing each step or task

3. The required completion date of each step or task

For each marketing plan, you may have between five and twenty action plans. The sum of all your action plans is your *milestone calendar* or *PERT chart*. A milestone calendar keeps you on target relative to timing. A PERT chart determines which completion dates for certain steps or tasks are the most critical and have to be watched most closely. These critical steps or tasks are the ones that influence the beginning of another step or task.

Keep your action plans in separate binders. Your Fact Book should also be in a separate binder. This will enable you to have a short, concise operational marketing plan that you can refer to each week. If your marketing plan is not operational, the preparation is nothing more than an exercise.

If you put your Fact Book on the computer, you may want to do the same for your plans. Put your objectives in a spreadsheet, your strategies in your word processing program, and your tactics in a time management program. However, you should have a hard copy on the top of your desk to be sure you monitor your plans frequently. That completes an overview on the six components of planning.

Look Out the Window

Whether you have a written plan or not, the key thing is to think about the market, competition, customers, and your business every day. Many managers put what they call their plans into three-ring binders, which is usually a combination of the plan, Fact Book, and action plans. It usually numbers 150 to 200 pages and the effectiveness is generally judged by how much the plan weighs. Most even emboss their company name in gold ink on the cover. After they present their plan, they put it up on the shelf someplace. It looks cool up there, but invariably no one looks at it until a year later.

When the year is up and the managers go into planning mode again, having neglected to keep the plan in mind and continually compare it to reality, they're already in trouble. They have been looking in the window at their own operation and made decisions based on what they see within the company—existing technology, type of equipment, processes, policies, employees, and current customers. Don't make the same mistake. This type of critique is only half of the planning process. You also have to look out the window to see who is passing by.

When you are looking out the window, keep asking yourself the following types of questions. Is there a change in what the customer looks like? Is he older? Younger? Is she richer or poorer? Does he still have the same importance in the buying decision? Have her needs, wants, or desires changed, as they have in medicine, stocks and bonds, the Internet, and telecommunications? Is the market growing faster or slower? Is my competition getting stronger or weaker? Do they plan to introduce new brands? Are they doing something I can take advantage of, like Intuit selling its software direct at a higher price than you can purchase it at retail. Am I competitively priced based on the value I offer? Is new technology available? Are fashion trends changing? Are there new lifestyles? Does my selling line really have a zing to it or can I improve it so it catches peoples' attention like Nike's "Just do it." Nike may have more marketing dollars than you, but that doesn't necessarily mean you need a lot of money to be creative.

Looking out the window means critiquing every strategy you see on television, hear on the radio, read in a newspaper or magazine, or encounter in the business world. The type of product or service is academic. What you are looking for is an effective strategy from another industry that you can steal, give a fresh coat of paint, and be the first to run in your market. That is the way to develop fresh and dynamic strategies. An example of the execution of a dynamic strategy is Netscape's introduction of their browser. They proclaimed in the media, "Use our software to explore the wonderful world of the Web." Not bad, but then they added the kicker "You can download it free." That was dynamite. Can you repaint that one for your business?

When you look out the window, you also want to be sure there are no emerging markets on the horizon that may replace yours. In his book *The Innovator's Dilemma* (Boston: Harvard Business School Press, 2000), Clayton M. Christensen talks about disruptive technologies precipitating the failure of many leading firms. He defines disruptive technologies as those that underperform established products or services in mainstream markets, but that have other features that a few, and primarily new, customers value. They are usually cheaper, simpler, smaller, and frequently more convenient to use. Consequently, they represent a new or emerging market.

One of the many examples he provides is the computer disk drive industry, where rarely did the market leader in one stage of technology become the market leader in the next. The reason was that at each stage of technology, the market leader's customers did not heed the continual downsizing of computers. For example, Winchester Drive led the market with the 14-inch disk drive. This was fine for their mainframe computer manufacturing customers, but then different manufacturers started making minicomputers. They needed a smaller-size disk drive. Winchester kept making the 14-inch to satisfy their current customers, but with the eventual shift to minis, Shugart Associates and Quantum became the leaders with the 8-inch drive. Then the shift was to microcomputers. Shugart and Quantum did not look out the window. Consequently, Seagate led with the 5.25-inch drive and Conner Peripherals with the 3.5-

inch drive. None of the above saw laptops and hand-held computers coming, so it is no surprise that they are not a factor in the 1.8-inch market. Ninety-eight percent of the sales for 1.8-inch drives are by new entrants.

The market leaders of tomorrow are those that are looking out the window today, so keep looking. Keep your plans on your desk and your head out the window.

PART TWO

DECISIONS TO BE MADE BEFORE DEVELOPING YOUR MARKETING PLAN

Chapter Two

Should You Link Your Business

to the Internet?

Your decisions regarding the use of the Internet are discussed here because they will influence your strategic, business, and operational plans, including your marketing plan. Developing your site and attracting visitors will be discussed in the marketing plan section, which is Part Four.

These is no question that the Internet has become a major information and distribution system and it, along with hand-held hardware, interactive TV, self-service kiosks, smart cards, and other related technologies, will continue to reshape marketing practices in the future. There is a question, though, that you have to answer—how will your company fit in and take advantage of these new high-tech business vehicles? Whether this question is one you are familiar with, or one just entering your thought process, you should arrive at the answer the same way you should to solve all challenges—by an all-encompassing analysis. This chapter is devoted to some of the factors I believe you should address in your thinking.

I believe many companies are going on the Internet just because the competition is there or they believe they have to be a participant in this red-hot new industry. Phil Worley, owner of Worley Hardware in Canton, Connecticut, started a modest Web site last spring with a modest goal: to bring in some additional sales for his small-town hardware store. After three months of advertising Weber grills at prices lower than most of his competitors, he had not sold a single thing. He stated, "I haven't seen much payback, but I feel like I need to be there, since so many in my industry are. I'm keeping the faith."[1] Let's discuss what you need in addition to faith.

The Advantages and Disadvantages of the Internet

The advantage of the Internet is that it offers greater possible distribution or presence for fewer dollars than any other marketing tool. It can cost only a couple of hundred dollars to put up a site where anyone in the world with Internet access can see your presentation. The disadvantages—maybe a better word is obstacles—are many. A major one is getting noticed, which will be discussed here. The others will be commented on later. There are two major ways to draw traffic, but they are both tough to execute. One method is to be selected when prospects insert words or phrases in search engine keyword boxes and the other is through the use of various promotional devices such as banner ads on other Web sites. The problem with the first method is that the different search engines such as Yahoo!, Excite, Lycos, and InfoSeek use different criteria for their listings. The second method has two problems—it can be costly and promotional strategies that work for one company's Web site do not necessarily work for another. Of course, this is true for promotional efforts in any medium. It just means promoting on the Internet is no piece of cake.

In case you are not yet an Internet participant, following is a brief description of search engines and banner ads. Search engines are programs that search the entire Internet for matches between keywords typed in by an Internet surfer and the text on the Web site. If you are relying on this method to be noticed, you want your Web site to be among the top ten listings shown when the search engine shows the results of the query. If you are not among the top ten, you probably will not be noticed. This is not easy to accomplish because some search engines scan just the first paragraph on your Web site to ascertain matches, some scan your entire site, while others put emphasis on your title, description, and keywords you insert in HTML, which is an Internet programming language. Therefore, one Web design may not work for all search engines. In addition, many of the search engines allow companies to purchase keywords so that they come up at the top of the search listings.

A banner ad usually has a rectangular shape and measures about 2 inches by 4 inches. They usually reside on the pages of a browser, a Web site, or search engine. A browser is an Internet program that connects you to all the computers (called servers) around the world that host the various search engines and other Web sites. Examples of such programs are Microsoft Explorer, which is owned by Microsoft and Netscape Navigator, which is owned by AOL. Banner ads contain a short sales message that the advertiser hopes will entice the viewer to click on to their Web site. The cost per thousand (CPM) for banner ads ranges from $20 to $200. Even at $20, this is more expensive than the CPM for prime-time network television. In addition, the industry average for people who "click" on the banner ad to go to the advertiser's Web site is only 2 percent. Some companies have successfully used banner ads while others state they proved to be too costly.

There are other means to draw traffic to your Web site, such as networking, newsletters, and catalogs, but the fact is that it is difficult to get noticed on this fast-growing medium.

It Takes Effective Strategies to Be a Winner on the Web

In addition to getting noticed, you need an effective marketing strategy to become profitable. Amazon (www.amazon.com) is probably the site most people consider as having the greatest success story. They are referred to as the retail Wal-Mart of the Web, although Wal-Mart is becoming a major presence on the Web, as will be discussed later. Amazon receives thousands of hits every day and they are being processed into millions of dollars in sales. The reason is their discounted prices and a huge inventory. Amazon began by selling books and continues to expand. Recent additions are music, video, gifts, and auctions. These products all lend themselves to marketing on the Internet because they have universal appeal and sell primarily on price. Undoubtedly, Amazon will continue to be called a winner. However, most of the items they sell have a low profit margin, and because Amazon discounts the price, and spends heavily on their infrastructure and marketing, the company has yet to show a profit. They will, say the financial gurus.

Dell Computer (www.dell.com) is one company that has made a profit selling on the Web. They pioneered the selling of computers and computer peripherals on the Web by offering two main benefits. One is price, like Amazon. The other is computers made to order. You can specify what components and software you want on their Internet order form and then the computer is put together and shipped to you. Because they have no warehousing costs, a marvelously efficient back office, and no middlemen, they can offer a low price and still beat the competition on profit margins.

Successful selling on the Internet, which is referred to as E-commerce, has not been limited to large companies. In her book *Striking It Rich.com* (New York: McGraw-Hill, 2000), Jaclyn Easton presents case histories of twenty-three profitable Web sites owned by small businesses. Some of these companies expanded their offline business to the Web. One is Coastal Tool and Supply (www.coastaltool.com), a retail store in

Hartford, Connecticut, which launched its Web site in October 1995 with a first year budget of $1,800. Earnings for 1998 exceeded $1.5 million. The store credits its success not only to massive inventory and deep discounts, but to the simplicity and ease of ordering from its site.

Others companies cited in her book started from scratch, selecting a type of business that related to their business background or interests. For example, Tim Carter, a home improvement adviser, started Ask the Builder (www.askthebuilder.com) in December 1995. His company's Web site, with himself as the only employee, contains hundreds of articles providing advice on every aspect of home improvement. In 1998 he received over 12,000 visitors a month and earned mid-six-figure annual revenues from manufacturers' ads on his site.

A few companies in Easton's book just selected a business they thought would be a winner. For example, the founders of The Knot (www.theknot.com), a site offering advice on weddings, selected this category because they believed the market was huge, advertising dollars large, and competition weak. Started in 1995, The Knot currently receives 320,000 visitors a month and ad revenue for the month of January 1998 was $187,000.

Probably the most surprising market category in Easton's book is steel. Weirton Steel (www.weirton.com) has filled 6,000 orders over the Internet since their launch and has averaged monthly sales in the $3.5 to $4.4 million range. They offer their excess and secondary steel products to customers through an auction process. They credit their success to market research—finding out who the customers were and what they wanted. The opening question in one of their surveys was: "What can we do to make your life easier?"

Those are a few of the winners. However, there have been many losers among companies trying to sell something—a loser being defined as one either now off the Web or still holding on to their site, but disappointed with the results.. Even among those currently considered successful, many have yet to make money. They usually state that they are still building infrastructure, but the investment market is becoming impatient with some of them. One of the companies that Easton profiles in her book as having a successful Web site now has a sign up reading, Temporarily Closed. Why have so many companies not achieved the results they expected? Well, I have already said that it is difficult to get noticed on the Internet and that you need a unique selling strategy, but I believe there is more to the story. Let's begin by discussing the various types of Web sites and what is required to make each one successful. You basically have six choices:

1. To sell your brand, referred to as a *transaction site.*

2. To promote your brand, referred to as a *promotional site.*

3. To offer information or advice on a subject, referred to as a *content site.*

4. To support or replace your customer service activities.

5. To purchase your supplies off the Internet.

6. Any combination of the above.

Should You Have a Transaction Site?

A transaction site is usually your first choice if you have a relatively inexpensive brand, a simple sales presentation, and an infrastructure that lends itself to direct selling. Previous examples were Amazon, Dell Computer, Coastal Tool and Supply, and Weirton Steel. The items for sale are relatively inexpensive and do not need a complicated selling presentation. The only one of the four that does not have an existing offline (bricks-and-mortar) business is Amazon and it is the only one that does not have a profitable online operation. What some companies going online without an existing business may be doing is underestimating the need and cost of a sound infrastructure. After all, online selling "isn't about the Internet and fancy technology," says Procter & Gamble's Rich Essigs, associate director of customer business development for North America, who works with online retailers, "it's about getting products from the warehouse to the consumer's home and still make money."[2]

Whether you are selling online to consumers or business-to-business, you need an infrastructure that includes order processing, warehousing, order fulfillment that also handles financial transactions, a security system, order tracking, processing of returns, and available customer service personnel. Setting up all these operations takes experience and money, factors that some companies going on the Web do not appear to be taking into account. If you are experiencing problems in these areas, you may want to turn to a systems integrator. You can get referrals from Information Technology Industry Association of America (www.itaa.org), Council of Regional IT Associations, which is accessible from the same site, IBM's commerce site (www.software.ibm.com/commerce/net.commerce), or Microsoft's site (www.microsoft.com).

If you have a current bricks-and-mortar business, which probably means you have an existing infrastructure that can handle the above factors, there are additional decisions to be made. Should you combine all aspects of this two-tier business or keep them separate? Should there be two separate brands? Should there be two separate marketing campaigns? Should inventory for the online operation be in your company's warehouse or at a supplier? Do you hire people from within your current organization to run your E-commerce operation or do you go to the outside? How do you compensate the sales force of the current operation for items sold from your Web site?

If all that is not enough, there is still the critical factor of brand recognition. As stated in Gardiner Harris's article in *The Wall Street Journal*, "Merck-Medico (www.Merckmedico.com), a division of venerable Merck & Co., is just the kind of stodgy, paper-dependent company that pesky Internet start-ups were supposed to crush." Harris continues, "But while Web rivals that started up last year amid much fanfare are struggling, Merck-Medico is thriving. It now has its own Web site, and its Internet sales dwarf those of its Net competitors." Harris concludes, "Creating an Internet site, it turns out, is the easy part. Getting customers to frequent it is the challenge. As a result, the ability to market an

Internet site to an established customer base has become an ace in the hole for Old Economy companies."[3]

America Online and Wal-Mart started a joint venture to promote each other's brands, as did Yahoo and Kmart Corporation, Microsoft and Best-Buy. Toyota sold their Prius hybrid automobiles only on the Internet for the first several months. The big companies, with strong brand recognition and economies of scale, are on to the Internet and that could be bad news for less known competitors.

Figure 2-1 shows Wal-Mart's home page. On the menu, notice the twelve different departments a customer can click on. Figure 2-2 shows the resulting page if you click on Apparel. There you will find nine subdepartments to select from, ranging from Baby Apparel to Watches. Eight of the subdepartments offer seventy further options, from Girls' Special Occasion Dresses to Women's Scrubs. It will be difficult for smaller-size competitors to compete against this wide array of merchandise at Wal-Mart.

Should You Have a Promotional Site?

Having a promotional site rather than a transactional one may be a better strategy if any one or a combination of the following factors exists: a several-step sales presentation; expensive merchandise; an infrastructure that doesn't currently exist; weak brand recognition; no unique strategy. For example, Back Roads, Inc. (www.backroads.com), sells active vacation tours that average $1,900 and the average sale takes two years to close.[4] Each tour provides alternate routes of varying difficulty so that family members of mixed athletic ability can enjoy the tour at their own pace. Because it takes so long to sell one of their tours, their site promotes interactivity. Every page ends with both a phone number and direct e-mail link to a trip consultant. The site also offers an electronic postcard service that customers can use to send messages to friends and family while on tour. The recipient needs to go to the site to retrieve the message. The company says it is a great way to obtain new customers.

PENgroup.com (www.pengroup.com) is another example of a pro-

Figure 2-1. Wal-Mart home page.

motional site. Their site is used to promote their consulting matchmaking services in order to build an online data bank of professional consultants as well as companies looking for consulting services. However, the actual matchmaking is done offline due to the personal nature of this type of activity. After a consulting firm pays up to $4,000 annually for a member-

Figure 2-2. Wal-Mart apparel page.

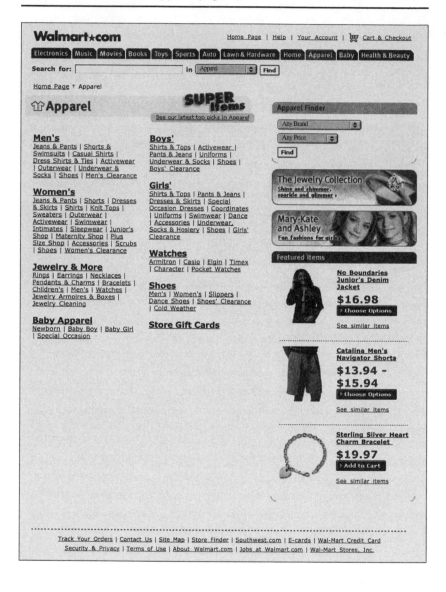

ship, PENgroup.com e-mails them consulting leads. The consulting firm then contacts the leads either by telephone or in person. PENgroup.com injects a powerful strategy into their marketing mix—if a participating consulting firm does not obtain a project or certain number of leads in its first year of membership, its membership is extended until PENgroup. com meets these criteria. Their home page is shown in Figure 2-3.

You can put your brochures, catalogs, and sales literature on the Web, either as a separate site, or in conjunction with a transaction or promotional site. It could save you a lot in printing and mailing costs. However, it is interesting to note that even with the explosion of Internet promotional sites, catalog mailings have increased 8.7 percent since 1995, according to *The Wall Street Journal*. It appears that the strategy of bricks-and-mortar companies is to have their offline stores, catalogs, and Web sites work in concert to give them an edge over companies just selling on the Internet.

Figure 2-3. PENgroup.com home page.

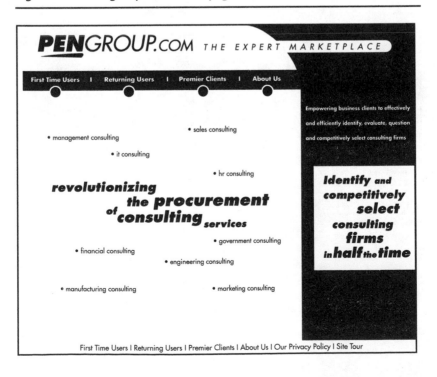

Should You Have a Content Site?

Your third choice is a content site like Ask the Builder or The Knot. Unlike choices one and two, where you use the Web to sell or promote merchandise, you use the site to sell your audience. You build your audience by offering knowledge or expertise. If you are successful in building enough traffic, you can then sell advertising space on your Web site to other vendors. Figure 2-4 shows the home page of Ask the Builder. If you click on Column Archives, you come to the page shown in Figure

Figure 2-4. Ask the Builder home page.

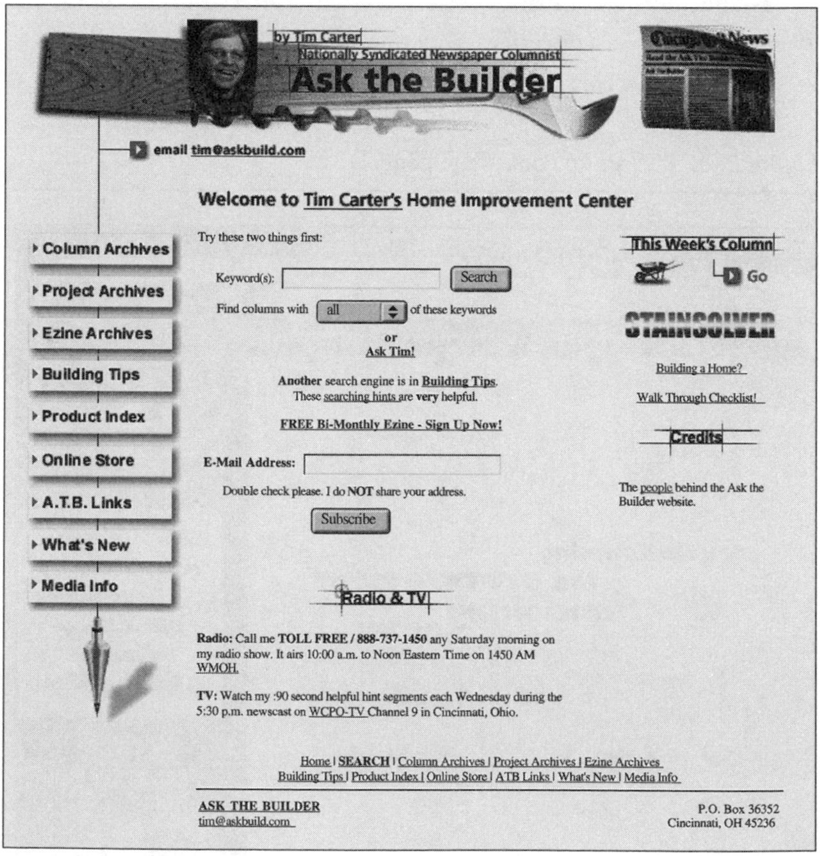

2-5. Notice the banner ad for Sanitary for All, Inc., with its blunt copy-line, "This toilet flushes."

A content site can also be a promotional site. *The Wall Street Journal*, *USA Today*, and *The New York Times* present their incumbent front pages in a format that contains breaking news with links to full articles. The Web sites for the TV networks—CBS, ABC, NBC, and Fox—provide program listings and biographies of their stars.

Figure 2–5. Ask the Builder column archives page.

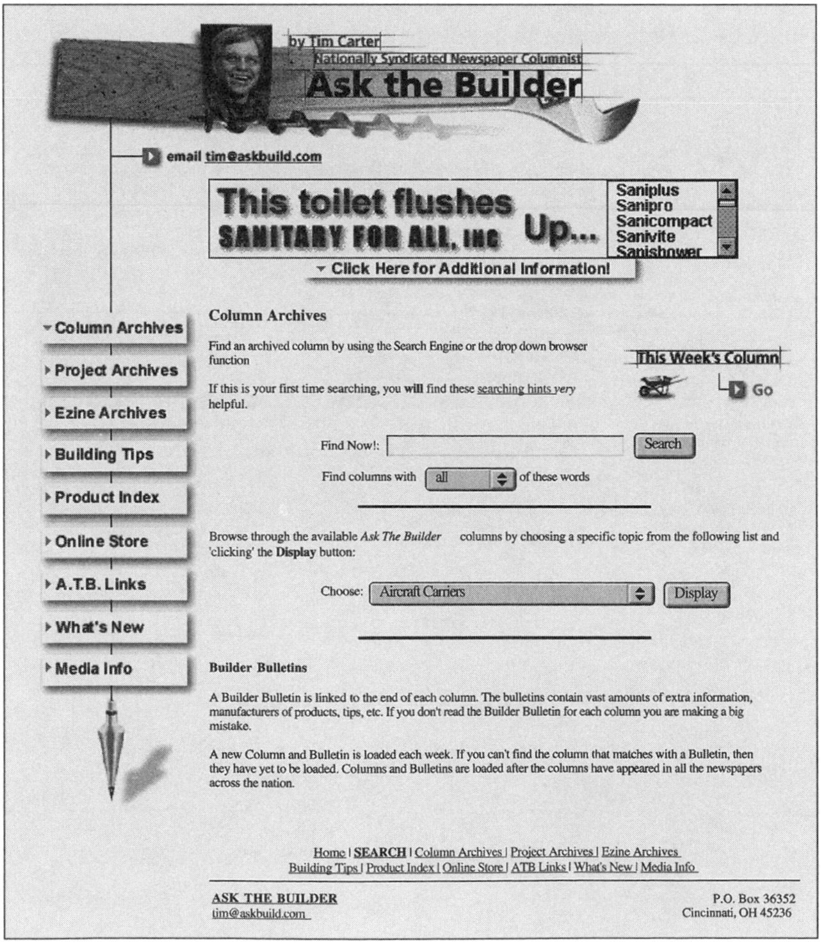

Should You Have a Customer Service Site?

Your fourth choice is to have your Web site serve as an extension of your customer service department. Probably the best example of this use is FedEx (as shown in Figure 2-6). On their Web site, customers can track their packages, check drop-off locations, look up rates, and request pickups. On bank sites, like Citibank, you can access online services such as viewing your checking, savings, and credit card accounts, paying your bills, making transfers, obtaining stock quotes, and rummaging through

Figure 2-6. FedEx home page for the United States.

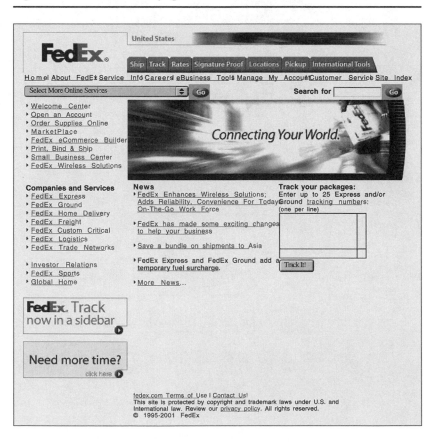

their frequently asked questions (FAQ) section. Insurance company Web sites like Amica allow online reporting of claims and losses as well as checking the status of your account. Stock brokerage companies like Charles Schwab permit you to do all your brokerage transactions online.

In the years before the expansion of the Internet, many companies shied away from markets that demanded extensive customer service representation because they knew they were incapable of providing good performance in this area of marketing. Today, many companies have abandoned this skittishness because they have been able to employ effective customer service functions on their Web sites. If your business necessitates customer service activity, which I assume it does, then this part of marketing should be addressed on a Web site. Just be sure that you prominently display a toll-free number for additional help. Having your Web site handle the bulk of your customer service functions is no reason why you can't answer your toll-free number by the third ring. And please do not play over and over that stupid recording that says how important your customers are to you, while the caller is frustratingly waiting for a live person to answer.

Should You Purchase
Your Supplies off the Internet?

General Electric was probably the first major corporation to begin purchasing from suppliers over the Internet. As stated in *Forbes* magazine, the system was launched by GE Information Systems in January 1997, and by April 1997 they had purchased $350 million worth of industrial products electronically. Their Web site enables General Electric employees to zap out request for bids to thousand of suppliers who can respond via the Internet. The company is currently purchasing several billion dollars of supplies over the Internet and sells the purchasing software they developed to other companies. "GE Information Services claims cost savings of 10% to 15%, thanks to more and lower bids. It also claims a five-day savings in order time, thanks to the immediacy of the Internet."[5]

Both General Motors Corporation and Ford Motor Company announced plans to set up massive online bazaars for all the goods and services they buy—everything from paper clips to stamping presses to contract manufacturing. "By the end of 2001, we're going to expect all of General Motors' purchases to go through this site, and we would expect all of our suppliers to be as actively engaged," said Harold Kutner, GM's purchasing agent. Both companies want their suppliers to use the Web sites to make their own purchases or sell excess inventory. A company that provides suspension parts to GM, for example, might use GM's virtual marketplace to get a more favorable price on steel by piggybacking on the automaker's enormous purchasing power.[6]

Unlike other types of Web sites, after the initial expense of setting up the system, purchasing off the Internet is a money-saving venue rather than a cost item. You should be onboard.

Should Your Web Site
Offer a Combination of Choices?

I believe the General Electric site (www.ge.com) is the best example of how to use a Web site to its fullest advantage. It is a transaction site where you can purchase such things as equipment parts and accessories; auto, life, and long-term care insurance; lighting equipment; adhesives and sealants; and electrical products. It's a promotion site for the company's aircraft engines, appliances, and other major equipment and vehicles. It's a content site in that it discusses such subjects as dynamic lighting; acquiring or relocating a business; business and industry solutions; reducing vehicle costs; and today's news headlines and financial stories. And it's a customer service site because it displays FAQ's, 800 numbers, and a site map of service centers. (See Figures 2-7 and 2-8.)

If you are not yet on the Internet or you are not satisfied with the

Figure 2-7. First part of General Electric's home page.

current performance of your site, give the above some thought. Your analysis belongs in your Fact Book and the resulting decisions made in your strategic and business plans. You definitely should try to handle at least part of your customer service activity on the Internet. Online purchasing from suppliers should be a high priority. If direct sales are

Figure 2-8. Second part of General Electric's home page.

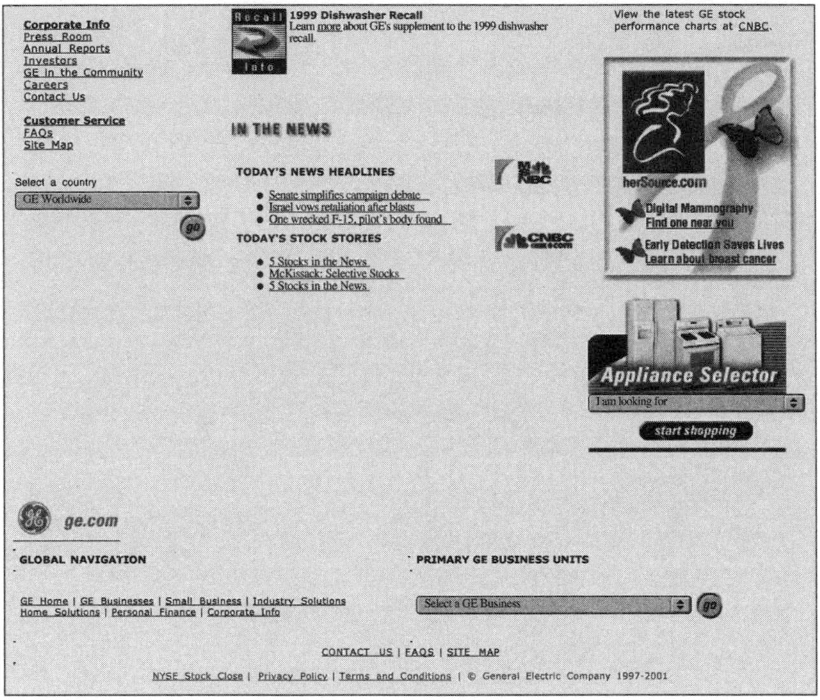

not appropriate for you, then you should add brand promotion to your customer service presentation and supplier purchasing. A fourth addition could be content if you have interesting news for customers and prospects.

Notes

1. *The New York Times* article, "Local firms going online require faith and patience," appearing in the *Minneapolis Star Tribune,* August 22, 1999.

2. Emily Nelson, "As Web Retailing Surges, Where's Wal-Mart?," *The Wall Street Journal,* May 17, 1999.

3. Gardiner Harris, "How Merck Unit Beat Dot-coms in Web Foray," *The Wall Street Journal,* April 13, 2000.

4. Claire Tristram, "Happy Returns," *Small Business Computing & Communications*, May 1999.

5. Scott Woolley, "Double click for resin," *Forbes*, March 3, 1997.

6. Gregory L. White, "How GM, Ford Think Web Can Make Splash on the Factory Floor," *The Wall Street Journal*, December 3, 1999.

Chapter Three

Your Strategic Plan Determines Where to Spend Your Marketing Dollars

The purpose of a strategic and/or business plan is to select which markets offer the greatest profit potential and then determine and fund the resources needed in these markets to build competitive brands. The purpose of the operating plan is to translate these resources into business strengths that will make the brands competitive. By business strengths I mean factors such as quality, price, method of distribution, packaging, and, of course, marketing effectiveness. By competitive, I mean brands equal to the competition in performance. All a marketing person can ask for is a competitive brand. Better mousetraps are few and far between. It is up to marketing to take a competitive brand and turn it into a winner.

When I use the word *market* I am referring to a group of prospective customers who now have or will have common wants or needs. The market should have a common profile relative to such factors as competitors, distribution, and packaging. Do your strategic analysis by market rather than by product or service because a product or service may be involved in more than one market.

For example, a company was selling frozen soup to restaurants, delis, and airlines. Like many companies, they pulled their profit and loss statements by product rather than by market. When they were asked whether these three groups of customers had the same needs and requirements, their answer was no. They said that the deli and restaurant customers were quite uniform in their needs, but the airlines requested new soup formulations monthly so they could advertise exotic new names on their menus. The airlines also demanded large price discounts due to their volume buying. Based on this information, the financial people were asked to pull a profit and loss for the deli and restaurant business and a separate profit and loss for the airlines. They were surprised to learn that they were making a profit on the deli and restaurant business, but losing money on airline sales.

You can select the right market, develop a competitive brand and still not be highly profitable due to ineffective marketing. Royal Crown Cola usually beats both Coca-Cola and Pepsi in blind taste tests, yet the brand is not among the top five in cola sales. We will talk about marketing effectiveness later. This chapter is devoted to selecting the right markets in which to spend your operating dollars and exert marketing pressure.

Five Possible Market Profiles

You can divide markets into five possible profiles based on an analysis of their profit potential and required business strengths. One is an unprofitable market due to characteristics of that market. A second is one that could be profitable, but is currently unprofitable because market participants are not exercising the right business strengths. A third is one that was profitable in the past, but now is not due to changes in customer usage. A fourth is one that is currently profitable to one or more market participants. A fifth is a new market.

Unprofitable Markets

Let's examine each one, beginning with a market that is unprofitable due to characteristics of the market. Two examples of this kind of market are airline carriers and restaurants. Airline carriers have lost more money than they have made since the two Wright brothers took off from Kitty Hawk in 1903. The overall market is so price sensitive that when one airline drops the price of their airfare, all the remaining airlines have to drop theirs. Although one segment of the market—the business traveler—is less sensitive to price, no single airline company can monopolize departure and arrival times, which are the main factors this segment uses to select a carrier.

Opening a restaurant may sound glamorous, but don't do it for the money. Restaurants are highly labor-intensive, and even if you solve this problem, obtain a perfect location, and luck out on selecting a menu that is preferred by many—it's a trendy business. Just when you think you have all your pots in a row and start to relax, you will probably see all your customers going next door to enjoy the latest "in" place.

Are you currently in any markets that match this type of profile? If the answer is yes, I recommend that you start thinking about how to phase out of them. It doesn't make much sense to work hard in markets where you can't make any money. And it certainly doesn't make sense to spend marketing dollars in them.

Currently Unprofitable Markets

Next let's look at a market that could be profitable, but is currently unprofitable because market participants are not exercising the right business strengths. An example could be the dry cleaning business. Ownership of dry cleaning companies seems to change every couple of years, probably because there hasn't been a change in technology in fifty years. The price for dry cleaning seems to increase each year and dry-cleaned garments may have a chemical smell. However, it seems that at least two companies have acquired the right business strengths. Morrisville Hangers has introduced a new cleaning method using liquid carbon dioxide that they claim will not only eliminate the chemical smell, but also trim long-term costs by eliminating the expense of adhering to governmental regulations regarding chemicals. Procter & Gamble is after the same market, but using a different tack. They offer an inexpensive dry cleaning product to use at home and claim there is no resulting chemical smell.

The question is: If you are in any markets that match this profile, do you have the business strengths to turn it into a profitable situation like Morrisville Hangers and Procter & Gamble are trying to do? If so, then this could be a great opportunity to build a brand with your marketing dollars. If not, don't waste your money.

Changes in Customers

Market profile three is one that was profitable in the past, but is not now due to changes in customers. Clayton M. Christensen's book *The Innovator's Dilemma*, which I referred to in Chapter One, contains several case histories of companies that lost sight of new customer demands. If your company is participating in this type of market, it could cause problems. Your management may insist on continuing marketing support, even though the market is no longer viable. This market or brand may have been responsible for the initial success of the business and for you to recommend that it be shut down could be a gutsy call. However, you only have so many marketing dollars and you want to spend them where you can reap the greatest reward.

Profitable Markets

That greatest reward usually comes from market profiles four and five. Profile number four is a market currently profitable to one or more market participants. You know money can be made here, so the first step is to be sure your have the right business strengths. The best way to do this is to review the five-step analysis of the customer, which is in the customer section of your Fact Book. This five-step analysis is covered in Chapter Four. You also want to critique what your competitors are doing. This information should be in the competitive section of your Fact Book.

Hopefully, you will not be up against powerhouse companies like a Cisco Systems or Home Depot. You want to become number one or two in *market share* in all markets where you are going to spend your marketing dollars. The definition of market share is your share of the total potential in a market. The total potential is the sum of annual sales in a market by all companies including your firm, plus potential customers that have not yet made a purchase. If the total potential adds up to $1,000,000 and your sales are $250,000, your market share is 25 percent. You may ask: How do I determine the total size of the market? It is an estimate and the estimate comes from many sources: your sales team, market research studies, government sources, searches on the Web, competitive analysis, online databases, etc. It's an estimate, but an important estimate, and the more accurate the better.

The importance of being a leader in market share is underlined by a marketing rule with the numbers 3 and 4. The rule was formulated by the consulting firm McKinsey & Company. The interpretation is that when a market matures, only the three companies with the largest market share will be making money and in order for the third largest company to be profitable, its market share has to be at least one fourth of the market leader's share. Jack Welch, CEO of General Electric, and considered by many to be the best manager in the world, will not stay in a market unless his brand is, or he believes it will become, number one or two in market share.

New Markets

The market where you should concentrate your marketing dollars is in new markets, once again, provided that the market offers profit potential and you can develop the right business strengths. New markets are your future. Without them, your portfolio of existing markets will eventually decline in profitability. They all do. The only question is how soon. Going back to market share, you want to maximize it during the early stages of a market when growth is the greatest. You want to become number one or two by the time the market matures because it is much more difficult to gain share when there is little growth. In a growth market, you can gain share and your competitors could still be gaining in sales. Most likely that will keep them happy and they will be less inclined to go after you. However, in a mature market the only way you can gain share is by taking business away from your competitors and that usually makes them fighting mad. If the market is too big for you to become a major player, you should consider a niche or segment strategy.

Market Characteristics That Influence Profit Potential

You may think the above is well and good, but are not sure how to critique your markets relative to profit potential. If that's the case, let me give you some help. Figure 3-1 lists thirty-eight characteristics that can influence whether a market can offer you good profit potential. An explanation of each is in Appendix B. It is not an all-inclusive list— just one to whet your thought process. You should go through this list, add ones I missed, and select three to ten that appear to have the greatest influence on whether your business can be profitable in a market. You can critique your markets using the selected characteristics to arrive at comparative scores.,

Figure 3-2 shows an example of how this can be done by using a hypothetical company, WML Company, in a hypothetical market, Market A. In the first column labeled Market Characteristic, insert the characteristics you have chosen. The first one for WML Company is pricing sensitivity. In the second column, Value, assign a value from 1 to 10 for each characteristic based on its status in a particular market. WML Company prefers a market insensitive to price and because Market A has

Figure 3-1. Thirty-eight market characteristics that can influence profit potential.

1. Pricing sensitivity	21. Promotion costs
2. Captive customers	22. Social attitudes
3. Customer concentration	23. Environmental attitudes
4. Economies of scale	24. Raw materials availability
5. Barriers to entry	25. Sales costs (% of sales)
6. Regulatory exposure	26. Distribution costs
7. Selling off the Internet	27. Customer relations costs
8. Promoting off the Internet	28. Service costs
9. Customer relations off the Internet	29. Demand cyclicity
10. Buying off the Internet	30. Demand seasonality
11. Foreign operations	31. Functional substitutions
12. Foreign investments	32. R&D costs (% of sales)
13. Opportunity to segment the market	33. Gross margins
14. Stage of the life cycle	34. Growth rate
15. Number of major competitors	35. Size of industry/segment
16. Level of technology	36. Need for capital
17. Value added (% of sales)	37. Aggressiveness of competition
18. Manufacturing costs (% of sales)	38. Trendiness
19. Investment intensity (% of sales)	
20. Inventory (% of sales)	

average sensitivity, they gave it a value of 5. If the market was insensitive to price, they would give this characteristic a value of 10. If it was very sensitive to price, they would give it a value of 1.

In the third column labeled Weight, assign each characteristic a weighting based on its relative importance to the other characteristics,

Figure 3-2. Analyzing market profit potential.

Market Characteristic	Value	Weight	Weighted Value
Pricing Sensitivity	5	10%	0.5
Aggressiveness of Competition	3	20%	0.6
Ability to sell off the internet	8	10%	0.8
Value Added	4	15%	0.6
Gross Margins	7	15%	1.1
Barriers to Entry	2	5%	0.1
Growth Rate	7	10%	0.7
Level of Technology	10	5%	0.5
Investment Intensity	5	5%	0.3
Raw Materials Availability	5	5%	0.3
Total Weighted Value		100%	5.4

with the total for all characteristics being 100 percent. WML Company believes pricing sensitivity is of average importance relative to the ten characteristics they have chosen, so they give it a weight of 10 percent. In the fourth column multiply column two by column three to arrive at each characteristic's weighted value. WML Company multiplied 5 (column two) by 10 percent (column three) to arrive at 0.5 for the weighted value of pricing sensitivity. The sum of column four provides a "total weighted value" of the market being critiqued. The total weighted value of Market A for WML Company is 5.4.

My interpretation of this total weighted value is shown in Figure 3-3. I have based this breakdown on my years of consulting experience, but I don't mean to imply that they are written in stone. Use your own judgment. You may also decide to evaluate your markets in a different manner than shown above. These figures emphasize the fact that you should not treat all markets the same way. If a market ranks low in profit potential, what are you doing in it? Market A is a loser for WML Com-

Figure 3-3. Interpretation of market scores for profit potential.

Market Value 8 to 10

Indicates extremely high opportunity to make money if you can obtain the necessary resources.

Market Value 6 to 8

Indicates a fair to good profit potential. You probably will not become a millionaire, but you should be able to pay the bills and then some.

Market Value 4 to 6

This may be a market you want to phase out of.

Market Value 1 to 4

Sell your assets in this market tomorrow.

pany, and in the real world, this type of situation would call for a phasing out of the market or a harvest strategy.

Where Should You Apply Maximum Marketing Pressure?

This chapter ends with an exam on where should you apply maximum marketing pressure. Suppose, as shown in Figure 3-4, that you have

Figure 3-4. Where to spend your operational dollars.

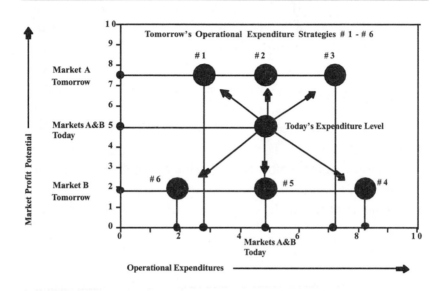

two markets, Market A and Market B. Last week while preparing your Fact Book, you decided that both markets currently rank about average in market profit potential. You inserted a dot for both on the *y* axis next to the value of 5. You considered your operational expenditures and resulting business strengths for both markets versus competition to also be about average. You inserted a dot for both on the *x* axis next to the value of 5. You then extended lines from the dots for each market and where they intersected, you inserted a big dot. Because the dots for both markets intersected at the same point, the two dots are on top of each other, at the intersection of 5 on the *y* axis and 5 on the *x* axis. It is labeled Today's Expenditure Level in the figure.

Imagine you are in a strategic planning session and you believe that the potential profit in Market A will dramatically increase during the next five years due to a change in customer needs. You set its new value at 7.5 on the *y* axis as shown in the figure and labeled Market A Tomorrow. The first question is, based on this change in profit potential for Market A, which strategy would you recommend?

If you chose strategy one, that indicates you plan to decrease operational expenditures. Insert a new dot for tomorrow on the x axis to the left of 5. Strategy one shows a dot at about 2.5. (If you drew a vertical line from tomorrow's dot at 2.5 on the x axis to where it intersects with the horizontal line drawn from the tomorrow's dot at 7.5 on the y axis, they would intersect where the dot labeled #1 is shown.) If you select strategy two, you are recommending no change in operational expenditures. (Leave the dot where it is on the x axis.) If you chose strategy three, you are recommending a major increase. (The dot on the x axis is at about 7.3)

I hope you picked number three. You want to apply the power where you have the most to gain. Strategy two may be appropriate (no change in operational expenditures) if you are unsure that the market profit potential is going to show an appreciable upward movement. Strategy number one does not make good business sense, but as you will see, it is too often mistakenly chosen.

The second question concerns Market B. In your strategic planning session you decide that there will be a dramatic decrease in the profit potential in Market B. You set the value for tomorrow at 2. What strategy do you recommend for this market—four, five, or six? Strategy four shows an increase in operational expenditures; strategy five no change; and strategy six a decrease.

I hope you chose number six. When the profit potential is going down in a market, you want to start decreasing operational expenditures and put these savings into markets with greater potential, including new markets. Sometimes management will want you to do just the opposite. For example, they might say, referring to a Market A situation, that the company is doing fine there. They could want you to pull back the company's operational expenditures in Market A and add those dollars to Market B's, where the company is not doing as well. You could not make a bigger mistake. The shaded area in Figure 3-5 illustrates the axis you want to be on in each of your markets. As market profit potential increases, you want to increase your operational expenditures, including marketing pressure, to gain market share. In markets declining in potential profitability, you want to pull back.

Figure 3-5. Ideal relationship between market profit potential and operational expenditures.

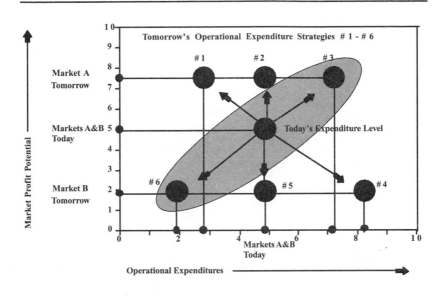

Follow the Money

To find the real culprits in a political investigation, they say you just have to follow the money. The same strategy applies to marketing. Follow the money. Spend your marketing dollars in markets where the profit potential is high. However, to make more money, you first have to spend more money. As shown in Figure 3-6, when you increase your operational expenditures to increase market share, sometimes referred to as *share penetration*, your current cash flow will not be sufficient to finance this type of strategy. You will probably have to buy more machinery, increase production time, buy more raw materials, hire and train new employees, and increase your marketing effort. You cannot do all this using the current cash flow from this market. Therefore, you have to borrow cash from some other market and this other market should be a Market B situation. Don't ever recommend a share penetration strategy to management without showing them where you will get the additional cash flow needed. Otherwise, they will say your plan is just wishful thinking.

Figure 3-6. Financing share penetration.

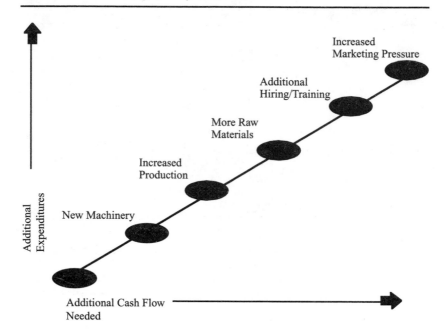

Chapter Four

Determining Who the Customers Are

and What They Want

Here are a few thumbnail sketches that illustrate why an analysis of who the customers are and what they want is so important:

- Five state colleges in Florida spent their entire recruitment budget on high school seniors until they discovered parents and high school guidance counselors have a greater impact on the choice of school.

- The male CEO of a women's contraceptive manufacturer allocated the entire promotional budget to doctors until a new female marketing director informed him that women make the brand decision.

- The American Cancer Society promoted sunscreen lotion to teenagers with the slogan "It saves lives" until they discovered the phrase was meaningless to their target audience. They successfully countered with, "Be more attractive in the sun."

• Levi Strauss & Company is closing half of their plants in North America because they didn't realize that cachet sells jeans not functionality.

Major companies like Procter & Gamble spend millions of dollars on market research to obtain the answer to who are the customers and what do they want. You too should spend money or your own time on market research. Let me take you through a five-step analysis that will help you, whether you hire an outside research firm to conduct the audit or do it yourself. This information belongs in the customer section of your Fact Book.

Five-Step Market Analysis

The first three steps define your target audience or anticipated heavy users. In other words, where you should be spending your marketing dollars. They are:

1. Segmenting the market

2. Establishing who participates in the purchasing process or buying decision

3. Determining the relative importance of the individuals involved in the purchasing process

The next two steps define your positioning statement. They are:

4. What features are sought

5. What features are delivered

Segmenting the Market

The first step is to segment the market. Segmenting the market means dividing it into sections that correspond to the different people involved in the purchasing process or buying decision. If there are different people involved in the purchasing process within each market, most likely they have different needs, wants, or benefits. You have to look at your markets by segments; otherwise you may deliver the wrong message to the wrong person. In segmenting your market, you may find it helpful to segment it in as many ways as possible and then go back to review each segmentation to determine which target audiences you can best serve.

If local hardware stores were to try to go after the Home Depot customer segment, who want large inventories to choose from at low prices, they would fail. Their target segment is the people who want good customer service. Likewise, Enterprise-Rent-A-Car didn't compete with Hertz and Avis head on in its climb to market leader. They went after the rental business at automobile repair garages—a market segment the giants had ignored.

You segment the market to determine the parts in which you want to concentrate for maximum profitability. That doesn't mean you turn down potential customers outside your niche. You just don't spend precious promotional dollars going after them.

If you are a consumer marketing company, you may segment by demographics. If you are dealing with industrial or business-to-business markets, you may segment either by Standard Industrial Classification (SIC), job descriptions, size of company, type of company, or some combination of these profiles. You can also use *psychographics*, which is the use of demographics to study and measure attitudes, values, lifestyles, and opinion.

After selecting the segment you can best serve, you then use the promotional vehicle that reaches the greatest concentration of your target audience. For example, you can purchase mailing lists based on demographic profiles, psychographic profiles, job descriptions, size of company, type of company, or SIC indexes. Most trade show promoters can provide SIC indexes or a list of the type of companies that attended past shows. Magazines have breakouts of their circulation by demographics, job descriptions, or SIC indexes.

When you segment by demographics you have such choices as age, education, income, sex, city size, county size, geographical location, nationality, and size of family to help you find the right market. Senior citizens have different needs and desires from baby boomers and the baby boomers don't know what they begot with Generation X. Generation Y customers are off on their own tangent. Levi Strauss & Company did not realize that Generation X males did not want to wear their fathers' jeans.

Although segmentation by SIC is a commonly used phrase, you don't actually segment by SIC. You segment by company and job description, then use SIC indexes as identification marks. These indexes are provided by the federal government. All United States industries are divided into two-digit classifications. For example, all businesses that are involved in electric and electronic equipment have a designated number of 26. The two-digit classifications are further segmented into three and four digits to reveal specific job descriptions within the two-digit classifications. If you are after a chemical engineer in the agricultural industry, that person has a four-digit number. These classifications are available from the United States Department of Commerce. You can also download the complete index from the Internet. Type in the keyword SIC or use a search engine to locate supplies. However, there are some problems using the SIC. Many corporations do not breakout their divisions, some of which may be involved in different markets. In these cases, you may get the SIC for just one or two of many markets in which the corporation is a participant.

There has been a considerable increase in the use of psychographic segmentation due to accumulating research that indicates strong relationships between peoples' lifestyles or personalities and their purchasing or shopping habits, the benefits that they seek in a product or service, and the message approach that is most effective. For example, would you use the same promotional strategies and tactics to market to former

Secretary of State Henry Kissinger as you would to NBC's weatherman Willard Scott?

In psychographics there are several techniques or classifications available. One is DISC, which enables you to classify people by one or more characteristics, each profile associated with distinctive sets of habits, attitudes, and traits. The D stands for dominant. (News commentator Chris Matthews?). I is for influence (MSNBC newscaster Brian Williams?). S is for security (NBC news commentator Jane Pauley?). C is for conformity (NBC newscaster Tom Brokaw?).

Another psychographic measure is VALS. VALS stands for values and lifestyles. A third is PRISM. PRISM divides the country into several categories based on the price of the homes or the condominiums. There is a specific descriptive category for each county of the United States. If you want more information on this subject, go to the Web and try one of the search engines using psychographics as the keyword.

USING SEGMENTATION

I will use two hypothetical companies to illustrate the use of segmentation as well as the four subsequent steps mentioned above. One of the hypothetical companies is LeanChem, which sells chemical compounds, and the other is a service company referred to as The Nerds. LeanChem sells chemical compounds mainly to medium-size companies in package sizes too small for larger competitors to handle. One possible segmentation could be based on potential customers' annual sales. For example, companies in markets that use their type of chemical compounds having annual sales between $250,000 and $1,000,000. This would be based on the assumption that companies with annual sales below $250,000 are too small to be profitable for LeanChem and companies with annual sales over $1,000,000 probably do not need small shipments.

LeanChem could then select the appropriate SIC indexes for company addresses. For direct mail and sales calls, the company would find a mailing house that could cross reference the SIC indexes with size of company. For trade show selection, they would have to base their decisions on SIC indexes regardless of company size. By the time this book is published, e-mail addresses will probably be available by type of company.

The Nerds is a computer support company that makes house calls when either a company's computers or peripherals are down. Like Lean-Chem, The Nerds probably would be better off concentrating on medium-size companies. Medium-size companies could be segmented further based on the number of digital machines a company has up and running. Having fifty clients averaging twenty machines would be more profitable than fifty averaging only five to ten. Because the company's customer base cuts across many industries, SIC indexes would probably not be helpful. However, analyzing demographic and psychographic characteristics may be advantageous if the company positioned itself in a style reflective of the company name. This type of positioning may appeal more to younger, computer-literate people with a Willard Scott personality rather than one like Henry Kissinger.

Purchasing Process or Buying Decision

After you have selected the segment that seems to offer the greatest potential, the next step is to determine who the people are involved in the buying decision or purchasing process. From this list you determine which ones should receive your promotional material. This type of information can be gathered by talking to your customers, reviewing sales call reports, searching online databases for articles about your customers, and visiting their Web sites.

You want to be sure to take into account all possibilities. There have been many cases where one or more of the individuals in the purchasing process have not been identified by companies. These companies kept making sales presentations, but nothing happened because they were talking to the wrong person or not to all of the key individuals.

Figure 4-1 shows a five-section matrix that will help you ascertain all the titles or job descriptions of individuals involved in the purchasing

Figure 4-1. Establishing who is in the purchasing process.

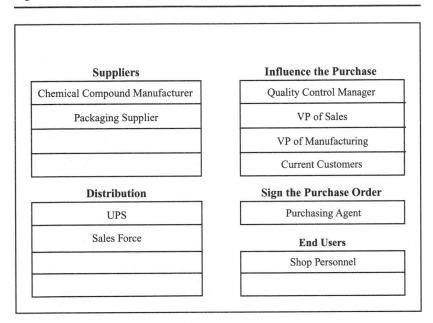

Suppliers	Influence the Purchase
Chemical Compound Manufacturer	Quality Control Manager
Packaging Supplier	VP of Sales
	VP of Manufacturing
	Current Customers

Distribution	Sign the Purchase Order
UPS	Purchasing Agent
Sales Force	**End Users**
	Shop Personnel

process. LeanChem's process is shown as an example. The five sections are:

1. Suppliers to the business, such as vendors of raw materials, and all business components outsourced to other businesses

2. Channels of distribution, such as a sales force, distributors, wholesalers, jobbers, and retailers

3. Individuals who sign the purchase order or write the check

4. Individuals who are the end users of what you are selling

5. Individuals who influence the sale, such as department heads, consultants, doctors, the press, and associations

Following is an explanation of each section.

SUPPLIERS TO THE BUSINESS

LeanChem has two major suppliers. One is the company that manufactures chemical compounds and the other is the company that supplies packaging material. There is no need for LeanChem to spend major promotional dollars on these suppliers, but it should let them know about any growth strategy. You always want your suppliers to believe you will be more important to them tomorrow than you are today. If instead of chemical compounds, LeanChem sold items such as toys and games, books, software, or fashionable clothes, promotion to suppliers would be more critical. In these instances, you want to be sure you are allocated a fair share of the "hot items" from manufacturers. When a craze hits, shoppers go to the stores they believe have the largest inventory.

Suppliers are a more important promotional factor to The Nerds than they are to LeanChem. When machines are under warranty, manufacturers only want approved vendors to fix them. If you cannot convince the manufacturers that your company is capable of handling these tasks, your positioning to customers is limited.

CHANNELS OF DISTRIBUTION

The second section of the figure contains the distribution chain. Lean-Chem's distribution chain is not complex because it sells direct, with the CEO being the only salesperson. Its shipping is done by UPS, which is a mainstay except for rare strikes. The Nerds also sell direct, but have a sales team consisting of twelve computer specialists. Even when you have your own sales team, motivating them is vital or their sales efforts will suffer. Ask the employees of a local drug store, clothing store, or restaurant how highly motivated they are to sell. If they are honest, they will probably say they are just watching the clock. Promotional activity becomes even more critical in the distribution chain when a company sells through distributors, jobbers, manufacturers reps, or retailers. If this is your situation, consider these companies or individuals as part of your own sales team. They should be involved in all of your planning, including the allocation of your marketing dollars and the design of your promotional material. They are in the field more than you and closer to the end users. They should be your eyes and ears in the marketplace. If you don't motivate them to do so, they will only talk and listen to themselves.

INDIVIDUALS WHO SIGN THE PURCHASE ORDER

The third process contains the job descriptions of individuals who sign the purchase order or write the checks. For LeanChem, like most companies that market industrial or business-to-business goods, it is usually the purchasing agent. For The Nerds, there is more variation. It could be the information technology (IT) manager, another department head, or even the end user. Promotional effort should be directed toward these individuals—the key question is how much? The ranking of importance of each individual in the purchasing process will be discussed in the next section of this chapter. For now, it is sufficient to say the ability to block a sale by the person signing the check varies greatly by market.

THE END USERS

The fourth section of the process contains the end users. For LeanChem, its end users are shop personnel, for The Nerds it is employees using computers. For The Nerds, employees in small companies could also be the ones who sign the checks. If this were true, they would become a major factor in the purchasing process.

When you are selling direct like these two companies, sufficient promotional effort can be easily applied to the end users. However, for companies that market through the trade, such as distributors, the question of how marketing dollars should be spent is not always easy to answer. In these cases, there are three basic ways to allocate your marketing dollars. The least expensive and the least effective way is to commit your dollars to the trade. It is the least expensive because there are fewer members in the trade than there are end users. It is the least effective because it won't build brand loyalty among the end users. If the trade leaves you, you have a serious problem. To allocate your dollars against the end users is more expensive and more effective. It is more expensive because you have more people to cover. It is more effective, because, if you do it right, you build brand loyalty. This will lessen the chance that the trade will drop you. The most expensive and most effective choice is to spend against both the trade and the end user.

Be careful if you are currently selling through the trade and are not spending marketing dollars on the end users. That normally is a short-term strategy. If you want to grow your business and not be dependent on outsiders, allocate funds to the end users as soon as you can afford to do so.

INDIVIDUALS WHO INFLUENCE THE SALE

The fifth section of the purchasing process contains the job descriptions of individuals who influence the purchase. Figure 4-1 shows four for LeanChem. They are: quality control manager; vice president of sales; vice president of manufacturing; and current customers. The quality control manager determines whether compounds offered for sale meet the company's standards. The vice president of sales has a say in the buying decision because she wants the ingredients of the company's products to have recognizable brand names she can promote in her sales presentations. The vice president of manufacturing is included because he wants to be sure the supplier will make deliveries on time.

The last category contains the current customers. They should be on the list for every company. The problem is, they are on very few. You have probably patronized a particular grocery store, restaurant, or drug store for years. Has anyone in these firms ever thanked you for being so loyal? Do they know your name? If AT&T thanked their customers for their business before the breakup, they probably would not have any competition today. Because they were so autocratic, their customers could hardly wait to jump ship. Conversely, when a company has thanked you for being so faithful, how many of your friends did you tell about the experience?

The value of cultivating current customers' goodwill is reinforced by research that indicates the most effective way to sell to industrial or business-to-business companies is by using testimonials. You must show a photograph of the customer and her name and address, otherwise the testimonial is not believable. To obtain customers' permission to identify themselves is usually difficult, so spending time to gain their goodwill is a wise investment.

The Nerds' list of influencers could include department heads not listed as the person signing the purchase order, such as IT, data processing, or operations manager; presidents of companies; and current customers.

Determining the Relative Importance of Individuals

After you have determined the individuals or job descriptions in the purchasing process, the next step is establishing priority in reaching them. Of all the individuals, who is normally the most important player? Who has the greatest impact on whether or not your brand is purchased? Who is normally number two? And so on. Once again, use research or your own sales experience to accomplish this task. This ranking determines how to allocate your marketing dollars. You don't want to repeat the mistake made by the five state colleges or the CEO of the contraceptive company. Budget first for the number one player. She gets the largest allocation. Next, you budget for the number two player. Keep going down the list until you deplete your total marketing budget.

For some brands, the people at the top of the priority listing could be doctors for drugs or consultants for computers. IBM says that the single most important player in the purchase of a mainframe computer is an independent computer consultant. It could be the actual purchaser, such as women for most, but not all, grocery items. Mom, and sometimes Dad, buys the cereal, but the children, the end users, are the number one players because they usually determine the brand.

Figure 4-2 illustrates the purchasing process priority for LeanChem. The CEO believes the vice president of manufacturing is the most critical roadblock for him to overcome to make the sale. The feature he offers is

Figure 4-2. Purchasing process priority list.

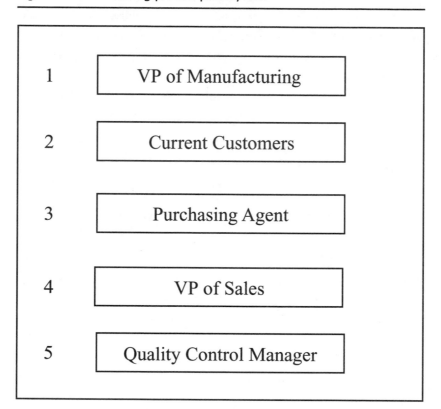

1	VP of Manufacturing
2	Current Customers
3	Purchasing Agent
4	VP of Sales
5	Quality Control Manager

delivery in small quantities, which ensures a saving on inventory costs. This is good news for a company, especially for the purchasing agent. However, the manufacturing head is more interested in being sure he has inventory when he needs it. The CEO has to convince manufacturing that he can deliver on time and is using the satisfaction of his current customers as the weapon. He lists current customers in the number two position. The purchasing agent is number three. Without her, no sale can be made. She enjoys the benefit of having saved the company money, thereby increasing her esteem, but manufacturing has to sign off before she can act.

The vice president of sales is number four. She would prefer a better-known brand name and voices opposition to unknown brands. But with the top three in his pocket, the CEO feels he can mollify her. The quality control manager is number five. He has to be satisfied that the compound meets company standards, but this is no problem for the CEO because he has the documents needed for approval.

For The Nerds, the priority could probably be:

1. IT or data processing managers

2. Sales force

3. Manufacturers of computers and peripherals

4. Current customers

5. Presidents of companies

The IT or data processing manager is usually The Nerds' primary contact within customer organizations. She is the one who calls in for help, approves the repair, and signs off for payment. The sales force is critical to repeat sales because if they don't perform, there will be no repeat sales. The Nerds must constantly promote themselves to the manufacturers of the equipment they repair in order to keep their status of "authorized repair dealer." Current customers are included in the priority list because so many companies complain they cannot find suppliers who know their equipment. Being able to merchandise their expansive knowledge, based on service contracts with current customers, is an effective tool to eliminate this sales objection. When such an objection is raised, the reply could be something like, "Why not call Sam at XYZ corporation. We handle fifty of his machines supplied by over ten different vendors." Presidents are listed because The Nerds primarily service small to medium-size companies where the president may be involved in everyday operations.

What Features Are Sought

This is the most difficult part of customer analysis. What does the customer really want? Sometimes common sense prevails over research. Research conducted by Ford indicated that people didn't want a second sliding door on minivans. Chrysler disagreed, concluding that all passenger cars and station wagons have four doors. They didn't do any research, they just went ahead and added the second sliding door. Now it is a standard feature.

Customers can be contradictory. According to an article by Gayle Sato Stodder in *Entrepreneur* magazine, we are dealing with a schizophrenic nation. She states, "They're healthy; they're indulgent. They're cynical; they're hopeful. They're having fun; they're working like maniacs. Are today's consumers nuts—or just trying to have it all?"[1] A gourmet takeout restaurant catering to the fitness-obsessed can't keep enough chocolate cake in inventory. A jewelry boutique owner states that she has customers who buy a pair of $45 silver earrings one week and a $15,000 strand of South Seas pearls the next. An owner of a high-end luggage shop points out, "That guy you don't like the looks of just might be the drummer for Mötley Crüe."

The reason I raise the fact that some research studies reveal customers respond one way when actually they feel another, or indicate customers act this way one moment and another the next, is to warn you about believing the results of any research study without first checking the validity of the study. Apply your own experience with customers and inject common sense. Research can be a valuable tool, but it is not an exact science.

Notwithstanding the above, features sought for the hypothetical LeanChem are illustrated in Figure 4-3. First insert in the matrix the various features offered by your brand as well as by the competition. Then have the various people involved select the feature most important to them. The ideal way to do this is to have a research company go out into the marketplace and ask potential customers. If you cannot afford to do this, use your best judgment.

Regardless of the brand, in practically all instances you will find a different ranking of features for each individual involved in the purchase process. This is critical information because you have to match up the

Figure 4-3. LeanChem features sought.

Features Sought	Rank of Features Sought by Individuals Involved in the Buying Decision				
	VP of Manu-facturing	Current Customers	Purchasing Agent	VP of Sales	Quality Control Manager
Company Standards					1
Brand Name				1	
Just-in-Time Delivery			1		
Adequate Inventory	1				
Appreciation for the Business		1			

features sought with the particular target audience. If LeanChem's promotional material to the vice president of manufacturing featured brand name or just-in-time delivery, it would be a wasted effort. All he is concerned with is adequate inventory.

When you ask people what they want or need, they will mention features such as adequate inventory. A feature describes what a brand will do. However, what they are really searching for are believable benefits—what an item will do for them. Therefore, knowing the feature, you determine the benefit. Then, when you design your promotional material, lead with the benefit and make it believable by supporting it with features.

Features sought by individuals in the purchase process for The Nerds are shown in Figure 4-4.

What Features Are Delivered

In this analysis potential buyers are asked to rank various companies on their ability to deliver on their features offered or promises made by

Figure 4–4. The Nerds features sought.

Individuals in Purchase Process	Feature Sought
IT Manager	Efficient repairs
Special Agents	Fun place to work
Manufacturers	Stay within warranty
Current Customers	Appreciation for the business
Presidents	Cost of repairs

using a form similar to a report card. They grade each company using either pluses and zeros, a scale of 1 to 10, or any other method that seems appropriate. Once again, the most accurate way to conduct this analysis is to use a research company, but if time or money is not available, do your own research or make your best guesstimate.

Knowing how you are perceived relative to features or promises offered enables you to fix what is not working in your marketing plan. Figure 4-5 illustrates this type of report card for LeanChem. Pluses and zeros are used for grading purposes. A double plus means potential customers perceive a company as doing an excellent job on delivering a particular feature. A single plus means an adequate performance and a zero means below average.

As shown on the figure, LeanChem is perceived as poor on delivering a brand name. This is because the company is small and relatively unknown. As the company grows and additional marketing dollars are spent, brand recognition should improve. The company receives just an adequate perception on just-in-time delivery and adequate inventory, once again due to its size and newness to the market. However, the CEO has an excellent relationship with his current customers and promotes

Figure 4–5. LeanChem features delivered.

| Features Sought | Customers' Perception of Companies' Ability to Deliver Features Sought | | | | |
	My Company	Competitor One	Competitor Two	Competitor Three	Competitor Four
Company Standards	++	+	++	+	0
Brand Name	0	+	++	++	+
Just-in-Time Delivery	+	+	0	0	0
Adequate Inventory	+	+	++	+	+
Appreciation for the Business	++	+	+	0	+

this fact in direct mail and brochures to help alleviate this marketing problem.

Competitor one is a medium-size company also offering minimum shipments, but with a better-known brand. This is the competitor Lean-Chem has to watch carefully because if they improve their quality and relationships with current customers they could be a major threat. Competitor two is the market leader, but does not offer minimum shipments. They will probably keep LeanChem from going outside of their niche. Competitors three and four are major firms, but without the marketing competence of competitor two.

The report card for The Nerds is shown without any competitive comparison in Figure 4-6. Leaving out competitive analysis is what many companies do. They just examine themselves. They don't look out the window. When you look at The Nerds' report card it doesn't look bad. However, if a competitor is getting double pluses on efficient repairs, appreciation for the business, and computers being operable, The Nerds could be heading for trouble in the future.

How to incorporate this five-step analysis into your marketing planning will be discussed in the next chapter.

Figure 4–6. The Nerds features delivered.

Feature Sought	Report Card
Efficient repairs	+
Fun place to work	+ +
Stay within warranty	+ +
Appreciation for the business	+
Computers being operable	+

Note

1. Gayle Sato Stodder, "Schizophrenic Nation," *Entrepreneur*, March 1999, p. 114.

Chapter Five

Aiming at the Right Target Using the Right Message

After you complete the customer analysis you should know:

1. Your target audience

2. Who is in the purchase process or making the buying decision

3. Their relative importance

4. What they want or need

5. How they perceive you

Knowing this information, start your marketing planning with the individuals or job descriptions that have priority in the buying decision (number three above).

Aim at the Right Target

You know their hot buttons (number four above), now the question is how to tell them you can deliver it. To make your selection, you should know their habits, such as are they reachable through your sales force, advertising, sales promotion, public relations, or some other form of marketing. You may have to use trial and error to determine whether your sales team can reach them. Either they will see you or not. The use of advertising and public relations depends on whether your target reads the appropriate print publications, watches television, or listens to radio broadcasts. Trade show attendance profiles will tell you whether this medium is viable. If you are thinking about using other types of promotion, you will have to do research or use industry knowledge to determine whether the vehicle is workable

As shown in Figure 5-1, first aim at the center of the bull's eye, which represents the group of individuals who are at the top of the buying decision list. If possible, you always want to use your most effective marketing tool to reach this group, which is a one-on-one sales presentation. If you think you may have trouble getting in the door, you

Figure 5-1. Targeting your potential customers in the buying decision.

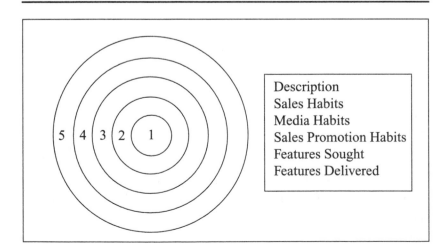

could begin your campaign with direct mail or advertising. If you do not have a sales team, or cannot reach this group in this manner, select one or more other promotional tools to use. After you develop your objectives, strategies, and tactics for this group, move on to number two. The number two group usually warrants contact with your sales team, too. After that contact, it probably is not cost-effective to use this tool. Then you kick in advertising, direct mail, trade shows, and other types of promotion.

If you want to get more for your marketing buck, don't use the same tools for each group year after year unless they are working extremely well. Try to come up with different types of promotion to add uniqueness to your plans. A common mistake marketing people and business owners make is that they say they can't use another industry's marketing tools in their particular industry. They say unfamiliar tools will only work for packaged goods, industrial goods, services, or whatever is not sold in their market. They keep using the same three or four promotional tools that have been around for years in their industry. As a consequence, there is no excitement in what they do. No surprises. And usually no big payoff.

You can use practically any type of promotion in any market. You may have to tweak a new technique here and there to make it work, but by so doing, you could be the first to use it to reach your customers. That's how to add promotional flair. This book covers a whole bag of promotional tools that have been used successfully by one or more companies. As you read these pages, keep asking yourself, can I use this one effectively, can I use that one, and so on.

Deliver the Right Benefit

In addition to selecting the right tools, you want to be sure you are delivering the right message. From your analysis of "features sought," you should know which feature is the most important to each person in the purchase process. Now you need to come up with the resulting benefit for these features because customers buy benefits supported by features, not features alone. To do this, write each of the appropriate features in one column, the resulting function in the next column, and the true benefit in the third.

Figure 5-2 illustrates some examples. If a company manufactures bronze bearings, the feature of what they are selling is the bronze the bearing is made of. Analysis of promotional material I have done in the past leads me to believe a company selling this type of product would most likely put this feature on the cover of their brochure. This would be a mistake. People don't buy bearings because they are bronze. The feature of a bronze bearing is that its harder surface creates less wear, friction, and heat. This message is stronger. This statement could go on the cover of the brochure in smaller type than the main message. It could be in the body copy of an ad. However, the main message should be what the product or service does for the buyer. That's the benefit. In this case, it is less down time and lower operational costs.

If you examine ten brochures, you will probably find at least nine

Figure 5-2. Hypothetical features, functions, and benefits.

Features	Functions	Benefits
1. Bronze bearing	1. Harder surface, less wear, less friction and heat	1. Less downtime, lower operating
2. Conditioner added to shampoo	2. Replaces natural oils removed by shampoo	2. Hair is shiny and more manageable right after shampooing
3. Torsion bar spring	3. Greater storage of energy per pound	3. Less weight and smaller space increase mileage and roominess in automobile
4. Aerobic exercise	4. Healthful and weight reducing	4. A more attractive person
5. American Express Platinum Card	5. Credit card with special privileges	5. When owner uses it, everyone thinks he/she is a big shot

that do not have a benefit on the cover. Some just show a picture of their plant and their company name. You wonder if they are trying to sell their plant. Others only show their name and list their products or services. This is a waste of the highest-read page of a brochure. The same mistake is made in advertising. Most headlines describe what the company does. Who cares? Tell me what you are going to do for me. Sometimes the benefit is buried in the body copy, which is better than leaving it out altogether. The problem is that only 20 percent of those reading a headline also read the body copy.

When you lead with a feature, the audience sometimes will make the translation to the benefit, but not always. Why gamble? One father didn't. He revised his young son's sales presentation so it opened with a benefit. During the snow and cold of a Minnesota winter the boy had been unsuccessful selling magazines door-to-door for a publishing company. He followed the publisher's recommended sales pitch of showing the covers of the three magazines he was responsible for and mentioning the lead article in each. Learning of his difficulty in making sales, his father gave him a few tips on marketing. The following week when a front door was opened after he rang the doorbell, the occupant of the house witnessed the boy's new presentation. He was still bundled up in winter clothes with traces of snow. But now his dog was sitting by his side as he made his revised opening statement, "Would you like an evening's enjoyment?" Within a month he was selling more magazines than any other salesperson in the state.

As previously mentioned, you need features to make a benefit believable. However, sometimes a marketer will present seemingly logical features for justifying a customer's purchase of a benefit. There is no logical business reason for paying $250 per year for an American Express Platinum Card. It has more features than ordinary credit cards, but their value doesn't come close to matching the platinum card's cost. It is a success because its owners believe everyone thinks they are a big shot when it is used. When they slam that card down on the counter, they are screaming, by implication, to everyone that can see the card, "Hey,

I've got a platinum card. You probably only have a green card. Obviously, I am more successful than you."

Even in professions like medicine, products are purchased based not on their features, but on benefits. A salesperson for a company that sells medical devices recently inserted the product into a patient's body. The doctor was standing by, but the salesperson did the actual insertion. In other words, the doctor purchased the machine based not on the features of the product, but on the ability of the salesperson to show him how to use it. Dell Computer is currently the number two and fastest growing computer-systems company worldwide. The reason is not that they have a superior product, but that they pioneered the build-to-order delivery system.

You can touch a product, a benefit you cannot. But do you buy a product because you can touch it or do you purchase it for what it can do for you? People don't buy homes based on whether or not the two by fours are straight. People don't discard their glasses and buy contact lenses to improve their vision. Even optometrists admit this. They wear them so they look more attractive. Saturn cars sell well because people love their customer relations.

In your planning, when looking out the window, when driving your car, keep asking yourself, "What can or will this brand do for our customers?" That's the key. You don't promote jeans by describing the fabric. You promote them by showing a model wearing them as she walks away from the camera. Develop messages that dynamically state the benefit of what you are selling in your marketing plans.

Chapter Six

Marketing Management

There are many questions among marketing personnel concerning their responsibilities, the relationship between their jobs and other departments in their companies, and the best way to set up a marketing department. This chapter provides information to help answer these questions.

In the past some companies had one individual who had both the responsibility and the authority for sales, advertising, sales promotion, public relations, customer service, and new product development. From a marketing person's viewpoint this was the ideal situation, because if you are responsible for something, you want to have the authority to run the operation the way you see fit. With one person as head of the whole marketing operation, coordination between the various marketing functions was good. There was also active coordination between marketing and other business functions, such as engineering, manufacturing, and processing. The title for this position usually was vice president of marketing.

It is a shame that many companies have gotten away from this form of marketing management. Various reasons are given, with most of them based on the belief that sales and the other remaining parts of marketing should be separated. The main rationale given is that selling is one area of expertise and all the other parts of marketing another; they can't be combined. Hence the phrase, sales and marketing. In many companies no one sees the sales plan except sales personnel and no one sees the other marketing component plans except those who write them. As mentioned in the first chapter, no company can be effective in marketing unless they get all six components—the sales plan, the marketing communications plan, the brand plan, the research plan, the customer service plan, and the Internet plan—working together.

To work together, you have to break down the fiefdoms within marketing. All six components should be developed together and their plans recorded in one place—the marketing plan. How else will you know how to reach a particular prospect? Whether you should use a sales presentation or an ad, a trade show or a brochure, an ad first and then a sales presentation, a trade show first and then a sales presentation, and on and on. This coordination is not happening in many companies since the demise of the vice president of marketing position.

Following is a discussion of the most prevalent forms of marketing management used today. Hopefully, you can coordinate one of these forms of management or a derivative into a marketing team.

The Product or Brand Manager

Many years ago two of the major consumer packaged-goods companies, Procter & Gamble and General Foods, concluded that because they were multiple product companies they should separate by brand the various marketing functions, such as sales, promotion, and new product development. Fearful that some of their brands would be lost in the shuffle and not receive the individual attention needed, they created the position of brand manager. Brand managers have authority over just one person—their assistant. They have complete control in only one area—promotion. Yet the brand manager is responsible for obtaining a profit for the brand. Through the sheer power of persuasion, the brand manager has to get all other components of marketing, as well as all other departments within the company, to work together on the execution of the marketing plan.

Brand management works at Procter & Gamble and General Foods because they hire only outstanding students right out of college so they can train them in their own methodology. They get them, too, because this position is one of the most sought after jobs in marketing. They hire individuals who have excellent communications skills and have the ability to persuade others to follow their recommendations.

Marketing departments in so many other companies are ineffectual because they copy the brand management concept from Procter & Gamble and General Foods, but don't hire the right type of people and don't train them. They just pull people from sales or advertising on a Friday and tell them that on Monday they have full responsibility, but none of the authority, for the brand. They sometimes change their titles from brand manager to product manager, but usually no help is forthcoming for making the transition from being knowledgeable about one component of marketing to being knowledgeable about all components.

Before a company sets up a brand management structure it should be sure that this is the best of all possible worlds. If it is, then management should be sure to hire an individual with the right type of qualifications, provide sufficient training, and set up clearly established areas of responsibilities and lines of communications between the brand manager and the various departments.

The Marketing or Market Manager

The marketing or market manager's role is very similar to that of the product, service, or brand manager except that the marketing manager's efforts are devoted to one or more products within one or more market segments. A marketing or market manager is normally hired when a company has many similar or closely related products or services that are sold in different markets. If this is your role in the company, like the brand manager, you are responsible for the success of the brands. Once again, you do not normally have direct line authority for all the various functions required to get the job completed.

The Marketing Coordinator

My recommendation for marketing management is that for each market there should be one person responsible for presenting the marketing plan to top management once a year. If your markets are relatively small, one person can handle more than one market. This person's title can be product manager, service manager, brand manager, or marketing coordinator. My preference is marketing coordinator.

After the marketing plan is approved, the marketing coordinator should have the authority to make most of the day-to-day operating decisions, including resubmitting the marketing plan when it is off target. The marketing coordinator does not write the plan. He or she directs and coordinates the input from individuals working within the six components of marketing. The marketing manager should have experience that includes some time spent within each of these functional areas. The marketing coordinator should excel in communication skills and have a persuasive personality. The marketing coordinator also needs an appropriate line of communication directly to the field to be sure that all aspects of the plan are quickly executed. The marketing coordinator's tasks should include the following:

1. Coordinate the completion of the marketing plan.

2. Establish measurements and controls.

3. Communicate the plan to the entire company.

4. Create and maintain enthusiasm for the plan.

5. Prepare a midyear report to management, as well as any necessary revisions.

The marketing decision areas where the marketing coordinator should have primary responsibility are:

1. Product/service

2. Packaging

3. Advertising

4. Communications research

5. Sales promotion

The marketing coordinator's tasks and decisions should influence the behavior and activities of most other departments within the company, including engineering, processing, manufacturing, research and development, marketing research, sales and customer service, finance and accounting, data management, Internet, and legal.

The marketing coordinator's interactions with engineering or processing are primarily interpretive. The coordinator conveys the needs of the market to these departments and monitors the product or service to be sure that changes in function, quality, and design are favorable. The marketing coordinator is the source of information about past and anticipated sales volume, which is used for developing production and manpower schedules. The marketing coordinator should balance market needs against cost when recommending inventory levels and should continually share information on brand performance in the marketplace.

In addition to suggesting market needs and brand concepts to research and development (R&D), the marketing coordinator also evaluates ideas from the viewpoint of market needs. Without close communication between marketing and R&D, the successful new brand development rate will be even lower than the pitiful national average of 10 to 30 percent. The marketing coordinator continually uses market research to measure market needs and the satisfaction of those needs by the company's brand as well as by the competition.

In dealing with public relations and customer service, the marketing coordinator serves as a source of information about the product or service line. For public relations he emphasizes that their activity should reinforce the image of the brand. The marketing coordinator can help customer service teams learn the functions of the brand.

When dealing with the sales force, the marketing coordinator is responsible for convincing them to execute the sales portion of the marketing plan, concentrating on profit rather than sales volume, and the long term rather than the short term. Therefore, they need to know the profitability of the various brands, long-run trends, threats and opportunities, customer and segment types, and constant market analysis.

The marketing coordinator's relationship with the Internet functional area should be of an informative nature. The marketing coordinator ensures that their activities are compatible with the offline brand personality.

The marketing coordinator plays a major role in obtaining the necessary financial support for the marketing plan from the finance and accounting departments. He should develop a thorough knowledge of the profit-and-loss statement, including a concern for net as well as gross profit. He should be on the lookout for arbitrary assignments of administrative or staff charges to the brand. Ideally, the marketing coordinator has the right to sign off on all administrative charges. That means that he can reject, for example, an assigned cost of $20,000 from a staff department. Of course, if he rejects the charge, the service is not provided.

All advertising and sales promotion activities should be cleared by the marketing coordinator during their developmental stages to prevent wasted time and expenditures. She should remember that the company's legal department is friend, not foe. As an individual, she can be prosecuted for misleading and false advertising claims and be fined or imprisoned, or both. It's not worth the gamble, so always check everything with the legal department.

The marketing coordinator should be the main contact with all marketing consultants employed by the company. This subject will be discussed next, but first you may be interested in knowing what top management usually considers the basic problems with marketing personnel:

1. They fail to provide sufficient factual information and they make unsound marketing decisions.

2. They do not understand the broad implications of marketing, especially relative to return on investment, strategic or long-range planning, financial implications, and manufacturing.

3. They spend too much money on advertising, considering that it is not as exact a science as finance and manufacturing.

How to resolve each of these three problem areas is discussed in different parts of this book. Parts One and Two, plus Chapter Nine on the product/service plan, address problem areas one and two. Chapter Ten, on advertising, and Chapter Eighteen, on research, address problem area three.

Conversely, you may enjoy learning the most commonly voiced complaints of marketing personnel about the people in top management:

1. They lack understanding of the marketing function, especially advertising.

2. They fail to explain the company's long-range goals and financial objectives.

3. They consider themselves advertising experts.

Relative to number one, it is up to you to educate them on the subject. Relative to number two, take the initiative and come up with your own long-range goals and financial objectives and present them to management for approval. If you do so, they will be impressed. The third item will always be a problem for you, but getting your creative strategy approved by management before you start on your ads will be a big help. This procedure is discussed in Chapter Ten.

Using Consultants

M arketing consultants can be helpful in setting up and running your marketing program if you use them in the right way. With the exception of the preparation of creative material, such as ads and brochures, you do not want a consultant to prepare anything in its entirety. This recommendation will probably get many consultants upset, but if you have a consultant write a plan, whose plan is it? It certainly isn't your marketing team's. Consequently, the internal endorsement of the plan will probably be weak. Use a consultant to educate you on the advantages and disadvantages of various marketing concepts and strategies. Have her help you develop your plans and programs, but make it a joint effort. No outsider should know your business better than you do. Take a consultant's advice, but be sure your marketing team's input is clearly evident.

There are several different types of consultants within the sphere of management and marketing. There are consultants on management and there are ones that can help you with your complete marketing program. They are usually referred to as *marketing consultants*. There are also sales management consultants, marketing communications consultants, advertising agencies, public relations agencies, sales promotion agencies, media buying services, and research companies.

Because your relationship with the consultants who prepare your advertising is ongoing and more complex than with the other types of consultants, they will be examined in detail here. You have a choice of either a marketing communications agency or an advertising agency. The advantage of a marketing communications agency is that they are responsible for all parts of your marketing communications, such as advertising and sales promotion, which include direct mail and public relations. The resulting benefit should be that you avoid the infighting for marketing dollars that you have when you use separate agencies for advertising, sales promotion, and public relations. The problem with many marketing communications agencies is that they do not have experts in each of these three fields. They may say they do, but they don't. Many advertising agencies bill themselves as marketing communications agencies. That's fine, as long as they know what they are doing in each of these areas. You want to use consultants who are truly experts in a specific field. For example, you don't want an art director who has been doing television storyboards for the last ten years designing your brochure or direct mail piece. If you find a consulting firm that can dramatically do it all, that's great. If not, seek out the individual specialists.

Regardless of what type of advertising consulting company you plan to select or are currently using, the following are areas that deserve special attention.

Selecting or Reviewing Your Current Advertising Consulting Firm

If you are looking for a new advertising agency, there is no precise method of compiling a list of potential agencies. Here are a few suggestions. First, analyze the advertising you see. When you notice what you consider an extremely effective campaign, something that really gets you excited, call the advertiser and ask for the name of its agency. Next, call the agency president and ask if he or she would be interested in discussing your future advertising plans.

Second, discuss your situation with various media representatives. Ask if they are familiar with any advertising agencies that are doing excellent work. Media people are anxious to help clients locate good agencies because it makes their work easier. A happy client makes a happy media representative. Third, go to your local advertising club. In some cities, the advertising club offers a good representation of the better advertising consultants. In others, it is primarily a concentration of advertising suppliers looking for sales prospects. You never know until you go to a couple of meetings.

If none of the above work, you'll have to send out letters of inquiry to all the advertising agencies in your vicinity. Send each a letter telling about your company, possibly including one or two of your major marketing problems. Ask if the agency is interested in discussing a possible relationship. From subsequent telephone and written communications, pare the initial list down to three to five for further discussion. At this point, you should either invite them to your office or set up appointments in their offices. Five items should be discussed: management, account service, media department, creative team, and compensation. These are discussed below. If you are using an advertising agency, you can use these items as the basis of a review of your current operation.

Advertising Agency Management

Managing an advertising agency is difficult. There are two distinctly different types of people employed by an agency and they are not always compatible. The type that is not unlike people you find in other types of companies is found in the account, media, and research groups. The account group consists of individuals who handle your account on a daily basis. They are the ones with broad marketing experience and are the liaison between you and the agency. The media group places your advertising in the various media and the research group handles your communications research.

Then there is the creative group—the copywriters and art directors who design your advertising. They are not like people you find in other types of companies. They tend to resist organization, conventional dress, and higher authority. Their lifestyle, in itself, is not the problem for agency management. In fact, sometimes the most unconventional creative people create the best work. What can be a problem for management is putting these two seemingly incompatible groups together in a structure where one does not dominate the other and neither loses its identity or contribution. It's not easy.

If the creative group dominates, and it does in many agencies, you usually find weak account, media, and research teams. In this situation, it is not uncommon for a creative person to show an ad to the account executive and for the account executive to state that it's the wrong approach. The creative person ignores this comment and instructs the account executive to show the client the ad and return immediately so production can begin. The account executive, possibly afraid of losing his or her job, shows the client the ad, stating that it's perfect for the current marketing situation. Many clients, not having the benefit of previous advertising experience and assuming that what is presented has the approval of all the professionals at the agency, will approve the ad.

Conversely an agency can be dominated by the account people. Excellent advertising campaigns can be vetoed by the account executive because of politics or a lack of imagination before the client ever gets the opportunity to see the ads.

Ask the president of each advertising agency you are interviewing how disagreement between the creative and the account groups over whether creative work should be presented to the client is handled. I would be wary of any agency that did not have a specific plan.

Account Service

The marketing expertise of an advertising agency can be invaluable to a client. The marketing people in an advertising agency are called account executives, account supervisors, and management supervisors. The account executives report to the account supervisors, who in turn report to the management supervisors.

Preferably, the account people should have MBAs. There is no comparison between business courses offered in undergraduate schools and those in master's programs, either in content or in the qualifications of the professors. A considerable amount of the material presented in a good graduate school can be used immediately in the day-to-day operations of a business. Many of the larger advertising agencies will no longer hire an account executive without an MBA.

Look for account people who have had experience solving marketing problems similar to yours. This does not necessarily mean that they should have past experience in your industry. Sometimes it is better that they don't. Too much familiarity can lead to stagnation. What it does mean is that if you are number one in market share in the industry, look for an account group that has handled another client that was the leader. If you are number two in share, look for experience in handling another number two. Products and services in the same competitive position, regardless of the industry, have similar natural marketing strategies. That's the benefit of working with agency people—they have marketing experience in executing strategies in other markets that can be right on target for your business. A good account team can also provide a much broader range of marketing activities than you would ever be able to obtain internally. No matter how hard you try, after years with a particular corporation, you develop tunnel vision. It's up to your account team to constantly broaden your perspective.

Liaison between your corporation and the agency is another responsibility of the account people. You should be able to discuss all your marketing problems with them, and they should get you the right help from within the agency. If you are having problems with other people within the agency, it is the account group that you go to for clarification and corrective action.

For these reasons, there has to be the right chemistry between you and the account group. Don't select an agency that offers an account group you don't feel comfortable with. You can usually tell when you first meet people if there is going to be a personality conflict. If you think there is, stay away from those people.

Your account group is also responsible for providing agency assistance in the development of your marketing plan. The account group helps determine your marketing strategies and plans and provides you with the services of all the other agency departments. For example, the media department should help prepare your media strategy, the creative group the creative strategy, and the production people your production budget.

Media

The media department of an agency is responsible for the development and execution of your media strategy and plan. These are discussed in Chapter Ten. The media function has become much more complex in recent years. One of the reasons is segmentation. Radio stations are constantly developing new formats to gain a niche in the listening audience. There are all-talk, all-jazz, and many other unique styles. A station may be folk music today and Latin music tomorrow. There is also the division between AM and FM. In the Los Angeles region alone, there are over 30 AM and 40 FM stations.

Magazine and newspaper publishers have also been forced to appeal to specific groups within the reading audience in order to deliver a target audience. There are magazines for every interest group, from organic gardeners to the Internet. Not only do the big daily newspapers publish regional editions to compete with the growth of the suburban papers, they've developed special sections on such subjects as science, the Web, cooking, travel, gardening, and health.

Buying time on the radio, or space in a magazine or newspaper is complicated today, but it may be easy compared to buying television advertising. In the past, you basically had the three major networks. Now you have four networks, super stations, cable, and satellite. It is becoming increasingly difficult to decide where you will get the best return for your advertising dollar.

When reviewing various agencies, ask to meet the media people who will be working on your account. Sadly, some still buy time and space depending on who bought them lunch, dinner, or drinks the previous day. But most media people do not operate this way, and it's best to avoid those who do. You should ask the media people about the innovative media plans they have developed for other clients. Also ask about their accessibility to computer data banks and their ability to program for the optimum media schedule for your account.

Don't overlook the importance of the media department. You can have a great creative campaign, but if it is being seen by the wrong people or with insufficient frequency, what good is it? Also, a sharp media buyer with experience is able to buy media time and space at rates lower than those shown on the rate cards. With the cost of media constantly increasing, you need all the experience and ingenuity you can get just to stay even.

Media Buying Services

If you have a relatively large advertising budget, there is a variation of an agency media department that you should check out. It's called a media buying service and all they do is buy media for clients. They can usually get better buys than an agency media department. The reason is that the employees usually have been buying media for several years. This is not the case in most agency media departments because this department is usually a training ground for agency employees. New employees are assigned to the media department, and if they do well there, they switch to their original preference, such as account service. Consequently, the experience of many media department employees can be limited.

Creative Group

The creative group, more than any other group in the agency, can make or break your advertising campaign. These people have the most influence over whether you get a dull campaign or one that is memorable. Never select an agency until you meet the creative team that will work on your account. Don't buy the common line: "We have many fantastic copywriters and art directors, and you'll get the best." Ask who they will be and look at their work. If you're not enthusiastic about what you see, then don't use that agency.

You should also make it clear that you only want to see creative work done by employees still with the agency. Agency employees, especially the creative staff, change jobs frequently. If you're not careful, you might select an agency on the basis of creative work done by people no longer with the firm.

Compensation

There are basically three factors that influence the amount of money an advertising agency should be paid. First is the number of ads that have to be prepared relative to the total budget. Obviously, it costs an agency more in time and overhead expenses to prepare ten ads for a $500,000 budget than to prepare five ads. This is one of the reasons that industrial advertisers generally have to pay their agencies a greater percentage of the total budget than consumer advertisers. Media costs for industrial trade publications are much lower than for consumer magazines. This means more insertions per media dollar, which in turn means a greater number of ads. Industrial advertisers also usually have a greater diversity of products or services. Once again, this means a larger number of ads.

The second determining factor is the number of agency services the client uses. A request for "full service" means the client is using the services of the account team, the creative group, the media department, the production department, and the traffic department. The traffic department is responsible for sending your creative material to the various media. These five services are normally provided if a client is paying on the standard commission basis, as discussed later.

If you do not use the agency's media department, you can lower your payments to the agency by 25 to 33 percent. Some clients use just the creative services; others use just the account group and the creative services. In these situations, clients pay the agencies less money, but, of course, they have to find somebody else to do the work the agency does not do.

The third factor that influences agency compensation is the number of approval levels that are required within the client's organization. In some corporations, only one person has to approve the agency's copy, layout, mechanicals, negatives, and proofs. (A mechanical is a pasteup of an ad's components—a step desktop publishing usually eliminates today.) In others, there can be as many as three or four approval levels. For example, the agency may have to present first to the advertising manager, then come back and present to the director of marketing. A third or fourth meeting may be necessary for discussion with top management. Under these conditions, more agency time is required. With time being more critical to an agency than for other types of companies—its complete inventory walks out the door each night and returns the next morning—you will have to pay the agency considerably more for this type of approval scenario.

There are three primary methods of compensating an agency: commission, retainer or fee, and cost-plus. With the commission system, the agency receives a certain percentage of the media budget. The amount was originally set at 15 percent, but today's national average is for consumer advertisers to pay 14 percent and industrial advertisers 21 percent. Most media give agencies a 15 percent discount off their rate cards for time or space. This is called *commissionable media*. What this means is that if the cost of an ad is $1,000, the agency is charged only $850. If a client hires an agency on the 15 percent commission basis, the agency bills the client $1,000 and sends a check to the advertising medium for $850. If the client is on a 20 percent commission basis, the agency bills the client $1,062 and pays the medium $850. The reason the amount is $1,062 rather than $1,050 is that agencies always take their commissions on the gross amount, not the net. This gross versus net billing will be discussed later.

This does not mean that agencies are the only ones that can receive discounts from advertising media. In years past it did, but this is no longer true. Today, it is illegal for any advertising medium to pay agency commissions to agencies and refuse to give the same discount to the advertiser.

When an agency is on a retainer or fee basis, it receives a set amount of money each month. It then returns to the client all commissions paid by the media. For example, if a medium gives the agency a 15 percent discount on a $1,000 ad, the agency bills the client only $850. Some clients are on a combination of commission and retainer or fee. This happens when the agency cannot make a sufficient profit on just the commissions, which sometimes occurs with industrial accounts or clients with small media budgets. Most clients are surprised that many agencies prefer the retainer or fee compensation system rather than the commission basis. The reason is that it gives the agency a known amount of revenue each month. It can be difficult to operate an agency with all accounts on the commission system because of the erratic cash flow. Agencies on the commission system can bill their clients only when the advertising runs. This can result in such wide swings as $500,000 in revenues one month and only $100,000 the next.

There are agencies, though, that still prefer the commission basis. The rationale is that they should be rewarded when they do good work. If they do good work, the client will increase the budget and they will then receive more money. One advertiser increased its media budget from $300,000 to $3 million within two years because the results were so spectacular. If the agency had been on the commission basis, its revenues would have increased 1,000 percent. If it had been on a retainer, at least theoretically, its revenue increase would have been zero.

The third and newest way to pay an agency is on a cost-plus basis. The agency adds up all its expenses, including rent, taxes, salaries, utilities, and other operating costs. Then you are billed for your share of the agency's total expenditures plus a predetermined profit.

When determining how to compensate your agency, ask them which method they prefer. If they opt for the commission basis and you have no problem with that, let it be commissions. If you think they will inflate budget requests on commissions, then ask for their second choice. The important point is to select a means of payment that is acceptable to both client and agency.

Regardless of whether the client is on a commission system, retainer or fee basis, or cost-plus, the agency will also bill the advertiser costs plus agency commission for production and out-of-pocket expenditures. Except for advertisers with very small budgets, the services of the account group are included in the commission system or retainer and not in the production costs. This is also usually true for the copywriter. However, most agencies include the art director's time in the production invoice. If an art director spends three hours preparing layouts for an ad and is billed out at $100 an hour, the client receives a bill for $300.

In addition to the costs of the art director, the agency will bill the client for all out-of-pocket expenses such as typography, artwork, photography, engravings, negatives, and proofs. The agency will also charge a commission on the out-of-pocket expenses, usually 17.65 percent. The reason for such an odd figure is that if agencies charged 15 percent on out-of-pocket expenditures, which is a net figure, they would not be receiving the same rate of return as they do on media, where they apply their commission on the gross amount. For example, on an ad with a media cost of $1,000, the agency makes 15 percent on the gross or $150. However, an agency's actual out-of-pocket expense of $850 is a net figure, therefore, you need a commission rate of 17.65 percent to earn $150 in commissions.

On production bills, you should demand details on all expenditures, including duplicate invoices from all suppliers. If there is a $500 photography charge, a duplicate copy of the invoice from the photographer in the amount of $500 should be attached to the bill. Clients that allow agencies to send them summary billing, such as $3,000 for copy, layout, mechanical time, and artwork, are offering the agency the opportunity to take a greater markup. It may be the rare agency that takes advantage of such an opportunity, but requiring itemized bills protects you against such agencies.

Making the Selection

Review the five factors (management, account group, media department, creative team, and system of compensation) of three to five agencies, then you should be in a good position to select the one that is best for you.

Be careful about requesting speculative presentations. First, it's expensive for the agencies, and the best ones usually will not participate. Second, the agencies don't know enough about your business at this point to advise you. If you buy their recommendations and they don't know if what they are saying is really right, then the one who suffers is you. Third, when agencies are asked to make speculative presentations, they sometimes hire creative talent from the outside. What they present may be spectacular, but after the agency gets the account, you may never see this creative talent again.

Base your selection on the agency people you meet—the people who will be working on your account. You can tell if they know what they are doing. Pick the best group—that should be your agency.

The Client-Agency Relationship

Once you have selected an agency, you should make everything it needs available to it. You have probably heard it before, but it's true—a client-agency relationship is like a marriage. If you start withholding information from each other, if you are not credible to each other, a divorce will be in the offing.

An example of how *not* to treat your agency comes from a person who was actually trying to show the disadvantage of in-house agencies. He said that whenever he had a critical deadline, it was difficult to make his own in-house creative director work over the weekend. Here was a person he had lunch with two or three times a week; on the weekends, their families even socialized together. How could he ask him to spend Saturday and Sunday in the office? He concluded that if he had an agency, he would just pick up the phone, call the agency, and tell the people there that if he didn't have the ad by Monday morning, he would find another agency.

No wonder he had an in-house agency. Probably no respectable agency would work for him. Antics like this destroy productive work between client and agency. Reward your agency when it does good work, and criticize it when it is sloppy or ineffectual. Many clients have a formal rating procedure that they use with their agencies. Some companies that use several agencies subject them to extensive performance reviews each year. If any of the agencies comes in last two years in a row, the company has the prerogative of firing it. Actually, most agencies prefer this type of review to sporadic, nonproductive criticism. Figure 6-1 shows an agency rating format that you can adapt to your own particular needs.

Plan with Hockey Sticks

I want to close this chapter and the first two parts of the book with my hockey stick analogy. The purpose of the hockey sticks is to run your business as if you were playing the game. Whether you ever get on the ice is academic. If you are the only employee in your company, go out and buy six hockey sticks for yourself. You will be the whole team. If you have six employees, you have one complete line. Buy one for each employee. If you have more than six employees, you have more than one line. Get them all a stick. The puck is your plan, the ice is the market, and the opposing team is competition. The name of the game is to get your puck into the opponent's net to complete the execution of your plan. As you move the puck down the market, opponents are going to try to take it away. Maybe it's a new promotional campaign. Maybe it's a new product or service. When this happens, you want to keep passing the puck to other employees or your consultants. Maybe you pass it to

Figure 6-1. Agency evaluation form.

Evaluation   _____
Position   _____
Date   _____

I.   Overall Performance

	5	4	3	2	1
A. Marketing					
General Knowledge					
Product Knowledge					
Strategy					
Plans					
B. Creative					
Development					
Execution					
Scheduling					
C. Media Plan					
General Knowledge					
Specific Product Area					
Development of Plan					
Execution of Plan					
Budget Control					

D.   Others

II.   Personnel Performance   (rating 5-1)

	Account Group	Copy Group	Media Group	Market Research	Other
Imaginative	_____	_____	_____	_____	_____
Takes initiative	_____	_____	_____	_____	_____
Able to communicate	_____	_____	_____	_____	_____
Cost-efficient	_____	_____	_____	_____	_____
Reliable	_____	_____	_____	_____	_____
Cooperative	_____	_____	_____	_____	_____
Professional	_____	_____	_____	_____	_____

III.   Strengths and Weaknesses: _____
_____

IV.   Recommendations for Improvement: _____
_____

marketing communications, maybe to R&D, or to sales. Maybe you pass to your advertising agency. If you keep passing the puck from one player to another, your whole team is involved in beating the opponents and getting the puck into their net.

The mistake many companies make is that although they have enough players for a team with one or more lines, they each skate down the market in their own groups or by themselves. They could all be centers or wings. Maybe a bunch of goalies. The sales team does their sales plan and doesn't show it to anyone outside of sales. The advertising manager does her plan and doesn't show it to sales promotion. The sales promotion manager does his plan and doesn't show it to advertising. Neither shows it to sales. Meanwhile, management is up in their ivory tower wondering what color the uniforms should be. When they finally decide to pass the puck, it takes days, sometimes weeks, to reach the other player. Meanwhile your whole team should be in front of their net.

When you go to a bank for a mortgage, you usually talk to a person who only does mortgages. If you want to talk to someone about investments, trusts, or checking accounts, you have to make separate appointments with different individuals for each bank offering. No passing the puck here. It's no wonder the primary reason for selecting a bank is location.

A company that has passed the puck is Compaq Computer Corporation. A member of each department was involved in the planning team from concept to marketplace. Compaq became a member of the Fortune 500 faster than any company in history. Their growth has slowed in recent months, most likely because they lost the puck.

As your company keeps growing in size, keep playing the game. According to research studies, more companies fail at the $5,000,000 sales level than at any other. The reason is that management becomes out of touch with the market, and fail to talk with their employees who are out in the field every day.

In summary, start your planning with the preparation of your Fact Book. Then divide your business into markets. For each, develop a *strategic plan*, followed by a *business plan*. Then go on to your *marketing plan* for each market. And don't forget to buy the hockey sticks.

PART THREE

Developing Your Brand Personality

Chapter Seven

Creative Positioning for Your Brand

Effective *positioning* of your brand—ideally one that is unique, memorable, desirable, and believable—is a critical factor in determining whether you can develop an effective marketing campaign. Positioning refers to how you are perceived by potential and current customers based on the various strategies you execute. You could be perceived as having high-quality merchandise like Liz Claiborne or great customer service like Nordstrom. Or your business could be perceived as being small and inexperienced.

Due to the importance of how you are positioned, there are two statements you should write. One is the *positioning statement* and the other the *statement of position*. The positioning statement states how you would like your business or brand to be perceived by potential and existing customers. It's the brand personality you want to develop. Your statement of position is how you are currently perceived. If you are currently perceived in a favorable way, your statement of position will be the same as your positioning statement. If this is true, you don't have to spend any time developing a "new and improved" personality. Whether or not you are satisfied with your current positioning, these next two chapters should provide you with some fresh ideas.

Use the Right Side of Your Brain

To be effective, your positioning should be a surprise to the industry, to the competition, to your customers. Customer reaction to your offering should be Wow! That's neat. That's cool. Why didn't I think of that? I want it. I need it. I'll buy it. The problem is that many people develop their strategies with the left side of their brain. That's where you juggle the everyday experiences of life; it's your pragmatic side. You have to use the right side—where many neurologists say creativity resides. You want to present a surprise. A surprise that is memorable, desirable, and believable.

You can spend all the time in the world developing your strategic and business plans, but if they don't include a unique personality for your brand, your chances of success are greatly diminished. The surprise could be x times faster, x times less expensive, x times less wear, more aesthetic, more convenient, more compassionate, more entertaining—all or any of which makes the customer's life or business richer. It should be presented in a manner that knocks the competitors' and customers' socks off. First develop your positioning statement and it becomes the foundation for all your strategies. If your strategies reinforce your positioning, your desired image becomes a reality.

That's a tall order, but you should remember the belief of Leo Burnett. He founded Leo Burnett Company, an advertising agency. His shop is renowned for effective advertising, including the Volkswagen's "Think Small" and "Lemon" campaigns and the current emotional Hallmark television commercials. His company's motto is, When you reach for the stars you may not quite get one, but you won't come up with a handful of mud, either.[1]

There are several large companies that have reached for the stars in developing their positioning. There is Neiman Marcus for products you yearn for; Bloomingdale's for classy merchandising; Marlboro cigarettes for freedom and wide-open spaces; and Nike for "Just do it."

Effective positioning is not limited to large businesses. For example, there is a computer support company in Minneapolis, Minnesota, by the name of Geek Squad. The company is patterned after the 1950s television show "Dragnet." Employees, called special agents, dress in black slacks, starched white shirts, white socks, and black shoes, and they carry a badge. Their vintage automobiles—the geekier the better—feature a large orange and black logo on the door, with the legend Geek Squad. Customers begin talking to a special agent within four to seven minutes after they run into a problem and repairs are completed as soon as possible. What sticks in the customer's mind are the geeks who wear badges, drive funny cars, and deliver reliable and fast service. Their positioning has resulted in a personality that is unique, memorable, desirable, and believable. "We are a living comic book and a profitable corporation," says the owner.[2] The company has twelve employees, about two thousand customers, and revenue has doubled every year.

Another example is a corporate jet refueler that offers beef to lure pilots to fill up. The company, Flower Aviation, offers low fuel prices and promises fast service. It also has two women dressed in short white skirts and sleeveless T-shirts waving bright orange flags to direct pilots to its facility. But the real attraction is what's in the brown paper bag the women slip to the pilot once they have pulled in to fill up—frozen Kansas City strip steaks. Pilots say their bosses like the fuel price, but they stop there for the steaks.[3]

These are just two examples of relatively small companies developing a personality that sells. It didn't take a lot of money. Just the right side of the brain.

Make It Easy to Complain

If you don't have superb customer service, resulting customer dissatisfaction will damage your brand personality. To have superb customer service, you have to make it easy for customers to complain. That means talking to them. It doesn't mean putting questionnaires in your store or in the mail. Who is going to take the time to fill out those impersonal queries? Besides, many people believe no one ever looks at the completed questionnaires unless it's for the personal data that the company sells to a mailing list firm. British Airlines has fifty people roaming Heathrow Airport in London who do nothing but help customers with their questions. Stew Leonard's dairy stores in Norwalk and Danbury, Connecticut, invite customers up to their second floor conference rooms every Saturday to ask them what they don't like about the store. And they act on the sensible suggestions. It is no wonder they have the most profitable dairy stores in the country. The best way to make it easy to complain is to ask your customers how you can improve your operation.

Making it easy to complain also helps you determine whether your positioning statement (how you would like to be perceived) is the same as your statement of position (how you are actually perceived). Inducing customers to critique your business is one of the best ways to obtain an unbiased snapshot of how they picture it.

Use Your Size to Excel

Usually the biggest advantage of a small company is its ability to move faster and to exploit custom requirements that large companies can't match. It's a great way to build unique positioning. HomeChef, a chain of eight cooking schools/kitchen stores has an effective strategy for competing against the large discount retailers in selling pots, pans, and electric mixers. Customers are treated to hot spiced cider and freshly baked biscotti while employees answer cooking questions. The company offers free one-hour cooking demonstrations and the owner, Judith Ets-Hokin, visits each store to mingle with customers. She refers to her stores as places that sell cooking experiences, not pots and pans.[4]

Bob Williams and Dave Ogborne renovate the interior walls of commercial jetliners. Usually airline mechanics do this type of work, but, according to these two, mechanics didn't like doing this work and didn't do it very well. The work is labor intensive and includes scraping off old wallpaper using heat guns and putty knives. Rather than creating a niche, Williams and Ogborne moved into a market where employees of large companies were ineffectual. The partnership had a slow start until the airlines started corporate identity programs, which included a unifying look throughout the cabin. That enabled the company to obtain contracts from several airlines to install "corporate identity" wallpaper designs. Sales shot up to $4.8 million in 1998.[5]

When determining which strategies you want to use to give your company a unique, memorable, desirable, and believable personality, keep thinking about what you can do that other companies can't or don't want to do. If you try to match them all, you become a blur. Successful companies become successful because they do something different from the competition. It can be a new type of brand like the one Steve Jobs and Steve Wozniak, founders of Apple Computer, Inc., built in one of their garages. It became the first successful personal computer. Or it can be a transformation of an existing market. Ray Kroc, founder of McDonald's Corporation, insured that the taste of the french fries you bought in Des Moines was the same as the ones you purchased in New York City.

Business Is Like High School

When you go to your high school and college reunions, at which one do you remember the most people and have the most fun? At which one do you have the closest friends? Most likely it's your high school reunion. The probable reason is that in high school, your relationships were less guarded and more intimate. The environment was less matter-of-fact, and you did not have that singular desire to achieve that is so common in college. You were not out to impress everyone, you were just pals exploring the world.

Ever wonder how some of your acquaintances succeeded in business although they did not appear to be that intelligent? It could be the high school factor. They took the time to establish a close relationship with their employees and customers. If two salespeople offer basically the same type of service, which one is most apt to get the sale: the salesperson who makes a professional presentation, but seems distant (like college) or the one who makes a satisfactory presentation, but seems interested in your welfare (like high school)? The smart money is on the latter.

This is not to imply that your business dealings and presentations should not be professional, but people buy from individuals they like. You should take the time to build in that high school relationship. For example, a young entrepreneur with a master's degree, has only one employee, who is the plant manager. He needs a plant manager because he is constantly on the phone and on the road talking to his customers. He golfs and dines with them. They don't play at country clubs because he tells his customers he can't afford them. They play at public links and the dining isn't at plush restaurants (Hey, I'm in high school!), yet he keeps taking business away from competitive companies much larger than his own.

Be Just One Thing

Most of us would have trouble dealing with a person with a split personality. People feel the same about companies that are involved in different and sometimes conflicting arenas. They don't know whether the personality is Dr. Jekyll or Mr. Hyde. Should an insurance agent also be your financial advisor? Conversely, do you really want to buy your insurance from a bank? Why does the world's largest seller of french fries and hamburgers keep trying to market bacon, lettuce, and tomato sandwiches? Why did the world's largest seller of soft drink syrup try to sell wine? Such diverse activities clutter positioning.

Line extensions can also be a problem. The American Marketing Association has established that 55 percent of line extensions fail.[5] You extend your line when you add to your main product or service an item with a different mixture of ingredients or uses. This type of promotion confuses customers. They wonder if the extension is better than the original and, if so, should they stop buying the original. Or they ask, "If the company said the original was so great, how come now they're coming out with something different?" Like anything else, there are exceptions. Clorox's extension, Clorox 2, is successful. Clorox 2 is for colored clothes.

Try to zero in on the one thing you do best and then keep promoting it. Let's say, for example, that you are faster than the competition and can make a statement like, "We can cut your inventory costs by 50 percent." That should be the headline in your ad and on the cover of your brochure. Maybe you also offer something else, like billing your customers' customers. If your positioning or headline now becomes, "We can cut your inventory costs by 50 percent and also handle your billing needs," you are making a mistake. You are making the statement less memorable. You added clutter. Nike's ads don't say, "Just do it and our shoes last longer." IBM's don't say, "We provide e-mail solutions and also have the fastest servers." Keep your positioning short and punchy.

If you are having trouble filling out your statement of position because you are not sure how you are perceived, get out in the field and start asking questions about your image.

Do the Research Yourself

Checking with your potential customers on how you are perceived is not that difficult. If you are a large company, you can hire a marketing research company to do the research. If you have a small to medium-size company, there is no reason why you can't do it yourself. Get into your car or on a plane and go talk to your customers. You may have to do some prying, because some customers may not want to hurt your feelings. However, if you keep asking them how you can improve your operation, most people will be honest in their replies. Some of their comments may be negative, and, if that is true, you have to address them. According to Bill Whitehead, chief executive of the Ted Bates ad agency, many companies overlook negative feedback. They try to solve the problem with advertising rhetoric.[7] No wonder so much advertising doesn't work.

An example of a company that has effective positioning and, consequently, a successful business, is one where the president finds time to call every customer at least once a month. She always begins the conversation with a question. That question is "What can I do to serve you better?" Sometimes a customer will acknowledge the question, but assume it is made in jest, and change the subject. The president listens to the customer, and as soon as he has finished talking, she asks again, "What can I do to serve you better?" She may go back to this same question four or five times until the customer finally concludes she really means it. Frequently the reply is something like, "No supplier has ever asked me that before." Based on the information she gathered from her customers, she has changed several of her strategies and plans and today she appears to be right on target. Still, she may make more changes. It depends on her calls next week.

Another example is a product manager who could not afford a market research company, so he decided to do the questioning himself. He only had the time and money to talk to ten customers, but nine made the same negative comment about his brochures. They said that there wasn't enough information about the conference rooms he was offering. Ten is a small sample, but when nine out of ten, or a large majority of any sample, agree on something, you should conclude that their comments need to be addressed.

When you do your research, you can use a form similar to Figure 7-1. Flower Aviation is used as an example. Notice that on the last two lines you fill in your estimated market share versus the competition's. These two lines have been inserted to keep you honest. If you conclude that you are effectively positioned, either in your own judgment or through research, but record a market share considerably lower than the competition's, you haven't gotten the story out or your strategies are not effective.

Flower Aviation moved out of a *commodity market* by offering free steaks. A commodity market is one in which all businesses are perceived as offering basically the same service or product. Flower Aviation's competitors offer what they believe are the basic needs, low prices and fast service, but nothing more. Flower Aviation, like the Geek Squad, has set itself apart by creative positioning.

Flower Aviation's statement of positioning (how they are perceived in the market) would be the same as their positioning statement (how they would like to be perceived in the market.) However, the hypothetical competitor in Figure 7-1 does not have as effective positioning and would probably have to rely on a low price strategy. That's what happens when you don't distinguish your business from the competition. You become a commodity. Your only weapon left is price discounting and that raises havoc with your bottom line.

Figure 7-2 shows another hypothetical example of a market— medicine—wherein most companies do not have effective positioning. The example used for illustrating poor positioning is a veterinary hospital, but it could be almost any hospital. The veterinary hospital believed,

Figure 7-1. Flower Aviation statement of position.

Question	Answer
Name of company:	Flower Aviation
Name of market:	Corporate jet refueling
Description of customer:	Owner of aircraft and pilot
Company strategies:	1. Free steaks 2. Attractive and fun employees 3. Reasonably priced fuel and fast service
As a result, research indicates the company is perceived as delivering:	1. Pilot: fun place to stop for refueling 2. Owner: reasonably priced fuel and fast service
Competitor strategies:	1. Reasonably priced fuel and fast service
As a result, research indicates the company is perceived as delivering:	1. Pilot: Fast service 2. Owner: reasonably priced fuel and fast service
Company market share:	35%
Competitor market share:	20%

Figure 7-2. Duke Veterinary statement of position.

Question	Answer
Name of company:	Duke Veterinary
Name of market:	Pet owners
Description of customer:	People in need of medical attention for their pets within an hour's drive of the facility.
Company strategies:	1. Provide excellent medical service
As a result, research indicates the company is perceived as delivering:	1. Unfriendly nonmedical personnel 2. Archaic billing process 3. Excellent medical services
Competitor strategies:	1. Provide excellent medical service 2. Treat patients like members of the family 3. Provide a simple billing system
As a result, research indicates the competitor is perceived as delivering:	1. Leading-edge veterinarian medical services 2. A friendly atmosphere
Company market share:	15%
Competitor market share:	30%

like most medical providers, that positioning itself as a leading-edge vet-erinarian service was all that was needed. Today that is not true. It may be the single most important factor in selecting a veterinary hospital, but other elements of the business can neutralize any resulting advantage this factor may deliver. For example, in this situation, they are perceived as treating pet owners in an unfriendly manner and having lousy billing procedures.

Notice that their competitor knows more about marketing in that they realize the importance of factors other than just good medical prac-tice. By offering good customer service, their medical practice shines through. Companies like Duke Veterinary Hospital have to understand that they can offer excellent medical services—or in case of other types of businesses, superior engineering, manufacturing, etc.—and still have unfavorable results due to other negative factors.

Watch out for negative factors in your business. Be sure your posi-tioning is believable. For example, if you are a small company you should not position your company as offering unsurpassed experience. Even if you do offer the most experience in your line of work, people probably won't believe you. Customers will conclude you are too small to match, let alone excel, larger firms in experience. However, if you promote your small-size operation as being able to give top management attention on each account, you will have a believable position and one that larger companies can't match.

In summary, your brand needs a creative personality to be successful. Fill out the statement of position illustrating how you believe you are currently perceived. Do your own research if you are not sure what to put down. If you don't like the resulting image, review your entire operation. Try to find something other companies can't do. Present that edge in a unique way that is memorable, desirable, and believable. This positioning or personality becomes the foundation of all your strategies. If you execute your strategies correctly, you will solidify your brand personality.

Notes

1. Leo Burnett Company Web site, www.leoburnett.com.

2. Chris Tomlinson, Associated Press, "Geek Squad bring law, order to computer glitches," *Minneapolis Star & Tribune*, September 3, 1997.

3. Scott McCartney, "We'll be landing in Kansas so the crew can grab a steak," *The Wall Street Journal*, September 8, 1998.

4. Carla Goodman, "That's Entertainment," *Entrepreneur*, December 1998, p. 94.

5. Timothy Aeppel, "Two partners find an unlikely niche inside commercial jets," *The Wall Street Journal*, January 12, 1999.

6. Bernice Kanner, "In stores, only the strong, fast and trendy survive," Bloomberg News, *The News & Observer*, Raleigh, North Carolina, March 17, 1998.

7. Ibid.

———

Chapter Eight

Strategies to Reinforce Positioning

Promotional Materials and Your Positioning Statement

Once you have established how you want to position your business in the marketplace, what its distinctive personality should be, you need to craft promotional messages and activities that reflect this personality and convey it effectively. Here are two examples of ads; one is effective and the other is not.

In every Kohler ad, their positioning statement of "The Bold Look of Kohler" is prominently displayed. Following is a summary of one of their print ads.

Headline: THE BOLD LOOK OF KOHLER
Visual: Photograph of an empty convertible pulled over on a dusty road in the desert with a road sign on the left reading, NEXT REST AREA 110 MILES. There are clothes hanging on

the corner of the sign. Behind the road sign is a man taking a shower in an elegantly tiled shower stall with a curved glass front. On the other side of the road is a woman taking a shower in another attractive shower stall.
Advertiser: KOHLER

No question who is selling what here. It is not every day you see beautiful shower stalls—Kohler calls them Body Spas—by the side of the road out in the desert. You do not even have to read the body copy to get the selling message.

Three other ads in the Kohler series are shown in Figures 8-1, 8-2, and 8-3. They are not as creative as the ads described above, but they effectively show the bold look of their merchandise. Notice the headline in each is THE BOLD LOOK OF KOHLER. Now, compare the Kohler ads with the summary of an ad by AT&T:

Headline: Out of the blue
Visual: Woman in bathing suit standing waist high in water with blue sky in the background.
Advertiser: AT&T

In the body copy of the ad AT&T states that you never know where your next business idea will come from, so carry an AT&T Direct Service wallet guide. (Would it not get wet in the bathing suit?) The Kohler ad contains a positioning statement for the company, while the ad for AT&T is for an individual brand. Still, ads for individual brands should contain their own positioning statement or reflect the positioning for the company. The AT&T ad does neither. The overall appearance of the ad does not project a unique personality. Maybe the message in the body copy is their positioning. The problem is, according to many research studies, only about 20 percent of individuals reading a headline also read the body copy.

(text continues on page 117)

Figure 8-1. First of three ads in Kohler series.

As I See It, #43 in a series
Lisa Charles Watson
"Tea Party"
Photography

THE BOLD LOOK
OF **KOHLER**®

The comfort of the curve is timeless. As is the Kohler Fairfax™ single-handled faucet. Its form and function elevate it far beyond the ordinary, but its affordability will relax and soothe. Kind of like a nice cup of tea. Stop by any Home Depot, call 1-800-4-KOHLER, ext. NU9 to order product literature, or visit kohlerco.com/fairfaxkitchen

©2000 by Kohler Co.

Figure 8-2. Second of three ads in Kohler series.

As I See It, #41 in a series
Charles Shotwell
"The One That Got Away"
Polaroid Transfer Photography

THE BOLD LOOK
OF **KOHLER**.

How do you capture a spirit? Look to an Artist Editions lavatory, tile and accessories. The Pheasant™ lavatory is inspired by 19th century illustrations. To revisit and reawaken the mastery of a time gone by. Don't let this one get away. See the Yellow Pages for a KOHLER® Registered Showroom, call 1-800-4-KOHLER, ext. NNN to order product literature, or visit www.kohlerco.com/pheasant

©2000 by Kohler Co.

Figure 8–3. Third of three ads in Kohler series.

As I See It, #32 in a series
Kenji Toma
"Reduce Speed, Curves Ahead"
4-Color Photography

THE BOLD LOOK
OF **KOHLER**®

Slow down and get a look at this. Our Finial™ faucets have taken creative license and come up with a whole new handle on line and design. Strong, striking and if that were't enough, they'll even turn on your water. See the Yellow Pages for a KOHLER® Registered Showroom, or call 1-800-4-KOHLER, ext. LD1 to order product literature. www.kohlerco.com/finial
©2000 by Kohler Co.

Probably the best example of a company's advertising reflecting their positioning is the TV ad campaign for Hallmark Cards. Each commercial has its own story, but each one reflects the company's positioning statement: "When you care enough to send the very best."

Everything you do should reinforce your positioning. For example, Flower Aviation is positioned as giving free frozen Kansas City strip steaks to pilots in a fun atmosphere along with reasonably priced fuel and fast service. It would be a mistake for them to run an ad or mail out a brochure that talks about anything other than these benefits.

If you plan to use outside help with your promotions, be sure they do not get too cute. Some copywriters and art directors are more concerned with winning awards than with developing effective strategies. Many times there is no correlation between these two factors. How often have you heard someone say, "I saw the greatest ad" (or direct mail piece, brochure, etc.). They continue, "I can't remember the company's name, but let me tell you about it. . . ." Leo Burnett believed that "lurking in every product which deserves success is a reason for being and a reason for buying which is deeply felt by the manufacturer and which, if captured and communicated, is the best of all possible advertising, because it is honest and believable."[1] Be sure your consultants—or whoever does your promotional work—know the reason for being and the reason for buying.

Strategies Based on Market Position

You should act your market share or you may lose it. And if your competitors don't position themselves correctly relative to their share, it may provide you with a golden opportunity, as it did for newcomers Apple, Dell, and Enterprise Rent-A-Car. First I will discuss how you should act if you are a market leader. Whatever you do, do it big. People have a tendency to judge the quality of a service based on the magnitude of the promotions for it, such as the size of the ads. A market leader should not run a half-page ad in a publication where competitors are running full pages. A market leader should not show up at a trade show with a less prominent exhibit than the competition.

A company that is the market leader, whether it is a large company in a large market or a small company in a small market, should not mention a competitor's name in their promotions. The market leader's name is usually the best known in the market. It normally has the highest brand awareness, which probably took years and a lot of dollars to build. Why then give competition free publicity? General Electric, which is the leader in almost all of their markets, doesn't compare itself with its competition. Conversely, Visa constantly mentions American Express in their television ads. In all fairness, American Express should donate money to Visa to help pay for the commercials.

Market leaders should position themselves as offering the greatest depth of line and the largest distribution network. Depth of line is the number of sizes, shapes, policies, models, etc., that you offer. Depth of line and distribution are two major factors that determine who wins when a market starts to slow down in growth or matures. Also, you don't want to leave any holes in the market where new entrants can pop in. An example of this all-encompassing positioning strategy is America Online Inc. AOL was a small company in recent 1995, but became the number one Internet service provider (ISP) within a few years. They then added their own Web site, AOL.com, and purchased another ISP (CompuServe Corporation). Next, they purchased Netscape Communications Corporation, which gave them their own browser. Recently, they purchased Time Warner.

AOL's strategy can be applied to smaller markets. A company that currently enjoys the largest market share in house painting within a city should offer both latex and oil paints in all possible applications, finishes and shades. It should run the biggest ads and submit the most professional brochures. Its employees should travel in new trucks, and dress in crisp company uniforms. A company that is the market leader in grocery sales within an area should offer the largest selection of meats, produce, dairy, bakery, and all other types of food and drink. They need pharmacy, bank, hardware, and flower sections. Their storefronts and interiors should be immaculate. Space should be allocated for children to play. They should be installing a system enabling customers to submit their grocery list to the store from their computer or from the chip in their refrigerator that keeps track of inventory. Home delivery should be available. In essence, there should be no holes.

If you are not currently a market leader, you may not have the desire to become number one. A number two position can be very profitable. Even a number three. Remember the "3 and 4" concept that was discussed in Chapter Three. However, if you are going for it, the only way you are going to become number one is to position yourself as delivering a bundle of benefits that are superior to the leader. This positioning normally calls for direct comparison—you versus the leader. One company that executed this strategy beautifully was Avis. Although it is a dated example, it was probably the most effective ad campaign of a number two company trying to become number one. Ironically, it led to one of the biggest marketing mistakes in history. Avis' ads proclaimed, "We're number two, we try harder." The campaign pushed the company into the black for the first time and it remained profitable until ITT purchased the company two years later. Harold Geneen, president of ITT, pulled the campaign, saying that no company of his was going to shout that they were only number two. Although the campaign ran fifteen or twenty years ago, many people still remember it fondly.

If you are a small company and not a market leader, what you should be looking for are holes in the market left open by the competition, large companies that don't position themselves against all segments. International Business Machines Corporation and Digital Equipment Corporation left the personal computer hole uncovered and in popped smaller Apple Computer Inc. Compaq Computer Corporation and IBM left the direct distribution hole uncovered and in popped Dell Computer Corporation.

Enterprise Rent-A-Car Co. Inc. found a hole and expanded all the way to market leader. The hole was making rentals available to people while they were having their cars fixed in a garage. Enterprise captured this huge market niche and by so doing became larger than Hertz. One of Enterprise's unique strategies is their arrangement to have pizza served for lunch one day a week to garage mechanics in companies offering Enterprise rentals.

Enterprise got its start by courting the airport passenger market. It could not afford to have space in the terminals, so their check-in facilities were located one or two blocks down the street. They countered this disadvantage by offering lower prices than Hertz and Avis. Their advertising campaign consisted of a photograph of a handsome male, well dressed, and drinking a martini. The headline was, "Before I started using Enterprise Rent-A-Car, I lived with my mother." After they built some mass, they moved into the garage rental market and switched their positioning to, "We'll pick you up." Their television commercials feature an automobile wrapped up like a gift package driving to the location of the person renting the car. The moral of the story is, regardless of how small your company is today, you can become a leader.

Look for market niches that larger firms have missed or can't handle due to their overhead or slowness in changing direction. Maybe it's a niche they don't think is important. Maybe it's a painting firm that doesn't do sand painting, a grocery store that can't handle computerized customer orders, or a components manufacturer that won't ship in small quantities or package in small units.

Critique All Markets

As discussed above, there is a correlation between a company's market position and the types of strategies it should execute. You should constantly review strategies being deployed by companies with the same market position, even those not in your market. If you are the market leader, you should be critiquing what other market leaders are doing. The type of product or service, market, or relative size is immaterial. What you are looking for are unique strategies that are increasing sales. Keep your eye on market leaders like America Online, Compaq, McDonald's, Enterprise Rent-A-Car, the various General Electric divisions, Citibank, Yahoo!, Cisco, NBC, and Home Depot. Who cares if these companies are in different industries than yours. If one or more of them are doing something that appears to be working, ask yourself, "Will it work for me in my market?"

For example, suppose you are the leader in a small or medium-size market. You have several smaller competitors that keep taking business away from you because they offer better service to customers. Home Depot is probably a larger company than yours, but their current strategy may be applicable. Home Depot is going after the small hardware stores with their rollout of Villager's Hardware. Now Home Depot is plotting to rub out rivals by challenging them on the only advantage they have left: service and convenience. The Atlanta-based retailer will soon begin an experiment with smaller stores that are "locationally convenient," as one company official put it. The idea is to entice customers who don't have the time or need to save a little money."[2] Can you adapt this type of strategy? That is the type of question you should keep asking yourself.

Let's assume you are not the market leader. You are in a position similar to the small hardware stores mentioned above. Hardware stores have taken their licks from national and regional chains, but their number is only down 12 percent from the mid-1970s. How are they staying in business? They buy from cooperatives like Ace Hardware Corporation and TruServ. They benefit from the loyalty of their neighbors. They concentrate on selling merchandise such as plumbing and electrical fixtures that requires patient explanation. (Did you ever receive a patient explanation about any item from a Home Depot employee?) Their inventory of odd-sized nuts, bolts, nails, washers, and screws is larger than the chains. For a do-it-yourselfer, it's no quick in and out here. It's fun to dig around in the stores' cluttered racks. Is there a lesson here for you?

Strategies designed to accomplish specific objectives can also be interchangeable. Durk Jager, CEO of Procter & Gamble, says, "The company needs to look outside its core business more often for inspiration." While visiting a photography store, he noticed that customers, with some help, were allowed to crop photos themselves. The visit prompted Mr.

Jager to wonder about the potential for a more interactive environment in mass-market retailing. "You learn more from the things that are not in the area where you normally operate," he stated. "Don't go to a Kroger [grocery store chain]. Maybe you should get to an outlet that sells furniture."[3]

Concentrate on 98 Percent

It takes time and money to improve your positioning. Be sure to concentrate in an area important to your potential customers and in which you can deliver at a level of excellence. You want to achieve a 98 percent approval level. I arbitrarily use 98 percent as a level of excellence because 100 percent is an impossibility, and less than 98 percent doesn't make you newsworthy. For example, Federal Express offers, "Absolutely, positively overnight." That's a home run for people who need speed and reliability for their documents. Customers believe in the company because they are good on their word practically every time. No one is going to beat them at their own game. The United States Postal Service is smart enough to know that. They don't compete on "absolutely, positively" because they can't deliver on a level considered excellent. They promote their cost savings, which is a significant benefit to a different segment of the market.

Bill Marriott, CEO of Marriott Hotels, keeps saying, "somehow we have to fix our restaurants." The reason for his statement is that when you go to a restaurant, you want great food, or if you are in hurry, quick service and something halfway decent to eat. Hotel restaurants can't deliver 98 percent of the time on either. They know they can't offer quick service so they promote the offering of great food. The problem is no one believes their positioning because they do not deliver on their promise. Conversely, McDonald's delivers on quick service and has decent food. In fact, their french fries are tastier than those served by most, if not all, hotel restaurants.

Hospitals know they have to become more user-friendly, but most just fake the strategy of improving patient relations. There are exceptions. Griffen Hospital, a small general hospital located in rural Connecticut, was losing business to larger hospitals. Realizing that hospital experiences were significantly more unpleasant than they ought to be, Griffen executives decided they had to improve its image to survive. Concentration would be on obstetrics, to catch patients when they were young, in the hope they would continue to come back in later years. To determine patients' desires, Griffen passed out questionnaires to their obstetrics patients, as well as to new and expectant mothers.

When the planning team from the hospital started examining the requests, they proceeded to eliminate one after another for being too goofy, frivolous, or downright dangerous to medical practices. Suddenly Patrick Charmel, the CEO, said, "Why are we doing this? We asked them what they wanted, and they told us. Now let's just give it to them." After a stunned pause, someone said, "You mean, all of it?" "Yeah," said Charmel. "All of it."[4]

Today the hospital offers double beds so husbands or partners can sleep next to the mothers. Rooms contain fresh flowers, have big windows and skylights. Jacuzzis are down the hall. Lounges are large, comfortable spaces where the family can gather. Families, including children, are allowed in the delivery room. Obstetric admissions doubled within two years after the changes were made. That's what happens to a business when you research what the customer wants and then deliver it 98 percent of the time.

Notes

1. Leo Burnett Web site, www.leoburnett.com.

2. James R. Hagerty, "Home Depot Raises the Ante, Targeting Mom-and-Pop Rivals," *The Wall Street Journal*, January 25, 1999.

3. Tara Parker-Pope, "New P&G CEO Jager Preaches Rebellion," *The Wall Street Journal*, December 11, 1998.

4. David H. Freedman, "Intensive Care," *Inc.*, February 1999.

PART FOUR

DEVELOPING YOUR MARKETING PLAN

Chapter Nine

Your Product/Service Plan Sets the Specifics of Your Marketing Plan

Your strategic plan sets the parameters of your marketing plan and the product or service (brand) plan sets the specifics of your marketing plan. These specifics include your pricing strategy, market variables needed to obtain your revenue projections, and marketing budget. Market variables include such things as awareness, distribution, sales closure rate, depth of line, packaging, distribution, and the introduction of new brands. If management provides you with *gross margins* (revenue or sales less cost of operations or goods), and administrative costs, you can also project your income from current operations.

Price Your Brand to Reflect Your Positioning

Your pricing strategy, like all other parts of your business, has to reflect your positioning. Your positioning determines how you are perceived and how you are perceived determines your perceived value. You want to do everything possible to obtain an estimate of your perceived value, because your market price should be the same as your perceived value. For example, if you are a small retailer, you cannot beat Wal-Mart or Home Depot on price. If you have to charge higher prices to survive, then you have to be perceived as offering something of value that they don't. The question is: What value will customers put on this something else you offer? The best way to find out is to go out into the market and ask your potential customers.

For example, assume the marketing manager for Ford Taurus knows he is losing sales to Toyota Camry. He conducts market research on perceived value by potential customers on these two makes plus two other competitors, the Chrysler 300M and Chevrolet Lumina. He charts the hypothetical perceived value versus the market price as shown in Figure 9-1. He then puts this data on a chart, as shown in Figure 9-2. McKinsey & Company refers to a similar type of chart as a "value map"[1]. Notice that Toyota Camry is to the right of the diagonal line, which means that customers put a higher perceived value in dollars on the car than the market price. Their perception was "you get more than what you pay for." Ford Taurus was perceived to be on the diagonal, which means a perception of "you get exactly what you pay for." Chevrolet Lumina and Chrysler 300M were perceived to be to the left of the diagonal, which means a perception of "being overpriced."

If this research truly reflects customers' beliefs, Toyota Camry should be gaining market share, Ford Taurus maintaining share, and Chevrolet Lumina and Chrysler 300M losing share. In order for Ford

Figure 9-1. Perceived value versus market price.

Make of Automobile	Perceived Value	Market Price
Chrysler	$31,000	$33,000
Toyota Camry	$26,000	$22,000
Ford Taurus	$18,500	$18,500
Chevrolet	$14,000	$18,000

Figure 9-2. Market price versus perceived value.

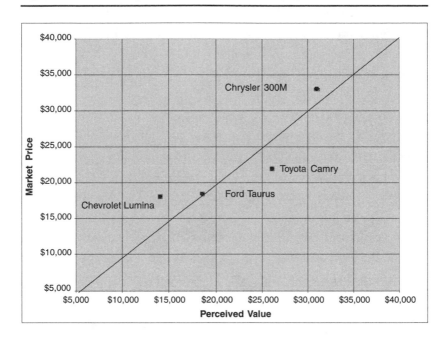

Taurus to increase market share, the manufacturer would have to either decrease the price of the car or increase the perceived value.

In this type of analysis, you must be correct in your judgment of what customers are looking for in the way of value or benefits. For example, a distributor of chemical compounds stressed the greater reliability of her products' formulas versus the competition. She concluded that due to this superior value, she could ask for a premium price and still stay on the diagonal. Confronted with weak sales, she did some research and discovered that technical support was the number one benefit sought. Reliability was important, but not to the degree she had anticipated. She was not on the diagonal as she thought she would be. She was to the left of it because the perceived value was less than the market price. She did not move her company's perception on to the diagonal until she started offering technical support; then she started making sales.

Another example of a company unknowingly being to the left of the diagonal was a golf course. It had beautifully manicured fairways and greens, which the owners felt justified a premium price. The problem was they were losing business to a course down the street that did not match it in attractiveness. It took the company two years to realize why. To keep its course in pristine condition, it insisted that golf carts had to stay on cart paths at all times. The competitive course allowed the golfers to drive their carts down the fairways. This benefit was more important to the customers than the exceptional beauty of a course.

If you do price your business to the right of the diagonal—offer more perceived value than market price—it can backfire on you. A case in point was the Mazda Miata. Mazda underestimated the appeal and the high perceived benefits of the sporty automobile. Consequently, the price was disproportionately low, diminishing the manufacturer's profit. The dealers recognized the mistake and claimed the surplus for themselves in the form of $2,000 to $3,000 "market price adjustments."

Your best bet is to set your market price equal to the perceived value, that is, on the diagonal. If you set your market price too high, you will lose sales. If you set it too low, maybe the competition will drop their prices and put everybody back on the diagonal. All you will have accomplished is cutting profit margins. Do your homework.

Use What-If Revenue Models

A what-if model is invaluable in helping to determine your marketing objectives and strategies, the resulting marketing budget, and projected revenue or sales. Insert into the what-if revenue model the market variables that you believe determine how much you sell. They could be such factors as the number of potential customers aware of your business, sales coverage, sales closure rate, and repeat sales. Using simple mathematics, you then look at the resulting sales objective. Using a what-if model, you can keep changing your variables—keep asking what if—and then look at the resulting objectives. Once you get the objectives to a level that you think is acceptable and obtainable, explain in your marketing plan how you obtained the numbers you used for the variables. If you execute your plan successfully, you will obtain your objectives.

What you are doing here is passing the puck among the various members of your company to ascertain your revenue or sales objective. Your sales team should not be the only employees of your company held responsible for sales objectives. The same is true for other promotional functions. Advertising should not be judged alone for sales results, unless you are doing direct response and no other marketing factors are being used.

To design this type of sales forecasting model, insert your objectives at the bottom of the model, then add all the variables that influence these objectives at the top of the model. Next, add formulas between the variables and the objectives relative to how the variables influence the objectives. The amounts or levels you insert for the different variables are estimates on your part. The more research you do on this subject, the more reliable the model. If you lack research, inserting a best estimate should give you a better idea of where you are going than just flying by the seat of your pants. Start with your best estimate, then keep making adjustments as the plan unfolds.

The necessary formulas for a what-if model are quite simple, as shown in Figure 9-3. Start with the estimated size of the market, which is the total number of potential customers. Next, set an estimated awareness level. This is the percent of the potential customers that will become aware of your store, what you are selling, etc. The next variable is sales closure rate or conversion awareness to trial, which is the percent of time you convert customers who are aware of your business into a trial or

Figure 9-3. What-if model.

Market	X	Awareness	X	Conversion	X
Distribution	=	Trial	+	Repeats	=
Purchases	X	Units/Price	=	Sales	/
Market	=	Market Share			

sale. If you average three sales transactions for every ten customers you reach or talk to, your closure rate is 30 percent.

Next, calculate the level of distribution. Your level of distribution could be the percent of total potential customers that can conveniently come to your store. If you have your own sales force or distributors, your level of distribution would be the coverage area of these individuals or companies divided by the total size of the market. After you insert these four variables into the model, calculate trial, which is the first purchase transaction by a customer. As shown in Figure 9-3, multiply the market size by your awareness level by your closure rate by your distribution level. The answer is trial or the number of first-time buyers.

The next step is to add estimated repeat sales transactions to the number of first-time buyers to arrive at total sales transactions. You then multiply this total by the estimated number of units per sales transaction to arrive at the sales forecast in units. Multiplying estimated sales in units by sales price provides the sales forecast in dollars. Go one step further to calculate your market share. Divide your units, revenue, or sales by total market size to determine your market share.

Of course you have to reach the level of the variables in your model to obtain the projected sales goal or market share. Examine each variable with other members of your company to arrive at the best promotional tool for each variable. Figure 9-4 illustrates some of the factors to consider

Figure 9–4. Factors influencing awareness and conversion.

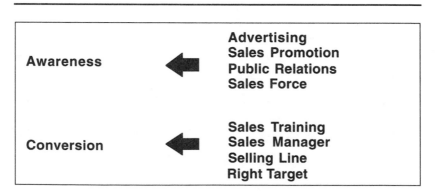

on how to increase your awareness and sales conversion. Figure 9-5 provides factors to consider to increase your distribution and repeat sales.

Figure 9-5. Factors influencing distribution and repeat sales.

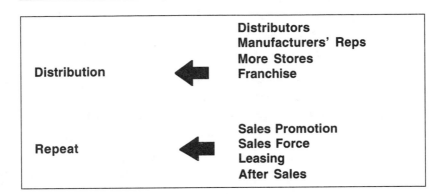

Appendix C has a detailed case history using a what-if model. The case history provides two sets of variables to illustrate how a small increase in the goals or objectives for your variables can deliver a pronounced increase in your sales forecast. In this example, it is a 41 percent increase in revenue.

This model was put to a test for accuracy by students in the business school at Michigan State University. They inserted the variables actually obtained by a product during a three-year period and the market share projected by the model was within one percentage point of the product's current market share.

Your Marketing Budget

Marketing budgets are usually based on either a percent of sales or an arbitrary amount given to the planner. A better method is to set a marketing objective for each variable in the what-if revenue model. Determine your strategies and tactics for reaching these objectives and add up the costs for execution. The result is your marketing budget.

For example, assume the most important players in the buying deci-

sion for brand distribution are the store managers of independent grocery stores. An objective to obtain stocking approval (approval to let you
put your merchandise on store shelves) on 85 percent of target stores is
set. Assume your resulting strategies and tactics involve personal selling
and advertising, then calculate the cost for these activities. Follow the
same procedure for your next objective and so on. Finish going down
the list, add up all the costs, and the result is your budget.

Doesn't that make more sense than calculating your budget based
on a percent of sales? This percent method is based on what is normally
spent in your market by the competition. How do you know the amount
the competition is spending is correct? Even if the amount is correct for
a competitor, it is most likely not correct for you. Using an arbitrary
amount to establish your budget is equally misleading. Where does this
amount come from? Perhaps from the company's owner while he is
shaving in the morning or when she is washing her hair. It could float
down from the heavens.

The only professional way to set your budget is to determine what
it will cost to reach your objectives. My experience suggests that you may
want to adjust the resulting costs in the following situations.

1. **A new product or service.** It costs more to build awareness from
   ground zero to an acceptable level than with an existing brand
   that may already enjoy this feature. If more than 50 percent of
   your product line is new, consider increasing your budget by 50
   percent. For example, assume you have been budgeting $30,000
   for sales management to meet your current brand's sales objectives. When introducing a new brand, consider increasing the
   new brand's sales management budget to $45,000 (a 50 percent
   increase) to cover the costs for more sales calls per prospect.
   Decrease your budget by 25 percent if you are not offering a new
   product.

2. **Premium prices.** If your service is premium priced, spend more
   to justify the higher cost. Consider increasing your budget by 30

percent. If you are priced below the competition, you can lower your budget by 20 percent. When you are competitively priced, you need make no adjustment.

3. **Low importance to the customer.** When your item for sale is not important to potential customers, you have to spend more to get their attention. If the purchase of your item accounts for less than 1 percent of the customers' total purchases, increase your budget by 35 percent. For 1 to 5 percent, make no adjustment. For over 25 percent, decrease your budget by 20 percent.

   An example would be introducing an item that is not a necessity for a buyer. You plan on using a direct-mail campaign and research and judgment tell you a budget of $20,000 will suffice. Using the less important factor, you should increase your budget to $27,000 (a 35 percent increase). You will need more elaborate or more frequent mailings to grab the recipients' attention because this type of purchase is not that important to them.

4. **A wide variety of products or services.** If you offer a broad depth of line, consisting of several sizes, models, policies, etc., it will take more money to promote each one. If this is the situation, increase your budget by 30 percent. For a narrow line, decrease it by 10 percent.

5. **Standardized product or service.** When your product is standardized, you need to spend more because what you are selling is probably not that much different from the competition. Increase your budget by 10 percent.

   If your product is customized, decrease the budget by 20 percent, because less time will be spent on promotional activity and more time on engineering and/or manufacturing specifications.

Note

1. Ralf Leszinski and Michael V. Marn, "Setting value, not price," *The McKinsey Quarterly*, Number 1, 1997.

Chapter Ten

Using Advertising to Build Awareness

Various research studies indicate that the average American is subjected to 2,500 to 3,000 commercial messages a day. How are you going to stand out? By developing an effective communications strategy.

Your Communications Strategy

Your communications strategy should include:

1. The target audience

2. Individuals in the buying decision

3. Benefits sought

4. Features supporting the benefits

5. Positioning statement

6. Basic selling line

Numbers one through five have been discussed in previous chapters. Number 6, *basic selling line*, is the message you deliver to your target audience. Select the target audience and determine the individuals involved in the buying decision and their priority. Using research or your own gut instincts, isolate the benefits sought by each key member in the buying decision. Based on this information, develop your basic selling line. If you market to consumers, you may have one basic selling line to the end users and one for the trade. If you are an industrial marketer, you are more apt to have several—one for the engineer, one for the purchasing agent, one for the operating officer, and so on.

Home Depot's positioning statement is probably: "A wide selection of brand name products for home improvement at prices below local and regional competition." Its current basic selling line is: "Where low prices are just the beginning." Successful positioning statements should not be changed unless there is a major change in the direction of the company or brand. Basic selling lines can be changed over time, but they should always reflect the positioning statement.

Developing Your Basic Selling Line

The purpose of the basic selling line is to interpret your positioning statement to the market—the individuals involved in the buying decision. It should contain the benefit sought by the particular person in the buying decision and, ideally, your company or brand name. This line becomes the headline in your ad. It should be on the cover of your brochure. Your sales presentation should be built around it.

After the basic selling line is determined, all types of communications to a target audience should contain it. By target audience I mean groups of individuals who are seeking the same benefit, such as mothers, fathers, engineers, purchasing agents, etc. A common mistake marketers make is saying one thing to their target audience in their ads, something different in their brochures, and something else again in their sales presentations. This is not effective communications. Remember that you are competing with 2,999 other messages directed at your target audience each day. You want to be consistent so that each additional communication reinforces the previous ones.

The basic selling line is discussed in this chapter because, ideally, it should be developed by creative advertising people such as copywriters and art directors. Copywriters are the wordsmiths in an advertising agency and art directors are the visual experts. The first five components of the communications strategy are business decisions to be made by the appropriate people within the company. When it comes to the basic selling line, you need people with a flair for the dramatic grouping of words and visuals such as Nike's "Just do it" and Microsoft's "Where would you like to go today?" Maybe you can develop an effective basic selling line yourself, but if you have any consulting money available, the best way to spend it is on creative people in an advertising agency. You don't have to use the rest of the agency's services, but hiring their creative people for this part of your communications strategy is a wise investment.

Try to get the best creative minds within the agency to work for you because some companies using advertising agencies have basic selling lines that I believe are ineffectual. Here are summaries of a few ads to help you critique your own advertising. As mentioned, analyze all marketing materials you see. There is no better way to improve your own material. Determine which ads you believe are on target and why, and which ones are not and why. When you start preparing your own material, you are less apt to make the mistakes others are making. Hopefully, you can duplicate, in your own way, the ones you believe are winners. Following is the headline (*basic selling line*), visual, and name of the advertiser for three ads that appeared in the April 1999 issue of *Entrepreneur* magazine.

Headline: Phillip Raclyn has a small business. He is a veterinarian.
Visual: Photograph of veterinarian with two dogs, one of which is biting his ear.
Advertiser: Microsoft

Even Microsoft makes mistakes. They were selling their Windows NT Workstation, but you would not know it unless you read the body copy. (Remember, only 20 percent of the readers of the headline read the body copy.) If you were a veterinarian, you might, but that appears to be a limited target audience. The fact that Microsoft's NT software is 30 percent faster than Windows 98 is buried in the body copy. Why isn't that feature in the headline? Why not put the benefit of that feature in the headline? Any reader short on time might have noticed.

> **Headline:** If this is your corner office . . . this is your network . . . AT&T personal network.
> **Visual:** Photograph of man on beach using mobile phone. Laptop and notebook computer also shown.
> **Advertiser:** AT&T

It appears that AT&T believes it is the only company in the market. The headline does not contain any reason for selecting AT&T. There is some meat in the body copy, but it is quite lean because the competition can match what AT&T says. As will be discussed later in this chapter, if you can't write a good ad, maybe the product or service is at fault.

> **Headline:** you inc.
> **Visual:** IBM computer monitor and keyboard on stepladder. Processor on floor.
> **Advertiser:** IBM

No wonder IBM lost one billion dollars on its personal computer business in 1998. They're lucky to be serving more than one market. It appears, like Microsoft, that they were going after a limited target. Maybe they were trying to reach only painters and electricians, because a stepladder is a weak symbol for any other type of new business. Like AT&T,

no reason for buying IBM was given except in the body copy. That copy was not unique; it had the same features the competition used.

Three ads from major corporations and not one contains a reason for buying—a benefit in the headline. Small companies do not appear to do much better with their ads. The following are summaries of two ads that appeared in the March 1999 issue of *North Carolina* magazine.

> **Headline:** Dog Story # 3
> **Visual:** Photograph of dog next to an archway inside a house.
> **Advertiser:** Wamble Carlyle (law firm)

Obviously, this law firm represents dogs.

> **Headline:** Do you have big plans for a great meeting?
> **Visual:** Photograph of huge dresser. It appears that a woman's brassiere and sock are hanging out of one of the drawers. A man a fraction of the size of the dresser is standing looking at the dresser.
> **Advertiser:** High Point, North Carolina, Convention Bureau

One would assume the purpose of the dresser is to convey the fact that High Point, North Carolina, is the furniture capital of the country. Did readers make that interpretation? What does that have to do with having a great meeting?

This small sample shows why management lost faith in advertising. They tired of the ineffective ads produced by or for their marketing people. Businesses are spending more dollars on sales promotion each year. Ten years ago 60 percent of advertising and sales promotion dollars were spent on advertising. Today it is the opposite. Sixty percent is spent on sales promotion. The problem with this shift is that, unlike advertising, sales promotion is mainly a short-term marketing tool and normally does not build customer loyalty.

It doesn't have to be that way. Although several magazines had to be searched to find them, following are basic selling lines that work.

1. "British Airways has the most comfortable international business class seat. Guaranteed." (British Airways)

2. "How to make your car invisible to radar *and* laser." (Rocky Mountain Radar)

3. "It's never too late for another great idea. What about something like lower prices?" (Compaq)

4. "You can pay taxes on your income now. Or you can pay taxes on your income later. Here's one vote for later." (John Hancock)

5. "Your biggest competitor just cut its prices by 10%. Is this bad news, or good?" (Microsoft)

The first two illustrate two completely different approaches to advertising layout. The British Airways ad contains a big, bold headline, with little body copy. (See Figure10-1.) The Rocky Mountain Radar ad is almost all body copy. (See Figure 10-2.) I do not know of any research done to judge the effectiveness of the British Airways ad, but I do know it created a lot of favorable talk value, and that is certainly beneficial. The Rocky Mountain Radar ad was a direct response ad, its effectiveness was directly measured, and the client informed me that it is a big money winner. The reason I am showing these two ads is to illustrate that a big bold headline containing a benefit can be powerful, but a smaller headline of interest with long body copy can be, too. Don't be afraid of long body copy as long as it is easy to read. Notice how Rocky Mountain Radar breaks up the body copy with subheads and photography. It makes the copy inviting.

Learn from Winners

You might want to know what were the five most popular television commercials since 1960, based on an initial selection of 20 favorites

(text continues on page 144)

Figure 10-1. British Airways advertisement.

British Airways has the most comfortable international business class seat.

Guaranteed.

Double miles and complete comfort. Or your next trip is on the Concorde.

If for any reason you don't agree that our Club World™ business class and especially our Cradle Seat™ are the most comfortable in the air, just write us — and the next time you fly Club World we'll put you in First or on the Concorde. Travel must be completed by June 30, 1998. And if you call before flying, you'll automatically receive double miles for your first trip. We guarantee it's worth a call.

1-800-480-1811
www.british-airways.com/Club-World

BRITISH AIRWAYS
The world's favourite airline

TERMS &CONDITIONS: To qualify, become a member of the Executive Club® USA and travel one transatlantic round-trip or two translatlantic sectors on Brotish Airways (BA) on a qualifying full-fare Club World ticket. Tickets must be purchased in the U.S. in U.S. dollars. Double miles are valid one time only during the promotion (March 4–June 30, 1998).Must pre-register for for mileage, To receive the certificate for the guarantee, write us by July 18, 1998 and tell us why the Club World experience was not satisfactory. Send your letter to BA Executive Club, P.O. Box 1784, Minneapolis, MN 55440-1784. BA is not responsible for lost or misdirected submissions. Only one certificate per member. valid for one east-bound transatlantic flight segment on or before March 31, 1999 from the U.S. to the U.K. in Concorde (Concorde available from JFK only) or First when you purchase a qualifying full-fare round trip Club World transatlantic flight on BA. Bookings in Concorde or First are subject to availability and may be made no less than 72 hours prior to departure.BA is not liable for the cost of connecting, interline or other transportation to or from a BA U.S. gateway city in connection with this offer. You may be required to produce proof of purchase for the flight which was unsatisfactory. This certificate is non-transferable, no cash substitutions and is only valid for the Executive Club member on the certificate; void if altered and will not be reissued if lost or stolen. Not available in conjunction with any other or promotion. Full terms and conditions of the Executive Club apply and are containedin the membership Handbook. ©1998 British AirwaysPlc.

Figure 10-2. Rocky Mountain Radar.

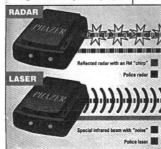

by 1,200 AOL subscribers. Bear in mind that this audience was probably skewed toward young adults. The ads were screened by 150 adults using hand-held meters to register their reactions electronically. The list appeared in the March 22, 1999, issue of *USA Today*.[1] Following is the ranking and the year the ad ran.

1. Wendy's, "Where's the beef?" 1984
2. California Raisin Advisory Board, "Lunch Box," 1986
3. Alka-Seltzer, "Spicy Meatball," 1969
4. Hallmark, "One hundredth birthday," 1990
5. Nissan, "Toys," 1996

The Wendy's commercial needs no additional description. The phrase "Where's the beef?" became a national cry for quality. Wendy's credited it with helping boost sales 31 percent and profit 24 percent in the first year. The problem with the commercial was that it was difficult to make into a campaign. You want to develop two or more ads or commercials, whether they are for print (newspapers and magazines), or broadcast (radio and television) that say basically the same thing. They should just be different renderings. That's what a campaign is; one ad reinforces the other.

A common mistake companies make is to run an ad talking about inventory control in January, then in March run an ad about quality control. When the closing for the June ad approaches, the company's ad manager may ask, "What haven't we talked about recently?" She is confusing the market as to what the company represents. Develop your positioning statement and a basic selling line to reinforce it. Design a series of ads or commercials that present your decisions, each one with a slightly different flavor.

The California Raisin Advisory Board commercial featured the dancing Claymation raisins. This commercial was part of a campaign that ran for several years. The commercials were so much fun to watch that in many households various members of the family would run into the television room when alerted that the commercial was being aired. No sales figures are available.

The Alka-Seltzer commercial was a commercial within a commercial. The commercial announcer kept flubbing his lines in his attempt to promote a brand of spicy meatball. After numerous takes—and bites of spicy meatballs—he gets heartburn. After he drinks Alka-Seltzer, he is able to deliver the line, but when he does, the oven door pops open and ruins the take. Some sources state that the commercial did not run a long time because Italian-Americans accused the company of stereotyping. Other sources stated that the commercial was pulled because it did not sell product. Research indicated that the public enjoyed the humor of the commercial, except when they had a condition calling for the product. Then the situation was not funny, and they purchased a competitive brand that did not use humor in their advertising. Be careful about using humor. When done right, it can be very effective. As long as the brand is compatible with a humorous situation and the reader or viewer remembers the name of the advertiser. When not done right, it can be a disaster.

Take special note of the Hallmark listing. This winner is from an emotional campaign that has been running for years. These commercials bring both tears of joy and smiles from ear to ear for some viewers. In addition to being extremely successful in selling product, they offer the best example of how to run a campaign rather than individual ads. Each one portrays the same selling line, which is basically: "When you care enough to send the very best." Every new commercial reinforces the previous ones.

The Nissan commercial aired in 1996. A G.I. Joe look-alike doll woos a comely girl doll away from a straitlaced male doll and takes her for a ride around the house. Although this "Toys" spot cost $1 million to produce, it did nothing to improve Nissan's lackluster sales. It is interesting that the co-creator said, "I believe if 'Toys' were part of a mix with more traditional car advertising, it would have been successful." This is an example of a commercial that was entertaining, but had no sales appeal. Many people remember the commercial, but cannot state the name of the advertiser. Don't be too cute if it gets in the way of your basic selling line.

To be effective, the basic selling line doesn't have to be in type or spoken. It can be a symbol that stands alone or in conjunction with the written or spoken word. The most famous example is the Marlboro cowboy, who never says anything. He took the brand from twenty-fifth in market share to number one in the world. Other symbols are the Pillsbury Doughboy, Procter & Gamble's Mr. Clean, Home Depot's Homer, McDonald's arches, and Nike's swoosh.

You may think you don't have the money to create a marketing symbol. Katrina Garnett, CEO of a small company named CrossWorlds Software, proved this theory wrong. She ran an ad that featured a glamour shot of herself in a provocative black cocktail dress. The ad didn't have a dynamic headline or spellbinding body copy. The headline was "Trail Blazer," and the text listed Ms. Garnett's attributes as younger than Bill Gates and older than Michael Dell. It also included the company's mission statement, "Build software applications that unite the operations of global enterprises."

It was the photograph that did it. A fellow CEO stated, "Everywhere I go, people are asking—who is this person? It must really be working." Indeed it did. Ms. Garnett and her company were featured in a half dozen newspapers, *Fortune,* and *Forbes.* She has been interviewed on CNBC, Fox News, and ABC. Most important of all, she received several calls from potential customers requesting more information on her business.

It doesn't take a lot of money to develop effective advertising. If you have a service you believe in, one that is better than the competition, just tell the story. Don't try to be cute. Be unique. The headline and visual should depict what the service will do for the buyer—the benefit. The body copy should contain the facts—the features—that make the benefit believable. Keep the format simple and easy to read.

Blame the Product or Service

You can't write a great ad for a product that doesn't contain the right benefits. Conversely, writing an effective ad is relatively easy for a product that offers a competitive edge. Determine the hot buttons for each key individual in the buying decision. Then the question is, can you deliver the benefits? If the answer is yes, writing the ad should not be difficult.

If you can't deliver the benefits, question whether you should be spending any marketing dollars on this brand. You can have a me-too brand and still be successful like Marlboro, Budweiser, and Coca-Cola. (Royal Crown usually wins blind taste tests over both Pepsi and Coca-Cola.) The successful brands have acquired a competitive edge through effective marketing. If you have a me-too brand, maybe you can do the same by running dynamic promotions on your brand or by creating a competitive edge by the way you offer technical support, terms, policies, delivery time, or customer service. If not, maybe the best thing to do is to fix the brand before you try to sell it.

Formatting Your Ads

If your objective is to reach the maximum number of readers per dollar, run small ads. A one-half page ad will reach more readers per dollar than a full-page. A full-page ad will reach more readers per dollar than a two-page spread. If your objective is to persuade people to try your brand, the opposite is true. A two-page spread delivers what is referred to as the "ability-to-persuade" index more than twice the index for a full-page ad. A full-page ad delivers an ability-to-persuade index more than double the index for a half-page ad. Therefore, if your objective is to persuade the potential customer to do something, go with the largest size ad you can afford as long as you still meet the frequency minimum, which is discussed later in this chapter.

Stay away from reverse body copy. Reverse body copy is white text on a black background. Using reverse copy sometimes improves the appearance of an ad, but it will drastically cut your readership. Put your headline in reverse as long as the type size is large. The same is true for a subhead—maybe even a few words of body copy. Beyond that, research indicates that you will lose up to 50 percent of your potential readers. The reason is that reverse type in a relatively small size looks hard to read. When something looks hard to read, many people won't read it. What you definitely don't want to do is put your entire brochure in reverse copy. Many companies do and it's a shame. What they are saying to the prospective reader is, "I dare you to try to read my brochure."

Stay away from surprinting, too. Surprinting is colored type on a different color background. If the contrast between the type and the background is pronounced, you may not hurt your readership. If it isn't, once again you are making your ad or promotional material hard to read. Consequently, many people will not read it.

Always have one dominant focal point when using print advertising, whether it is for a magazine, newspaper, or a brochure. The purpose is to give the eye someplace to land. Usually the focal center is one photograph or artwork with the headline next to it. Do not use two or more photos or artwork of the same size or intensity in an ad or, what is often seen, four photographs of the same size on a brochure page. These techniques confuse the eye, which doesn't know where to start looking. If you want to show more than one major element, make one larger than the rest.

Research indicates that ads with photographs obtain higher readership scores than those with artwork. Lowe's, the nation's second largest home improvement center, reached a similar conclusion. Their research indicated that people would prefer pictures of employees rather than the cartoon characters they were using in their ads. The customers said they would prefer that Lowe's present itself as authoritative rather than amusing. Nonetheless, Home Depot is continuing to use Homer, its cartoon mascot in print advertising and brochures. He is the one with the Home Depot hat pulled halfway over his eyes.

The ad format that receives the highest readership scores is one that has a large photograph or artwork at the top illustrating the benefit of the brand, followed by a headline containing the benefit and the name of the brand or company, then the body copy containing features that support the benefit and make it believable. (See Figure 10-3.)

Figure 10-3. Ad format receiving highest readership scores.

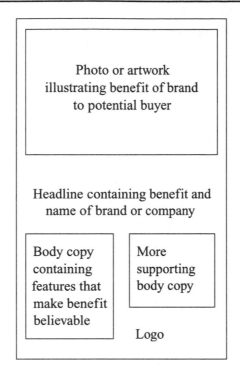

Because this format receives the highest readership scores does not necessarily mean that every ad you run has to match it. However, I recommend that you not vary from this format unless you have a good reason for doing so, such as the Rocky Mountain Radar ad. Art directors might change the format just for the sake of change and by so doing come up with a design that is hard to read. Sometimes they put the headline at the top of the page, the body copy in the middle, and the photograph at the bottom. The problem is two focal points, one being the headline and the other being the photograph. The reader's eye may jump back and forth between the headline and photograph, and eventually the mind may settle down to an analysis of the page. Then again, the eye may bounce back and forth, with no registration in the mind. When this happens, the eye usually leaves the page. In contrast, the format above has just one dominant element or focal point, which is the photograph and headline combined. Normally the eye will glance at the photograph, and if the mind finds it interesting, continue down to the headline. If the mind finds the headline beneficial, then, hopefully, it will take the eye down into the body copy.

Developing a Creative Strategy

You need to develop a *creative strategy* before you start developing your advertising material. A creative strategy is the outline or summation of your marketing communications. It contains your basic selling line and the copy points that support the statement. It can also state the tone or flavor of your communications, such as humorous or businesslike. There are two purposes for this document. One is the opportunity to get management to sign off on the ingredients of the marketing message before designing the creative material. When you show an ad, brochure, or sales presentation to management and they want to add extras, such as a picture of the company founder, you can prevent it by reminding them that ingredient was not in the approved creative strategy.

The other purpose is to provide a directional document that can be used by all members of your marketing team, so that all your material has that common thread. Creative strategy like your basic selling line, should be developed by copywriters and art directors. An example is shown in the marketing plan outline in Appendix A.

Determining Your Advertising Budget

Basing your budget on an arbitrary number of insertions or spots is not a reliable method. The reason is that one insertion in one particular magazine could reach twice as many target customers as an insertion in another publication. As previously discussed, using a percent of sales is equally misleading because what you spent last year or what your competitors are spending should not be a basis for what you should spend this year.

The best way to determine how much to spend on advertising is by using *reach* and *frequency* because it is based on your advertising objective. If the terminology of reach and frequency is new to you, you may need some help with the calculations. Ask your advertising agency or media salespeople, look up the subject at the library, or go on the Internet and type in the words in a search engine keyword box.

There are three factors used in the calculations: *reach*, *frequency*, and *the gross number of impressions. Reach* is the number or percent of your target audience that has the opportunity to see or hear your message at least once. It is an unduplicated number. You can only count a person once. Therefore, you want to know the amount of audience duplication in the media you have chosen. There is a considerable amount of research available on this subject such as estimated audience duplication of various types of radio, television, and magazines. Your ad agency or media salesperson can provide this information. There might not be information for the audience duplication of trade magazines having a relatively low circulation. If that is the case in your market, go with your best estimate.

The *gross number of impressions* is the total number of times the target audience has the opportunity to see or hear your ad. For print, the gross number is calculated by multiplying each insertion of an ad by the magazine's or newspaper's circulation. For broadcast, multiply each spot by its estimated audience. These are easy mathematical calculations. If possible, use circulation and audience figures that only include members of your target audience.

Don't confuse the *gross number of impressions* with *reach*. The *gross number of impressions* is a gross number. A person is counted each time he or she has the opportunity to see or hear your ad. *Reach* is a net or unduplicated figure. You count a person only once, regardless of how many times they have the opportunity to see or hear your ad.

Frequency is the average number of times a member of your target audience has the opportunity to see or hear your ad. Your goal should be a number between five and ten. To arrive at this number, you use an equation. This equation is the gross number of impressions equals reach times frequency. This equation is mathematically correct because multiplying the unduplicated audience (*reach*) by the average number of times they see or hear the commercial (*frequency*) equals the gross number of times (*gross number of impressions*) the audience sees or hears the commercial.

Knowing two of the three factors—*reach* and *gross number of impressions*—you can determine the third, which is *frequency*. The *gross number of impressions* you can calculate yourself. The *reach* figure is provided by research. Just as in your algebra class in school, when you solve for an unknown in an equation, you want this unknown by itself on one side of the equation. In this case, you are solving for the value of *frequency*, so to isolate this factor, you divide both sides by *reach*. The equations are shown in Figure 10-4.

To calculate *frequency*, divide the *gross number of impressions* by *reach*. For example, an advertiser obtains 100,000 *gross number of impressions* from running four insertions in three magazines. Research done by the magazines reveals that the three magazines have an unduplicated circulation or *reach* of 40,000. The *frequency* is 2.5 (100,000 divided by 40,000).

Calculating the Budget

Let's move on to calculating the budget. The first step is to set an objective. Let's say your objective is to obtain an awareness level of 50 percent. To obtain an awareness of 50 percent will require a *reach* of about 70 percent because not everyone who has the opportunity to see or hear your ad will remember it. If your objective is an awareness level of 70 percent, you will probably need a reach of 90 to 95 percent. Therefore, the second step is to set your *reach*.

The third step is to set your *frequency*. According to past advertising research, you should normally have a frequency between 5 and 10. The

Figure 10-4. Solving for the value of frequency.

Original equation................ Gross # of impressions = reach x frequency

Divide both sides by reach... $\dfrac{\text{Gross \# of impressions}}{\text{reach}} = \dfrac{\text{reach x frequency}}{\text{reach}}$

Reach cancels out on the
right hand side and the $\dfrac{\text{Gross \# of impressions}}{\text{reach}} = \text{frequency}$
equation becomes................

---

period within which to obtain this frequency varies by media. For monthly magazines, it is a year. For weekly magazines, it is ninety days. For daily newspapers, radio, and television, it is thirty days. This is why effective television advertising is so expensive. To obtain a national frequency of 5 on television for one month would take about 20–25 spots in prime time (8 P.M. to 11 P.M.) per week, and cost between $4 to $5 million.

There are several factors that influence when you can stay at the lower ends of the preferred frequency level and when you should stay at the high end. Five of these factors are: creativity; newness of the brand; aggressiveness of the program; inherent interest of the brand category; and the size and color of your ad or length of the commercial. For example, if you believe you have a very creative ad, you can stay near the lower end of the frequency spectrum such as the fives and sixes. If your ad is just mediocre, then you should stay at the higher range of 8, 9, or 10. If you have a new brand, stay at the higher end. If advertising is going to play a very important part in your marketing program, then stay at the higher end of the range. If you are in an exciting brand category like fashion, cosmetics, or food, you can stay at the lower end. If you are selling nuts and bolts, stay at the higher end. If you are running full-page, four-color ads or 60-second commercials you can stay at the lower end. If you are running less than a full-page ad or 30-second commercials, stay at the higher end.

Once you know the desired reach and frequency, keep adding insertions or spots to your media schedule until you reach these goals. After you determine the number of insertions or spots needed, cost them out. That's your budget. If the budget is too high, lower your reach and frequency requirements, which in turn, lowers your objective. That's a fast overview of reach and frequency, so if this interests you, which it should if you are spending advertising dollars, obtain detailed information from the sources mentioned above.

Three key things to remember are:

1. Have a greater *reach* than the awareness level you want to obtain.

2. Repeat the message enough times (a *frequency* between 5 to 10) so hopefully most potential customers will remember it.

3. Build *frequency* first and then add *reach*. Use sufficient number of spots or insertions to obtain your frequency requirement and then add as much audience (reach) as you can while still maintaining your required frequency.

Selecting Your Advertising Media

There are three factors to consider when selecting advertising media. They are:

- Type of message

- Budget

- Audience profile

If your target audience is the general public, you have a choice of radio, television, consumer magazines, newspapers, or outdoor advertising. If your story requires an extensive or scientific explanation, you probably will be limited to print—newspapers and magazines. If your story can be told in six words or less, outdoor advertising, where available, is a good possibility. Six words or less is the maximum for an effective outdoor poster. When sound effects enhance your message, radio should be considered. Television advertising should normally be saved for brands that require a demonstration or action to tell their story and used by companies that can afford to use it correctly. Television is the most effective media selling tool. It is also the most expensive. Because of its high cost, many television advertisers cannot afford to reach the minimum frequency of 5. Consequently, they may be wasting all their media dollars.

For companies advertising to other businesses, trade magazines covering their particular markets are usually the best selection, regardless of the type of message, because mass media has too much wasted circulation. Large companies, with more budget freedom than smaller ones, sometimes use trade magazines plus mass media. The wasted circulation is larger for the mass media, but as you will see, the *cost per thousand* (CPM) is lower.

CPM is the cost to reach each one thousand people using a particular size ad or length of commercial in a particular medium. Use CPM to help determine your media selection if more than one meet all other criteria. In addition, after you select your media, use CPM to determine which media you will use, such as individual stations or magazines. To calculate CPM, divide the cost of the medium by its audience, measured in thousands. Audience figures are furnished to you by the medium and are based on the numbers supplied by various research companies. You want to calculate your CPM based on your target audience, not the entire audience, although these numbers are not always available.

Following is a discussion of various media in order of ascending CPM. CPM is given for a local market—Raleigh-Durham-Chapel Hill, North Carolina—as well as national averages to illustrate that the CPM for individual media companies can vary substantially from market to market. Check your own local market for comparison before making any decisions.

Outdoor Advertising

Of all advertising media, outdoor 30-sheet posters—the large paper posters you see along highways and streets—offer you the lowest CPM. In the Raleigh-Durham-Chapel Hill metro area, the CPM for adults is approximately $1.25. The national average is $1.80. To use this medium, your message is printed on paper and then an outdoor company pastes the sheets on the wooden panels. There are also painted bulletins. These are larger than the 30-sheet posters and the message is painted on the wood panels. You usually contract for a painted bulletin for a three-year period.

If the individuals in your buying decision are members of the mass audience and your selling line can be stated in six or fewer words, think about using outdoor advertising. The production costs for printing the sheets to be posted may be relatively high, but you can use the same sheets for several months. If the printing costs are too high, even for multiple use, consider painted bulletins.

Mass Audience Magazines

The second most economical media are mass audience magazines such as *People,* with an average adult CPM of approximately $3.00 for a one-page, four-color ad. The problem is the total cost of an insertion. Besides, a national mass audience is probably not your target. However, most of these magazines offer regional buys. This means you can run your ad in specific parts of the country, although the CPM will be slightly higher. If you are going after a large audience in specific sections of the country and your selling line requires a photograph or artwork in beautiful color, this could be your medium of choice.

Radio

The third most economical medium is radio. For example, the CPM for adults for a 30-second commercial on a local station in Raleigh-Durham-

Chapel Hill is approximately $11.50. This is extremely high; the national average is only approximately $3.50. (A good example why you should always shop around for the best media buys.) This is for spot radio, which means individual stations. For network, it is only approximately $2.50. A network buy consists of a group of stations across the entire country. Radio is called a frequency medium, which means you can reach a relatively small group of people many times. For example, a four-week schedule of fifteen spots per week will deliver a frequency of about 4, but with a reach of only about 10 percent.

To use spot radio, your target audience should be concentrated in the listeners of one or more stations and your selling line should lend itself to music such as a jingle or song, or some type of special sound effects. Radio stations have specific audience profiles due to their different formats of talk and music. The individual stations can provide you with this information, including demographic, and possibly psychographic, profiles. The advantage of radio commercials is that spots can be bought locally on individual stations at a low CPM and the production costs are relatively low. If radio delivers your audience and you or your agency are creative with sound, radio should be your first choice.

Spot Television

The fourth most economical medium is spot television. The CPM for adults using a 30-second commercial on a local station in Raleigh-Durham-Chapel Hill is approximately $5. The national average is approximately $6 for early evening time and $10 for late evening news. Television is a reach medium compared to radio, which is a frequency medium. This means with TV you can reach many people a few times. For example, a four-week schedule of fifteen spots per week will deliver a frequency of only about four, but a reach in the range of 80 percent. The same schedule on radio, which would only cost about 20 percent of the television buy, will also deliver a frequency of about 4, but a reach of only about 10 percent.

Television is the most effective advertising medium because it combines sight with sound. The problem is that the production costs alone could exceed your entire media budget. Production costs for a 30-second commercial start at around $25,000 and go up to several million dollars. However, like everything else, there are exceptions. Engineered Protection Systems Inc. has seen sales climb from $350,000 in 1997 to $1.8 million in 1998, and they attribute the leap primarily to their ads on local cable television. This Houston-based commercial electronic-security company claims their ads only cost $200 to produce and cost $10 per placement. However, the commercials are scheduled late at night when total television viewing is light. They compare these costs with a half-page spread in the local business journal that goes for $5,000 per insertion. And they claim just one 30-second spot on AM talk radio runs around $150.[2]

Direct-response television (DRTV) is another possibility. Smart-Mop, a unique Finnish mop with a self-wringing twist action had sales of $1.8 million in 1993. Using DRTV and subsequent expansion into retail stores, the company grossed $44 million in 1994. The company produced a 28-minute infomercial in 1993 and orders poured in every time it aired. During a five-month period, they received almost three million orders. When the frenzy died down, the company commissioned a distributor to obtain distribution in retail stores. Within days, the mop was in Wal-Mart and Kmart.[3]

In reality, only the minority of the consumers who see an infomercial actually call the advertised toll-free number to purchase an item. Most wait until the product is on the shelves of local retail stores. "Direct-response TV ads only account for 9 percent of all sales of an advertised product," said Anand Khubani, president of wholesale operations for TeleBrands. "While we generate a revenue stream through direct TV, we are more interested in building a huge, pent-up demand for the product in the retail marketplace. Since we know that 91 percent of consumers prefer to purchase the products at a retail outlet, we first demonstrate the product on direct TV to create consumer awareness and demand.

Then a few months after the ads go off the air, we start shipping to retail stores."[4]

Home shopping channels like QVC are another possibility. Scott Ellis, a buyer for QVC, says only products with "great demonstration quality" work with the QVC format. "Some items sell very well on store shelves," said Ellis, "but if you have a product that requires a demonstration to be understood or appreciated—especially if it's a new gadget no one has seen before—QVC may be your best bet."[5]

Newspapers

The fifth most economical advertising medium is newspapers. For example, the CPM for adults for a one-third page, black and white ad in the *Raleigh News & Observer* in North Carolina is approximately $5. This is well below the national average of approximately $9. Daily newspapers offer the opportunity to get an ad out to the public in less than a week, especially if it is in black and white. You can produce a black and white newspaper ad in a day or two if it has a relatively simple design. Many times the newspaper will produce it for you, free of charge. Four-color ads take longer to produce—one to two weeks. However, newspaper closing dates are just a few days in advance of publication, regardless of whether the ad is black and white or in color. A closing date is the last day you have to deliver your commercial or ad to the medium. In comparison, radio and television commercials can take several weeks or months to produce. The same is true for magazine ads. Radio, television, and magazines usually have closing dates several weeks in advance of air time or publication.

Be careful about running four-color photographs in newspapers that still print using letterpresses. This type of press only prints 65 dots per square inch, which means the reproduction will not be good. In contrast, magazines use offset presses that print a minimum of 120 dots per square inch. Some newspapers, especially those with a small circulation, have now gone to offset presses.

Trade and Specialty Magazines

Trade and specialty magazines have the highest CPM. The average CPM for a full-page, four-color ad for trade magazines is approximately $50. This may appear to be extremely high compared to the CPMs for the other media, but their CPM only includes individual households or subscribers. The reason is that normally only one person per household or subscription reads a trade magazine. The CPMs for the other types of print media are for total adults per household plus pass-along readership.

The average CPM for specialty magazines aimed at men is approximately $12 and for magazines with selective women's interest, $9. Like trade magazines, these CPMs are high, but you have little wasted circulation. Using these types of magazines in comparison with other media is called a *rifle approach*. You can zero in on your target without wasting any ammunition on nonprospects. All other media, with the possible exception of radio, are shotgun approaches. You spray your message out to the entire audience, just as a shotgun fires a spread of pellets, hoping that you will hit some of your target audience. Be careful when you compare CPMs. The only audience that counts is your target audience.

Testing Your Advertising

When you spend money you always want to know what you receive in return. With advertising, that's hard to do. Procter & Gamble spends millions on concept, copy, and commercial testing, but for smaller companies, that's not in the budget. There is a way to test your advertising that won't cost you anything. It is not as scientific as the way the major corporations do it, but it will provide you with some valuable information. This inexpensive method is to include a telephone number, coupon, or some element that requires reply action on the part of the reader in your advertising.

Assume you have two different concepts or ads you want to test. Call them A and B. Also assume you are going to use your telephone number as a measuring device. You run them both and the results are ten phone calls from A and forty from B. What you have proven is that of those who called, more were interested in what you said in ad B than in A. Therefore, you can assume that among all those that did not call, they also preferred B. It is highly unlikely that those that did not call have just the opposite preference from those who did call.

Consider adding a telephone number, coupon, or some other type of tracking device in every promotional activity you run. It's an affordable method of testing each program's effectiveness. Advertising research will be discussed in greater detail in Chapter Eighteen.

Notes

1. Melanie Wells, "Top ads tickled, tugged at heart," *USA Today*, March 22, 1999.

2. Marc Ballon, "TV for the rest of us," *Inc.*, March 1999, p. 83.

3. David Doran, "Station Breaks," *Entrepreneur*, September 1998, p. 147.

4. Ibid.

5. Ibid.

Chapter Eleven

Using Direct Marketing to Sell

or Produce Leads

What Is Direct Marketing?

The Direct Marketing Association (DMA) in their promotional material states, "Direct marketing is an interactive system of marketing which uses one or more advertising media to effect a measurable response and/or transaction at any location." Based on this definition, you might think that direct marketing is limited to direct mail and telemarketing. That is a mistake. There are many benefits to be gained from trying to make all of your promotional tools interactive. It helps build your database. It indicates which activity is working best. It will increase your interactivity with customers, and nothing precipitates sales faster than one-on-one relationships. Include a coupon or reply card, an 800 number, and a Web address in all of your promotional activity. Display this information in your print ads, mention it in radio and television commercials, highlight it in your trade show exhibit, and include it in your press releases. It doesn't cost you anything extra.

An example of how direct marketing can improve the effectiveness of your complete promotional program is the strategy used by Bose Corporation. Bose uses print, radio, and television to interest music lovers in their radios and CD players, coupled with a request to contact them. Once a person responds, they use direct mail to close the sale. They test and retest mailings to ensure each piece is getting the highest, most targeted response. One variable is isolated in each mailing to see if it improves response. They conduct phone interviews with mail recipients to find out which messages are most meaningful. Bose then uses that information to modify their ads, commercials, and future mailings.

Another example of how direct marketing can help you test your programs is the experience of Printronix, a small company that produces a range of line matrix, laser, and thermal printers. They determined that one form of interactive marketing, direct mail, delivered the lowest cost per *qualified lead*. (A qualified lead is one that has been contacted by the company to verify its legitimacy.) Through interactive research Printronix learned that other marketing programs did, in fact, bring in more qualified leads than direct mail. When they measured the cost per lead, direct mail once again did not win. However, when they took a look at the cost per qualified lead for all promotions, they found that direct mail was the most cost-effective by a large margin.

Establishing a Database

To get your interactive promotional program rolling, you need a database. Following are some suggested fields in your database:

1. Name of individual

2. Mailing and shipping address

3. Telephone number

4. Size and type of company or family

5. Job description

6. Demographics and psychographics

7. Ranking in purchase process (see Chapter 4)

8. What features/benefits are sought (see Chapter 4)

9. What features/benefits are delivered (see Chapter 4)

10. Sources of inquiry card/or order

11. Date of inquiry/or order

12. Cost of inquiry/or order

13. History of purchase
    a. By date

    b. By items purchased

    c. By dollar amount of purchase

    d. By cumulative dollars

14. Geographical or segment grouping

How you acquire this information depends on your business and resources. If you compile it yourself, like Bose Corporation, you will have what marketers call the cleanest or heaviest concentration of target customers. Regardless of what source you use, add your current and past customer base to the database.

Three good sources for business-to-business databases are trade show attendees, association members, and trade magazine subscribers who are directed at your industry. For consumer mailing lists, your best bet is individuals who have purchased something else direct in the past. If you have ever purchased direct, you probably noticed an immediate increase in the direct mail you received from other direct marketers. You are now considered a hot prospect to buy direct, regardless of the category. The reason is that those who buy direct keep buying direct versus those who will never buy direct, even if you give away the product.

Obviously you want to build your database mailing list from the former, not the latter. Although those who buy direct do cross over into different categories of goods, your optimum list will include those who have purchased an item similar to yours.

If you need assistance in acquiring data, there are many companies that offer mailing lists and some of these will help you with your complete campaign. To review their offerings, use the keywords "mailing list" in an Internet search. You may also want to try "direct mail." Also try the Yellow Pages. Look under the headings mailing houses and mailing list consultants.

If you are selling business-to-business, three companies that you definitely want to check out are:

> Dun & Bradstreet: telephone: 1-800-879-1362, extension 3030; www.dnb.com
>
> InfoUSA: telephone: 1-800-321-0869; www.lookupusa.com
>
> Metroville: directory.metroville.com

If you are selling to consumers, check out:

> Metromail Corp., which is now part of Experian: telephone: 1-800-831-5614; www.experian.com
>
> Nationwide Data Services: telephone: 1-800-579-5478; www.nationwidedata.com
>
> SRI: Offers Vals 2, which uses psychographic market segmentation: telephone: 1-650-859-4600 for the western U.S. or 1-609-734-2048 for the east; sri.com/vals/valshome.html; e-mail: info@future.sri.com

If you use an outside source for your mailing list, be sure that the names and addresses are current and the profiles are correct. Dun & Bradstreet claims that everything else being equal, a valid mailing list contributes 60 percent to the success of a direct mail program. They add that the offer is responsible for 20 percent, copy 15 percent, and format 5 percent.

There are many different types of software programs that can help you compile your database. A relational database, such as Microsoft Access, is probably the best for direct marketing. This kind of database allows you to ask invaluable questions such as: "Which customers have purchased in the last three months?" "Who bought brand X in the last six months?" This information helps to determine whom to call next week, whom to include in your next direct mail or catalog mailing, and what and to whom you should be *cross selling*. Cross selling is marketing an item to a customer who has already purchased another item from you.

Using Direct Mail

Once you've created a database, you can try direct mail. You'll want to create what is called a mailing piece. The mailing piece should consist of:

1. An outer envelope or self-mailer

2. A brochure

3. A letter

4. An order or reply form

5. Gift slips and other enclosures

The most critical part of your mailing piece is probably the envelope. If the recipient doesn't open it, all is for naught. According to Bob Stone in his book *Successful Direct Marketing Methods* (Lincolnwood, Ill.: NTC Business Books, 1996), the envelope should:

Dazzle readers with color or graphics and with promises of important benefits if they will open it.

Impress readers with its simplicity and lead them to believe that the contents must be important.

Tease the readers and so excite their curiosity that they simply must open it.

Simplicity is usually the most effective approach when selling business to business. This holds true for the contents as well. The dazzle and the tease should be saved for reaching the consumer. For consumer mailings, consider adding a selling message next to the address panel. You know it will be read. Stay away from using a postage meter if you can. First-class stamps are best, but if that is too expensive, consider pre-canceled third-class stamps. When you use pre-canceled stamps, you only pay for the stamps actually used or sent through the mail.

Direct mail research indicates that the most effective inside package is a combination of a brochure and a letter. Each piece should do a complete selling job. Don't talk about your offer in one and dedicate the other to another subject such as a list of products or prizes. Keep the two pieces compatible in design. Add color if it is appropriate. The cost of adding color is usually less than the resulting increase in profitability of the mailing. A combination of artwork and photography on your brochure and letter usually works the best.

Ideally, you should open both the letter and the brochure with a benefit, just as you should with an ad or commercial. The beauty of direct mail, unlike an ad or commercial, is that you can alter the benefit in the pieces that you send to various individuals in the purchase process or buying decision. After you play up the benefit, describe exactly what the recipient will be receiving, including size, color, weight, and sales terms. Don't scatter this information throughout the contents. Tell the complete story up front in both the letter and brochure.

Support your benefit with features as discussed in previous chapters. Testimonials by current customers are the most effective method of selling business to business because you are adding a third-party endorsement. It makes the benefit more believable. You need to include the customer's name, address, and picture. Without this information, the believability of the testimonial is greatly diminished.

Be sure to end with a call to action and support it with a benefit to the reader, using either the one mentioned at the beginning of the letter and brochure or a different one. After your signature, add a postscript. The first sentence of the message and the postscript usually receive the highest readership scores. The postscript should contain a special offer or additional support for the call to action.

If you want a specific format for writing sales letters, Robert W. Bly recommends a five step approach in his book *Power-Packed Direct Mail* (New York: Henry Holt, 1996). He refers to the five steps as the "motivating sequence." They are:

1. Get attention.
2. Show a need.
3. Satisfy the need.
4. Prove your superiority.
5. Ask for action.

The first paragraph should get the reader's attention by talking about a problem she most likely has encountered. The second paragraph shows the need to solve the problem. The next paragraph(s) demonstrates how to satisfy the need. Next, is a paragraph(s) on why you are the best supplier to solve that need. At the end, ask for action.

Your call to action should include having the recipient fill out and mail an order form, request more information by calling an 800 number or submitting a reply card. Henry Cowen, a direct marketing specialist, stated in a speech, "There are direct mail manuals around that recommend simple, easy-to-read order forms, but my experience indicates the mailer is far better off with a busy, rather jumbled appearance and plenty of copy. Formal and legal-looking forms that appear valuable, too valuable to throw away, are good." Putting as much information as you can on the order form or reply card is good advice because many people read only the first two or three lines of your letter and then skip to these forms.

If your call to action is an order form, include all the necessary features of your products or services, including prices. The order form or reply card should be a self-mailer or include a self-addressed envelope in the package. Either way, include postage on the form. You can obtain a business-reply permit (BRP) from the post office, which enables you to pay the postage on only those forms that are actually returned.

If using a reply card, give the recipient one question to answer and three choices or check boxes to mark. The question is: When are you expecting to make the purchase? The three choices are:

Have a consultant call.

Send more information.

Not interested.

Notice that the first option is to have a consultant call the customer. Do not use the word salesperson because many people believe that means they will be subjected to a hard sell. You are better off using a title like consultant, technician, or engineer.

Adding a not interested choice can actually increase the number of closings. If someone takes the time to check not interested, there must be some interest in the product or service category, but your presentation is not on target. However, an objection has been identified and if you can overcome it, a sale could be made.

When sending material to answer a request for more information, be sure to include a bounce-back card. Make it easy to complete by the use of check marks and include return postage. Questions on the bounce-back card should include whether the information furnished satisfies the recipient's needs, and, if not, what else is needed, as well as asking again when the person anticipates making the purchase.

Whenever a bounce-back or reply card states an interest in purchasing near-term, this information should be noted in the database and the prospective customer contacted immediately. Always qualify your leads before giving them to a salesperson. If you give a salesperson just a couple of unqualified leads, you lose the salesperson's trust. He will throw all subsequent ones in the trash. The best method to use to qualify leads is by telephone. If the prospective customer is not immediately in need of the brand, but still shows interest, this information should be inserted in the database and passed on to the sales team for follow-up.

Gifts can have a tremendous impact on the response rate, sometimes increasing it 25 to 50 percent. However, offering the right gift can be tricky because some have actually reduced the response rate. If possible, always test your offer in a limited number of mailings before you expand it to your complete database. Another insert to consider is a small sheet of paper folded over with a message on the outside reading something like, "Only open if you plan not to accept this offer." Practically all recipients will open it up and that is where you tempt them with another sales message. Research indicates that this strategy can increase your returns by 10 percent.

Something that you think may not work, actually does. It's the postcard deck. These are the bundles of 40–50 postcards that you receive in the mail. They measure $3\frac{1}{2}'' \times 5\frac{3}{8}''$, and have a selling message on one side and the return address on the other. Book publishers have stated that postcards are one of the best selling tools they use. There is only a small area on one side of the card for your message, so your format should be similar to what you use for outdoor advertising. In outdoor advertising you have a huge space to work with, but you have to catch a person's eye as they whiz by your poster. For postcards, you only have a small space, but you have to catch the reader's eye as they quickly shuffle through the deck. Participating in a postcard deck costs about five cents per unit, whereas a direct mail piece usually costs about 50 cents each. It's definitely worth a try.

Direct mail can be used to reach just about anyone, even chief executive officers of major corporations. For example, a computer software company was having trouble selling a new piece of software that cost $250,000. Their salespeople called on the vice presidents in charge of computer systems at the division level. Invariably, the prospects would say they liked the new system, but could not sign off on such a large expenditure. The prospects would suggest that the computer company's salesperson go to the corporate level. The salespeople did and got the same response. Even prospects at the corporate level could not sign off for such a large amount. They suggested that the salespeople contact their chief executive officers (CEOs). When one of the company's salespeople tried to obtain an appointment with the CEO, the reply was, "See my computer system personnel." They were getting nowhere.

The challenge for the computer software company was how to get the CEO and the computer system employees together for a joint presentation. Their thinking was that if they could do this, the computer systems employees would say they wanted the new software and the CEO would ask how much. To execute their strategy, they decided to use—of all things—direct mail.

The direct mail campaign consisted of four mailings. Each was mailed to a CEO in a plain brown envelope with no indication of the advertiser. On the inside of the first three mailings was an attractive brochure with a note clipped to the cover. The note read, "Opportunity comes frequently to a businessman, but great opportunity comes rarely. Our decision to seize an opportunity presented, or to reject it, affects each of our businesses irrevocably. That moment of great decision is always most difficult. In this folder, we have recreated an opportunity that presented itself to a businessman in the past. If that businessman were you, how would you have reacted to this opportunity? In a future mailing, we will tell you his decision and the eventual outcome."

In the first mailing, the only copy on the cover of the brochure was "Opportunity #1." The inside of the brochure described the case history of an investment opportunity that had been pursued by famous investor Bernard Baruch and the financier J.P. Morgan. All the details were given and then the copy asked the reader what he or she would have done under a similar circumstance. There was no mention of the advertiser.

The next two mailings contained similar case histories and in each the recipient was asked to match wits against the final outcome. The second mailing had the words "Opportunity #2" on the cover of the brochure and the third "Opportunity #3." Still no mention was made of the advertiser. In the fourth mailing, the cover of the brochure was labeled "Opportunity #4," and the note clipped to the cover of the brochure now had a different message. It started out by saying that the actual outcome of the case histories presented in the first three mailings were inside. The note ended with: "You will also find Opportunity #4. This one is for you."

The inside of the brochure contained the final outcome of the three case histories plus an envelope inserted in a pocket of the brochure. The message on the cover of the envelope was "Opportunity #4 (This one is for you.)" When the reader opened the envelope, the copy stated that the company had a specialized program of information processing services tailored to the needs of major corporations. It concluded: "We would very much like to present this opportunity to you and your staff. In a few days, I will call you to see if a mutually convenient meeting might be scheduled." At the bottom of the card was the company's logo, the first and only time the name of the advertiser was shown.

When the company called the recipients of the direct mail campaign, over 30 percent agreed to the meeting. That's not a bad return when you consider that the average for a specific mailing list purchased from a supplier is only 1 to 2 percent. A specific list includes just your target audience. Even a mailing to a company's own customers will only average 3–5 percent. The lowest average return results when you use a general list that isn't specific to your target audience. The average return is only one half of 1 percent.

As mentioned above, it does not necessarily take a lot of money to develop effective promotional material—just creativity. Even a trade magazine that could not afford its own sales staff obtained a major increase in ad pages as a result of just one inexpensive direct mail campaign. It included a nutty German scientist who was going to make the recipients—media buyers at advertising agencies—rich by giving them stock in his new company. Seven witty letters were sent by the mad scientist, each including, in an indirect way, reasons why advertisers should use this particular trade magazine. In the sixth letter, the scientist told the American media buyers he was leaving Germany tomorrow to join them. The seventh and last letter was forwarded from the Bureau of Missing Persons with a note of condolence to the addressee. The enclosed letter, whose edges were burnt off, stated that he was coming across on the Hindenburg zeppelin and he was bringing a torch with him for use in a demonstration.

Production costs for direct mail should no longer hinder its use. With the advent of desktop publishing, there is no reason why you can't do all the work yourself, with the possible exception of photography and printing. The same is true for print material. If you are not handy with a computer, hire a teenager. You give her direction and let her do the technical stuff.

Before you start designing your direct mail piece, always make a trip to the post office. Contact the person in charge of bulk mailing. Discuss your plans and go through all their requirements relative to size, weight, etc. The requirements for the various postage rates are tricky, too. Get a thorough explanation of each. Always show your contact a copy of your final design before you go into production for final approval.

Be careful about how you handle the payment to a photographer. Normally, you only have the right to use the photos for the specific use mentioned at the time of the shooting. To get around this, get a release in writing for subsequent usage. Another choice is to buy the negatives, then you can use the pictures any way you want.

Telemarketing

If you insert an 800 number in all your promotional material, you will be involved in telemarketing. Use telemarketing as an advertising medium just like print and broadcast. Telemarketing's popularity and effectiveness are confirmed by the fact that it accounts for the largest promotional expenditure within direct marketing. Probably the reason for its extensive use is that research indicates prospects responding by phone result in closure rates two to three times higher than prospects responding by mail.

Telemarketing can consist of:

1. Giving information and taking telephone orders

2. *Outbound marketing*, which means making telephone calls to prospects

3. Multidisciplinary promotion that combines product and price testing with electronic direct mail, telephone, and print selling plus order fulfillment and collecting

If you are only going to give information and take telephone orders, you can handle it in-house or you may want to get some help from a standard telemarketing service bureau. As detailed in Fred E. Hahn and Kenneth G. Mangun's book *Do-It-Yourself Advertising and Promotion* (New York: Wiley Small Business, 1997), a standard telemarketing service bureau will assist you in the following ways:

1. **Consultation at the Marketing Plan Stage.** What is a feasible result of using telemarketing? What are some alternatives? How long will it take to plan, test, and do, and what will it cost? Many telemarketers will meet with you for this kind of discussion without charge.

2. **Consultation on What the Project Is to Produce.** Will the telemarketers only take the orders? Deliver a message? Answer questions?

3. **Scripting, Testing, and Training.** Writing for telemarketing is an art in itself. But successful scripting is more than that. It requires testing to see whether the script works, modifying where necessary, and then training staff for a particular project. In telemarketing, how something is said is as important as what is said.

4. **Continuing Evaluation and Reports.** Every telemarketing project will become more efficient as its operators become more com-

fortable and proficient at their assignments. Reports should include:

a. Number of operators involved and how long.

b. Number of calls made or received.

c. Average time per call per operator.

d. Results.

e. Operators' comments, both impressions and hard facts.

f. Service bureau or department evaluation and recommendations.

When selecting people for your telemarketing program, do not consider any of your successful salespeople because they thrive on face-to-face encounters. You want someone who has good communications skills, can take rejection, has a pleasant-sounding voice, and can adapt to different personalities.

For those of you who are considering or are currently doing outbound telemarketing, following is a seven-step selling process, compliments of Bob Stone in his book *Successful Direct Marketing Methods*.

1. Precall Planning

    a. Reviewing client information.

    b. Planning objectives for the call.

    c. Psyching—getting mentally ready for the call.

2. Approach/Positioning

    a. Identify who you are and where you're from.

    b. State the purpose of the call.

    c. Create interest.

    d. Build rapport.

    e. Get through the receptionist/screener.

    f. Reach the decision maker.

3. Data Gathering

    a.   Gain general understanding of the client's business.

    b.   Move from general to specific types of questions.

    c.   Questioning techniques.

    d.   Identifying a client business need.

4. Solution Generation

    a.   Tailor communication solution to specific client need.

    b.   Ask in-depth questions to test the feasibility of the solution.

    c.   Gather data for cost/benefit analysis.

    d.   Prepare client for the recommendation.

5. Solution Presentation

    a.   Get client agreement to area of need.

    b.   Present recommendation in a clear and concise manner.

    c.   Use benefits.

6. Close

    a.   Timing—when to close.

    b.   Buying signals.

    c.   Handling objections.

    d.   Closing techniques.

7. Wrap-Up

    a.   Implementation issues.

    b.   Thank client for the business.

    c.   Confirm client commitment.

    d.   Leave name and number.

    e.   Position next call.

If you use the multidisciplinary setup, you will probably need some help from a total service telemarketing bureau. You can obtain a list of local telemarketing companies by calling the Direct Marketing Association at 212-768-7277. You can also check trade magazines devoted to telemarketing. The *Bacon's Magazine Directory* lists and describes 76 telecommunications publications. They can be reached at 800-621-0561.

———

Chapter Twelve

Using Trade Shows to Demonstrate What You Are Selling

Advantages of Trade Shows

Like other promotional activities, trade shows are only effective when they reach the individuals in the purchase process or buying decision for your brand. To research this requirement for using trade shows, two good sources on the Internet are: www.tscentral.com and www.exhibitornet.com. They contain over 10,000 listings of trade shows and exhibitions, seminars and conferences, and conventions and meetings. Using their databases, you can find which trades shows cover your markets and a description of those attending the previous year. The descriptions will be either by SIC codes, job descriptions, or demographics.

When trade shows do meet your requirements and you have a brand that requires demonstration and/or you are looking for qualified sales leads, this type of event could be the most effective promotional tool in your bag. The Center for Exhibition Industry Research, a lobby for this industry, had Simmons conduct a research study for them. Simmons is best known for its readership studies of magazines. The study indicated that executives who authorize or approve purchases rate trade shows as the best source of "extremely useful" purchasing information.

The research study also indicated that these executives rate trade shows number one for:

1. Providing the best opportunity to see exactly what a product looks like

2. Providing the best opportunity to evaluate how a product works

3. The easiest way to evaluate competitive products

4. The most convenient way to find out who makes the types of products they want

The American Business Press, a lobby competitive with the Center for Exhibition Industry Research, states that their research indicates specialized business publications rank highest as the "most useful" marketing media. However, they rank trade shows second, ahead of salespeople, conventions, seminars and direct mail.

Not surprisingly many companies use the advantages of trade shows very effectively. Studies have shown that for some companies, up to 80 percent of qualified trade show leads become orders. On the other hand, some companies that rent trade show exhibits reveal that over 50 percent of the booths, when returned by businesses, still contain the attendees' business cards collected at the show. These companies are not marketing savvy or are scattering their shots too widely. Select a few tools that are the most appropriate for your business, then concentrate on using them correctly. The following will help you decide whether trade shows should be one of them.

Determining Whether to Use Trade Shows

If a trade show appears to be a viable promotional tool, you'll need to know what it costs and if you can you afford it. The first cost item is the space for your booth at the show. The minimum booth size is usually ten feet wide by ten feet deep. There are three layouts to choose from: back wall; peninsula; and island. Back wall booths are lined up in a row, either against a wall or another row of booths. This is the most inexpensive space. Peninsulas have aisles on three sides and usually are at the beginning or end of two rows of back wall booths. Because they abut two rows, they are usually twenty feet wide by ten feet deep. Peninsulas cost at least twice the amount for one back wall booth. Island booths have aisles on all four sides and are the size of a peninsula booth or larger. They are the most expensive sites.

Knowing the cost for the space, the next step is determining the cost for your exhibit. The cost for your space includes a sign with your company name and a curtained backdrop draped from a pipe. To hold down costs, you can skip a custom-built exhibit and just rent a couple of chairs and tables from the organization sponsoring the trade show. Sometimes the chairs and tables are included in your space cost. To the rental cost, if there is one, add estimated expenditures for dressing up your booth and displaying or demonstrating your brand.

Next, add travel and living expenditures for you plus one other person. You will need at least two people to man the booth. You will want to promote to potential customers two to three weeks before the show, so allow money for this activity. Add all these costs together—space, exhibit, travel, and promotion—that's your minimum expenditure. Compare these costs with other possible promotional choices to see if trade shows are feasible. If they are feasible at this minimum expenditure level, do further research and planning, including whether you can afford to spend more on your space, exhibit, and promotion.

Before the Trade Show Begins

After you have selected a trade show, the first decision to make is the type of exhibit you will use. You can go with the minimum discussed above or select from the following:

1. **Custom-Built Displays.** Custom-built displays give you one of the most impressive presentations at a show, but will also cost you the most money. You should not go this route unless you are convinced that trade shows are your most effective promotional tool and plan to attend several shows. However, companies that build custom displays can also act as your agent for all dealings with the show sponsor, except for renting the space. Get the display company involved from the very beginning so they can give you advice on the design.

   The display company will also ship your exhibit to a show, supervise the installation, dismantle it after the show, and store it for you until the next use. You can obtain names of display companies in the Yellow Pages, trade magazines devoted to trade shows, and from the Internet. Two trade magazines you can review are *Exhibitor Magazine* (507-289-6556) and *Tradeshow Week* (310-826-5696). On the Internet, use the search words "trade show exhibits."

2. **Rental Displays.** Many display companies have displays that can be rented and customized to meet your needs. If your design is not too elaborate, this may be the way to go.

3. **Off-the-Shelf Displays.** Off-the-shelf displays are smaller units that can fit into the trunk of a car or van. These are also available from display companies.

4. **Leave-Behind Displays.** These are nonelaborate, inexpensive units that you purchase or make yourself and then leave behind when the show is over. The cost for shipping, assembling, dismantling, and storage can quickly add up, maybe to an amount greater than the initial expense for construction. If you don't need an elaborate display, this may be your best choice.

Regardless of the type of exhibit you select, consider making it modular in design so it will fit in different size spaces. This gives you flexibility in case you want to contract or expand your booth space. It will also lower your costs for shipping, installing, and dismantling. If your exhibit is relatively small, consider having it shipped to your hotel and then taking it over to your booth on a handcart. This will save you from paying extra handlers to store and deliver your material. Pre-wire as much as you can to save the $75 plus per hour cost of electricians.

Your exhibit is an attention-getting device first and a sales tool second. Incorporate a dramatic graphic into your display, so people will notice you when they come down the aisle. This graphic should be the focal point of your exhibit—and it should convey a benefit. Treat the display as you would an outdoor poster. Ideally, the benefit should be stated in six words or less. Keep in mind that trade show attendees may be buying or critiquing your brand for another person in the buying decision. If this is true, your displayed benefit should reward the attendee for foresight as well as convey the efficacy of your brand to the boss or ultimate decision maker.

Once you decide to buy space at a trade show, do everything possible to let your prospects and customers know you will be exhibiting, and provide them with a reason for stopping by. Try to mention the fact in all your promotional activities. See if you can get some free publicity in an industry publication, then send reprints to your customer and prospect lists. If you are running ads in trade journals, be sure to devote a block of copy to the upcoming event. Highlight it in your commercials if you are using broadcast media. Add it to your telemarketing presentations. You may even want to prepare a special direct mail piece highlighting the benefits of attending. You could also offer a brochure or maybe even a video of your exhibit to those unable to attend.

As always, be creative. For example, a product manager was going to display at a trade show in Chicago. He purchased fifty cardboard garment bags and had a special message printed on the sides. He then mailed them flat, with specific instructions to his fifty salespeople who would be flying into the Chicago airport to attend the show. The salespeople, following their product manager's instructions, assembled the empty garment bag, packed their own bags, and headed for their local airport. They checked both bags to Chicago and hopped on the plane.

As they arrived at the Chicago airport throughout the day, they went to the baggage carousels and picked up their own bags. They left the empty garment bags on the carousels. As the rest of the trade show attendees arrived and went to get their checked baggage, on every carousel there were the twirling garment bags displaying the reasons no one should miss the product manager's exhibit.

Before the show, prepare as much of the material you will need after the show as you can. This will enable you to follow up on your leads as quickly as possible. For example, if you plan to send out covering letters with promotional material to customers and prospects that stopped at your booth, prepare those letters before the show. Decide whether you will have one version for "hot" or A prospects and another for B's and C's. Have everything ready to go, including envelopes and postage.

The main reason for exhibiting at a trade show is to obtain leads for future sales presentations. If that is your situation, you may want to talk to the show's lead retrieval contractor. The contractor can supply software and a scanner to scan the business cards you receive from prospects right into your computer's database. Some shows even provide attendees with badges imprinted with a magnetic stripe or bar code containing the visitor's relevant contact information. These badges enable you to scan this information directly into your computer.

During the Trade Show

If you have done all the planning discussed above, you can concentrate on meeting your prospects and customers during the show. Neither you nor anyone helping should ever sit down in the booth unless it is with a prospect or customer and someone else is standing at the front of the exhibit. You want to be standing up front surveying the crowd for a lead. Be ready first with a handshake and then the beginning of your presentation. Don't forget to obtain contact particulars from all individuals interested in your brand and try to qualify the lead right there. For example, first verify that they are potential customers. Try to ascertain how soon they will be in a position to buy. This will enable you to grade them A, B, and C, etc., so you know which plan of action to take for each as soon as you get back to your office. If you plan to reach them by phone after the show, ask them when is a good time of day to call.

After the Trade Show

Don't let your leads get cold. Most likely your competitors also exhibited at the show. You want to reach your leads before they make a purchase decision. Send out your letters and/or make telephone calls immediately. Whenever you send out mail, try to have it arrive on a Tuesday, Wednesday, or Thursday. Mondays are bad because your prospects are preoccupied with the upcoming week. On Friday, they are thinking about the weekend. After you make all your contacts and have a few minutes to breathe, calculate the cost of obtaining the leads. When your selling cycle is over, calculate the approximate profit resulting from the leads. If the profit exceeds the costs, you have got yourself a winner. If not, consider other trade shows or a different type of promotion.

—

Chapter Thirteen

Using Merchandising and Sales Promotion for Incremental Sales

Merchandising Is Coming Back

Effective merchandising is finally coming back. Merchandising has been missing from promotional plans for many years. Merchandising is what you do at the point of purchase or in the store to increase sales. Merchandising was prevalent in grocery and drugstores. A brand manufacturer or distributor did not encounter difficulty in convincing a retailer that its displays would increase volume. Retailers did not have accurate numbers on individual brand sales and basically left it up to manufacturers to control shelf and display space. Today retailers' increased knowledge about brand sales causes them to strictly control the access to all merchandising. If and when a manufacturer is allowed a merchandising event, the manufacturer pays dearly.

The ups and downs of merchandising have happened in other types of businesses, too. Department stores presented their merchandise with flair, restaurants welcomed their customers by name, and medical personnel realized you were a human being. That has changed due to volume and discount stores, chain operations, and HMOs.

Effective merchandising is beginning to come back as more and more business people realize that customers are tired of the slam-bang-buy-the-merchandise operation. Following are merchandising strategies that produced good results for various businesses. See if any fit in to your scheme of things.

Shoppertainment

Just for Feet, an athletic-shoe retailer, has indoor basketball courts, walls of video screens, laser light shows, hot dog restaurants, and athletic event viewing in their stores. This three-ring approach has a simple goal: Get shoppers to smile. "When they walk in, they're not happy. They're about to give you their money. But when they leave Just for Feet, they're smiling," says founder and CEO Harold Ruttenberg.[1]

At Country Hobbies, a California hobby store, shoppers can ask employees to build models for them so they can see and feel them. The shoppers are allowed to fly model airplanes using a computer simulation program. Customers are invited to display their finished airplane and glider models from the store's rafters; the store then sells them on consignment.

Newman Outfitters, a retail store that sells backpacking equipment, treats its shoppers to a steady stream of special events. The store has sponsored a special viewing of the Banff Mountain Film Festival, which presents the best outdoor films. It also hosted several slide shows presented by notable mountain climbers.

These are all examples of what is called "shoppertainment," blending entertainment with merchandising. "There are infinite ways to mix entertainment and retailing to create just the right shoppertainment concept for your store," says Howard L. Davidowitz, chairman of Davidowitz and Associates Inc. "Whatever you do, however, make sure it's appropriate for your store and customers. Next, be interactive. Customers want to participate in what's going on. Some of the best ways to inspire customer participation are the easiest. Serve coffee, show videos, let customers swing a bat or hit a few golf balls. Let children play computer games."[2]

Here are some similar concepts. See if any of these fit into your operation. A diner in Houston offers its patrons movie tickets at cost. The diner's management thought this would make customers feel less rushed. It turns out they were right. Sales of appetizers and desserts increased considerably. A bank in Maine presents home buyers with handcrafted models of their new house—perfect replicas down to the paint color and landscaping at mortgage closings. A retailer's operators announce a special word to customers while they are on hold, and when they get connected, if the caller mentions the special word, the caller receives 15 percent off on whatever he or she buys.

Sales Promotion

Sales promotion has not experienced any down years. In fact, the amount spent on sales promotion has increased every year for the last twenty years. A general definition of sales promotion is short-term promotional activity that lowers the price of the brand in pursuit of an immediate increase in product or service sales. The definition itself reveals the reason for its popularity—to increase sales tomorrow. With the possible exceptions of selling on the Internet and one-on-one sales presentations, no other promotional activity produces immediate sales. With business owners and managers constantly wanting more sales, it is no wonder marketing people put the sales promotional tool high on their list.

The problem is, if you are not careful when planning, the sales promotion increases sales while the promotion is running, deflates sales for several weeks after the event is terminated, and has no effect on long-term sales rates. If that happens, you have wasted the sales promotion cost. To avoid this situation, examine the various types of buyers to determine what kind of event will reach which target in anticipation of retaining their business. There are five groups to consider.

1. **Loyal to Your Brand.** This group will appreciate the sales promotion offer, but would have purchased from you with or without the deal. You may induce them to buy more at one time or earlier in their purchase cycle. Unless they increase their use of the brand, you are simply loading them up. That means they will be out of the market longer than usual.

2. **Loyal to Competition.** This group and non-users (#5 below) are the keys to the success of the event. Any initial sales gained are a definite plus. If you can then retain their loyalty, you have a successful program. That's tough to accomplish with only a price discount as a factor.

3. **Non–Brand Loyal.** These customers will buy from you, but only while the promotion is on. Then they are likely to switch to another product or service offering a price promotion. Retaining them as loyal customers is extremely difficult.

4. **Price Buyers.** Price buyers are similar to the non-brand loyal, except they only purchase the cheapest brand available. They won't buy your brand when there's a sales promotion, unless it makes your product the lowest priced. Forget about this group.

5. **Non–Users.** This group (and #2 above) should be one of the primary targets for your sales promotion activities. However, this group normally does not purchase items in your market category. It usually takes advertising, direct mail, or public relations to get them on board.

Keeping these groups in mind, let's consider various promotional tools and their effectiveness in obtaining long-term commitments from each.

Sampling

Research indicates that sampling is the best tool to produce *trial* or first-time buying, but until recently it was only used in the packaged-goods industry. For example, when Procter & Gamble comes out with a new or improved soap or toothpaste, it always distributes samples. Lee Iacocca, former president of Chrysler, broke that exclusivity. He offered a thirty-day return policy and many people thought he was crazy. They said a person will purchase the car, drive it for thirty days, then return it. Chrysler would then have to resell the car as used and lose a fortune. Very few customers returned the cars. Companies of all sizes and shapes are now using sampling for brands that vary from cable and satellite television to construction equipment such as backhoes.

There are many ways to sample your brand. You can hand out samples to prospects at their site or in your store. If the sample is not too heavy, use direct mail or have it attached to newspapers or magazines. At trade shows, hand out the sample from your booth or as you walk through the crowd. Check the Web to see if there are any co-op sampling programs to participate in. Co-op sampling is the distribution of samples of several noncompetitive brands together. If you can locate one, it will save you money.

In most cases, sampling is the only sales promotion tool that will work against non-users (customer group #5). As mentioned, they have a problem with your market category, but if they taste or try your brand, you may hook them. Sampling also works quite well against the loyal-to-competition group, if your product or service is superior upon trial. Sampling will not work for a me-too brand. Expect little renewed action from the non-brand loyal and price buyers groups. Those customers loyal to your brand will just smile.

Coupons Can Be Used for Any Brand

Coupons once were used exclusively by packaged-goods companies. Not anymore. A car dealer ran a full-page newspaper ad in his hometown newspaper. It consisted of one large coupon with the message that you could deduct the value of the coupon from the price of the car. The ad created so much talk value that it increased awareness of the dealer to unprecedented levels. Ensuing sales set a record. What was the value of the coupon? What amount do the packaged-goods companies usually offer? Usually around 25 cents and that is the amount the dealer used. The dealer's ad said, "Buy one of my $15,000 cars and you can have it for $14,999.75 when you redeem the coupon." What difference does it make if you are selling a tube of toothpaste or an automobile? You may not want to copy the above strategy, but it worked for this dealer. However, coupons are being used extensively, especially buy-backs: A customer purchases the item, and then mails in a coupon for a refund. It is a great way to build a customer database of names and addresses. Shiseido, a Japanese cosmetic company, built a database of 15 million users of cosmetics with this strategy. It is priceless information. The company sends catalogs to this group every quarter and special mailings in between.

If you use a low value coupon, you will probably get one-time sales from the non-brand loyal group. If you use a high value coupon, your chances of picking up the loyal-to-competition and non-users greatly increase. Some Internet service providers (ISP) offer $400 off the purchase of a computer if you sign up with them for three years. You have to pay $400, but if you need the service or are currently paying another ISP, in essence, you save $400. Many loyal-to-competition customers are switching. That means new three-year contracts for the participating companies. In addition, the offer received a lot of free publicity—just what you want for any of your promotional ideas.

One of the neatest strategies in target marketing is the use of electronic coupons. As a customer's merchandise gets scanned during checkout at a grocery store, any competitive brand to participating manufacturers triggers the electronic system and out pops a coupon from the manufacturer. For example, if Campbell Soup were a participant, any time a competitive brand, like Heinz, was scanned at the checkout counter, a cents-off coupon on Campbell Soup would pop out of a machine and be handed to the customer. This eliminates the waste of giving coupons to customers who would have purchased your brand with or without the coupon.

The Value of Premiums

M cDonald's and other fast food companies have proven that if you offer the right *premium* to the right audience, they will come. A premium is an item other than regular merchandise that you offer to customers either as a gift or at a supposedly special price. Customers obtain your premium either at the point of purchase or through the mail. McDonald's is famous for offering premiums kids will love, and consequently there is no way Mom or Dad can get out of taking the family to the nearest location.

Many marketers offer *self-liquidating premiums* in their ads. A self-liquidating premium is priced at the breakeven cost—you charge the buyer the same amount of money you paid for the premium. To be successful, it is key that the self-liquidator is of unusually high interest to your target and not be available from any other source. If the premium contains your brand name, such as on clothing or utensils, it is a major plus.

Effective premium strategies are not limited to consumer brands. A manufacturer of heavy earth-moving equipment mailed out miniature electric train cars to prospective customers. In a series of mailings, the prospects received various train cars used for hauling, such as a tanker, then the caboose, and finally the engine. After the completion of the mailing, the manufacturer's sales force had little problem setting up appointments with the recipients, especially the one-third that kept the complete train set on top of their desk.

The effectiveness of a premium resides almost completely in its uniqueness and value. If it is exciting, one-of-a-kind, a good deal, and if the recipient has to submit proof of purchase to claim it, a premium can increase your sales to all five customer groups. How many customers you retain is another question, but at least you have induced trial.

Sweepstakes and Contests

Sweepstakes or a contest offered to prospective customers may help you sell some merchandise, although many times the entrants forget who sponsored the event as soon as it is over. In addition, you cannot require the entrant to purchase your brand to participate when running a sweepstakes. The reason is that no skill is required and making people spend money to participate legally transforms a sweepstakes into a lottery. Running a lottery is illegal for a for-profit business. With a contest, however, skill is involved. It is not considered a lottery and you can require a purchase.

Probably the biggest payback from running a sweepstakes or contest is the free publicity you may obtain. To get covered by the media, you have to offer the unusual. For example, Mars ran the M&M's Color Campaign in 1995 and collected millions of dollars worth of free publicity. Participants had a choice of selecting purple, blue, or pink as the color for a new variety of M&M's. The announcement of the winner— the color blue—was carried on most of the television networks' news programs as well as David Letterman and Jay Leno. The company had the Empire State Building lighted in blue at night, resulting in wide coverage by print media. How it affected the five customer groups or even how much total product was sold, was not reported, but the publicity certainly resulted in increasing the brand's awareness.

Other Promotional Concepts

In the past, event marketing was used by companies selling beer and cigarettes to "Joe Six-Pack." But event audiences have changed through the years. Today women account for about 40 percent of the attendance at football games and stock-car racing. Golf and tennis tournaments draw a large percent of high income males and females. Like sampling and couponing, event marketing is now being used by companies with such divergent products and services as insurance, television networks, and automobiles. The beauty of event marketing is that the right event will enable you to spend time meeting your prospects face-to-face. Many event marketers conduct exit surveys and other forms of on-site research to determine the profile of the attendees. This makes it easier for you to select which ones to participate in. Try to be unique by having no on-site competition. Check out co-op advertising or other on-site promotional activities. Can you offer a giveaway? How about buying a poster that will be shown on site? If you can't afford any of these ideas, then buy a bunch of tickets to the event and give them to current and potential customers.

Providing information to customers is another promotional avenue. Salespeople often assume customers know far more than they do. Becoming known to customers as a reliable source of unbiased information can really pay off for your business. Consider setting up a method to keep your customers informed. You can fax or e-mail the information, or send out a periodic newsletter. Tell customers about new innovations, opportunities for outsourcing, and new trends. It's a promotional tool to you, but it can be a trusted resource for them. Keep up with technology advancements to determine whether any new gadget will help you sell more. For example, a sales manager put his entire catalog on a CD and sent it to current and potential customers with instructions that they could complete their order on their computers. After a customer completes the order form, the software on the CD looks for the computer's modem. After finding it, the order is transferred from the customer's computer to the sales manager's shipping department.

Have you thought about adding audio and motion to e-mail sent to customers? For example, many people send greeting cards that bounce around and sing on the recipient's computer. Why not add this excitement to your online promotional material?

Perhaps investing $7,000 to $10,000 in an electronic kiosk—in a few years they will probably cost half this amount—makes sense in order to increase sales and possibly cut your sales costs. For example, Wild Oats, a chain of natural foods grocery stores, has been using electronic kiosks to organize and deliver health and nutritional data in its stores. "People come to our stores because they want to learn," says the company's Webmaster. "They might want to know about the history and composition of dietary supplements, or how different herbs fit into various conditions and remedies, or the latest news about allergies, alternative therapies, government regulations, or research studies. We need to make all that available."[3]

Another company offers best-selling CDs through kiosks. A customer listens to the music, swipes a credit card through a reader, and the CD is mailed to his home. A five-location car dealership now uses kiosks to locate specific automobiles on their various lots. In the past, salespersons had to phone around to find out what was available at any given time. Because the inventory was large and often changed, this procedure was very time-consuming. Today customers select the desired model, make, color, and other criteria on the kiosk. It comes back with specifics, including location and color images of matching vehicles. A travel agency has a kiosk that accompanies visuals with aromas. For example, if a customer is checking out a wilderness tour, the kiosk might exude a hint of pine, then switch to gardenia to promote a tropical sunset sail, or to coconut for a beach resort.

You may even want to reconsider your current business title to add promotional flair to your operation. Traditional titles such as president are considered stuffy and unmemorable by some entrepreneurs. A Kansas City coffee wholesaler owner is officially known as "Bean Baron." In Bethesda, Maryland, a co-owner of a tea manufacturing company chose as his title, "President and Tea EO." The owner of a graphics firm in New York City uses the title "Empress" on her business cards, state registration, and tax records. The last example, but probably the most audacious, is the title used by the founder of a computer company. His business card reads, "Head Mouth."

Notes

1. Carla Goodman, "That's Entertainment," *Entrepreneur*, December 1998.
2. Ibid.
3. Fred Hapgood, "Death of the Salesman," *Inc.*, Tech 1998, No.3.

Chapter Fourteen
───

Using Public Relations for Free Ads

What Is Public Relations?

Public relations include all your involvement with the public—the government, financial institutions, stockholders, community, employees, and the media. It includes your financial reports, seminars, press parties, open houses, and other community activities. It also includes what I refer to as *interior marketing*, or how you market your company to your own employees. The most beneficial use of public relations from the standpoint of marketing is in promoting your brand directly to potential customers through the use of press releases or customer-attended events. A press release is a written or recorded story you would like the media to print or air. This type of public relations is discussed first.

Press Releases

When you receive a favorable review about your company or brand in a newspaper or magazine, or on radio or television, how many ads is it worth? You may reply, "I am not sure." This is a reasonable answer, but another one that is equally reasonable is, "At least more than one." In addition, the price is right. Your only cost is your time plus possibly a few incidentals. Whether you are running a small-size business or a large one, you are short on time, but you are probably shorter on money. Therefore, press releases should be one of your major promotional tools.

Daily newspapers have to fill their pages with news every day. Magazines must do so every week or month. Broadcast media (radio and television) have to fill their news times throughout the day. All of the media are constantly searching for interesting news they believe their readers or listeners will enjoy. They don't care who released the news—just as long as it's intriguing. As a result, much of it is given to them by others. Even in prestigious business magazines like *Forbes* and *Business Week*, over 40 percent of the articles do not originate with their reporters or editors. They originate with public relations employees of the companies being written about. How do you get written about? I suggest you follow the five-step procedure recommended by the Public Relations Society of America. They are: situation, research, planning, execution, and evaluation.

State the Situation

The situation details the brand's current situation relative to problems or opportunities you believe may be solved or enhanced through public relations. For example, a company named Purple Moon was interested in launching computer games for girls. However, the situation was that the only successful interactive software offered for girls featured Mattel's Barbie. In spite of the success of Barbie, the industry believed that the girls' market would never become profitable. The reason was the belief that girls don't like computer games.[1]

Another example is a group of physicians running a Medicaid managed care program who tried to improve immunization rates and use of other preventive care services for children and pregnant mothers. The problem was that Medicaid members were more interested in getting adequate food, shelter, and clothing than in keeping medical appointments.[2]

That is the first step. State your situation, opportunity, or problem. Are you introducing a new product or service? Are you trying to increase awareness or sales of an existing brand? Whatever it is, put it on paper.

Research

After considering your situation, decide if you have sufficient information to solve or take advantage of your situation. If you do, then you can start writing your plan. If not, consider research. For example, Purple Moon conducted research to determine why girls' computer games would not sell. The answer was that previous girls' games were simply boys' action games dressed up in female clothing. Girls thought they were boring, and said it was silly always to end the game by killing everybody. They were interested in computer games, but in ones that create realistic social situations and that gave them the opportunity to solve real-life challenges.

The physicians obtained the idea for their plan indirectly. Their research was directed at how to improve their member newsletter, but the results became the basis for a successful public relations campaign. Their annual survey sent to Medicaid members was expanded to include an open-ended question asking what issues they would like to see in the member newsletter. The answers included asking for help finding inexpensive clothing.

Your questions may range from who is your target audience and what is it they want or need, to—as with Purple Moon—is your brand or an extension viable. If you cannot afford independent research, go out into the market and ask the questions yourself. When you have your answers, write your plan.

Developing Your Public Relations Plan

The purpose of your plan is to detail how to solve or enhance your situation by offering the press a story it believes will interest their readers. For example, the objective of Purple Moon's plan was to create awareness and demand for their new CD-ROM, "Friendship Adventures for Girls," during the critical sell-in to the trade and sell-through to consumers. Figure 14-1 shows the cover of the CD-ROM sampler they included in their press kit. Their strategy was to take advantage of their new type of computer game and the market's demand for girl-specific

Figure 14-1. Purple Moon CD-ROM sampler cover.

titles. The objective of the physicians' plan was to increase the frequency of immunizations, prenatal care, and dental exams; educate members about the importance of preventive care; and satisfy the need for clothing. The strategy was to give articles of clothing to those willing to have an exam or immunization.

Notice that the strategies of both companies lent themselves to intriguing press releases. A plan that is not creative may deliver a story in a trade magazine in which you advertise, but you won't get extensive play in other media. To add creativity to your plans, you should critique what other companies are doing to obtain media awareness. Their actions may trigger an idea you can use. As mentioned in Chapter 13, Mars, the manufacturer of M&M's, used a chocolate candies color campaign, that allowed the public to vote on which new color they would prefer for M&M's. The plan netted the company millions of dollars in free publicity.

Sara Lee obtained over a million media impressions and one hundred telecasts for their new Wonderbra. They had models ride on the running boards of armored trucks down Park Avenue in New York City and major streets in other top markets to deliver the first shipments to the department stores. They commissioned supermodel Eva Herzigova as their spokeswoman and included the photograph shown in Figure 14-2 in their press kit.

The Dow Chemical Company was affected by a decline in the number of college graduates with degrees in chemistry, which made it difficult to recruit new employees. As a result, they presented a high-tech, live science theater production that used music, comedy and an interactive format to show the vital role chemistry plays in everyday life. The production toured middle and high schools in one hundred cities in the U.S. and Canada. (See Figure 14-3.)

Executing Your Plan

If your plan is well thought out, the execution is relatively easy. Purple Moon had an exciting new product in an exciting new category, so their

Figure 14-2. Supermodel Eva Herzigova displaying the Wonderbra.

major thrust was to get the story out to the trade and to the public. In their press releases, they positioned girls' software as the hot new toy and the arrival of Purple Moon as an innovative new girls' entertainment company. They received extensive coverage that included articles in *Time* and *Fortune* magazines, and appearances by company representatives on TV panels and talk shows.

Figure 14-3. Dow Chemical's Dow Chem TV.

A high-tech multimedia education program that motivates students to reexamine chemistry in their everyday life.

Dow Chem TV uses live music and videos to illustrate the issues facing the world and urges students to be part of the solution.

Vicki Lake Show - A humorous TV talk show uncovers the "chemistry conspiracy". Chemistry is used to create everything!

A rap song explains the scientific method: forming hypotheses, challenging ideas, making observations and creating solutions.

ChemTV presents the periodic table. The elements are shown as the building blocks for everything in our world.

Check it out! - ChemTV's game show challenges students to test their knowlege of chemistry and the exciting areas related to it.

ChemTV illustrates how rapidly technology changes and how chemistry is the power to change the world we live in.

The audience rock n' rolls down the information superhighway learning how to stay ahead of the technological revolution.

ChemTV challenges students to take action and become a part of the solution through chemistry and other sciences.

Chemistry textbooks, using examples which students can relate to, are available at no charge. A ChemTV video is also free.

The physicians used press releases to induce grocery stores, other physicians' offices, schools, crisis centers, and the news media to distribute flyers and display posters publicizing the events. The events were billed as "swap meets," where Medicaid members would receive free clothes in exchange for allowing the doctors to give them exams and immunizations. Volunteers conducted clothing drives, washed, folded, and boxed the clothing, and offered space in their buildings for the events. As a result of all this activity, the physicians were able to conduct nine "swap meets."

When you write your press releases for print media, as well as broadcast (radio and television), use what is called a *pyramid style*. This means that you put the most important facts in the first paragraph, the next most important facts in the second paragraph, and so on. Do not write a press release as you would a story. In a good press release, the headline and first sentence alone, or at least the first paragraph, should be enough to convey your message. You want a news editor to be able to cut it from the bottom up without jeopardizing the meaning. Press releases are inserted in print media after all the breaking news is covered. For example, an editor has five column inches left on a page, and is considering inserting your release, which measures ten inches. If she can chop your article at the five-inch mark without a rewrite, you are probably in. If she has to rewrite, you are probably out. The same is true with broadcast. If the news editor has to rewrite the release to fit it into a given time allowance, your release will probably not get aired.

In the first paragraph, cover the who, what, where, why, and when of your subject. Elaborate on these factors in subsequent paragraphs. Try to make your statements intriguing, but don't use superlatives and be sure what you say is believable. At the top of the release, have the name and phone number of the person the media can contact for more information. Below that information, type in capitals in the center of the page, "FOR IMMEDIATE RELEASE," unless for some reason you want to delay the message. Below "FOR IMMEDIATE RELEASE" insert a headline for your article that will be provocative to editors as well as to readers.

Research indicates that an article with a photograph is eight times more apt to be read. Therefore, whenever possible, include a photo along with your release. It should be an action shot, not a still shot of your brand. The photo should be either a 5″ × 7″ or 8″ × 10″. Type a caption on paper and paste it to the white border on the bottom of the photo.

Try to personalize each release you send. For example, when Hewlett-Packard introduced their 1.3 inch Kittyhawk computer disk drive, they did not pitch the same release to each magazine. Rather, they developed seven different themes or *angles* as they are commonly called, and pitched each one to a separate reporter/editor on an exclusive basis. To give you an idea of how to develop more than one theme on your next press release, here are the seven themes Hewlett-Packard used.

1. HP is a computer innovator . . .

2. HP outmaneuvers disk-drive makers at their own game . . .

3. HP executive proves that lightning can strike twice . . .

4. Kittyhawk will be an extremely profitable product for HP . . .

5. The battle of the Big Three—HP, IBM, and DEC—extends to the disk-drive arena . . .

6. HP's engineering expertise shrinks computer technologies . . .

7. HP fuels the power of sub-notebook computers . . .

Two companies, Bacon's Information Inc. and Editor & Publisher, publish directories that list all major newspapers and magazines, both domestic and international, including the names and phone numbers of the editors for each department or area of news. They also have information about domestic radio and television stations. This information is available on CD-ROM, too. Bacon's Information Inc. is located in Chicago, and Editor & Publisher in New York City.

If you haven't met your local editors and reporters, do so as soon as possible. Give them a press kit that contains all the pertinent information about your company. Include background on your company, a description and photograph of each product or service in action, and biographical sketches of all your officers. Then, when you have breaking news, and are short on time, or when the press needs more information, it is already in their files. If possible, follow the same procedure for editors throughout your complete distribution area. Call them. Talk to them. Send them a press kit.

A press party, during which you announce your news, can be beneficial, especially if you are launching a new product or service. It is relatively easy to get local and trade magazine reporters/editors to come as long as you have legitimate news. If the news has local flavor, your chances of local coverage are even greater. Determine the best time for the reporters to attend. Stay away from hours close to their press time. Give them advance notice and then a follow-up. Try to select a site convenient for them, but also a place they would enjoy visiting. Getting reporters from national media to attend is difficult, unless the news has impact on the whole country or industry. However, it never hurts to try.

The advantage of holding a press party is that it has a tendency to add importance to the press announcement, and a sense of gratitude on the part of the press toward the host. The press is not going to come to your party and then not run anything in their media, unless you have no real news. The disadvantage is that breaking news could keep the press from attending.

Performing the Evaluation

One advantage of using public relations as a promotion tool is its relatively low cost. Another is that you can normally measure the results. The physicians measured their own results. Diphtheria, tetanus, and pertussis vaccine rates went up 6.9 percent. Oral polio vaccine rates improved 5.0 percent; and measles, mumps and rubella vaccine rates improved 5.4 percent. In addition, 15 tons of clothing were distributed to approximately 13,000 people. Purple Moon traced 487 million media impressions through more than 845 local and national broadcast, print, and online placements. Their first two CD-ROM's outpaced sales of four leading Barbie software titles from Mattel. Not bad results, especially considering the low costs of the programs. If you 're worried about having a small promotional budget, don't overlook the leverage of public relations.

Other Types of Public Relations

Obtaining product or service publicity, as discussed above, is the primary marketing use of public relations. However, if you ever have a brand public relations crisis, follow the lead of Johnson & Johnson and their handling of the scare when foreign objects were found in a few Tylenol bottles. Even though it was believed the problem was limited to one store, the president immediately announced on network television that the Tylenol in all stores would be removed. As a result of the president's honesty and overly cautious command, the public never switched brands and, consequently, Tylenol never lost any market share.

Your company probably has an impact on your local environment, so community relations should be a high priority. Don't miss the opportunity to be a speaker at local events. If you become involved in an open house to show off your jazzy new quarters, following are some pointers.

1. **Set your objectives.** Like all promotional activity, decide what you want to accomplish. The objective of an open house is usually to convey to customers that you are in business to stay. Or you have bought some new equipment, systems, or stores that you want to show off. The key thing is to have a clear objective. Otherwise, your activities will not be focused.

2. **Set your strategies.** You have complete control over your presentation with no interference from competition. Take advantage of this situation by dramatically presenting the benefits of what you are selling. You also want to use the event as a springboard to place feature stories and interviews.

3. **Set your tactics.** Here are a few items you may overlook:
   a. Check with other local events to avoid conflicts.

   b. Invite the press in advance and follow up on invitations the day of the event.

   c. Set an alternate date in case of bad weather.

   d. Distribute follow-up news releases and photos while the event is in process.

   e. Send follow-up photos and letter to those attending.

The last subject discussed in this chapter is internal marketing. Several years ago, the employees of Delta Airlines gave their CEO a present. It was a new Boeing 757. The reason the employees said was just that he was a nice guy. They paid the $30 million price tag by having weekly deductions taken out of their pay checks. It is a shame that these same employees would not even consider such action today, but back then, the employees and management had a camaraderie that made them the preferred airline for business travelers. That is the power of internal marketing.

Be sure everyone is working toward the same common goal. One of the best ways to achieve this objective is to have all employees on a reward system. Don't limit it to your salespeople. Set goals for everyone—all pointing toward your major objectives—and when they're achieved, pass out the rewards.

Some companies are giving every employee the same title to facilitate everyone pulling in the same direction. Others have eliminated all office walls. Still others have eliminated all managerial perks. Whatever it takes, make sure every employee feels as important as the next and all feel proud of your company.

Notes

1. "Launching a New Concept in Girls' Entertainment," Purple Moon with Ketchum Public Relations, San Francisco, *The 1998 Silver Anvil Competition*, Public Relations Society of America.

2. "Kids Clothes Swap Meets," Arizona Physicians IPA, Inc., *The 1998 Silver Anvil Competition*, Public Relations Society of America.

Chapter Fifteen

———

Using the Internet for

Instant Distribution

Developing Your Web Site

Developing a Web site is not difficult. The easiest way is to have an Internet company do most of the work. This is referred to as vendor hosting. All you do is fill in the blanks on one of their templates. One of the least expensive is the small-size business package offered by Yahoo! (www.yahoo.com). It only costs $29.95 a month plus a $70 registration fee for your *domain name* or universal resource locator (URL). Your URL is the name of your site, such as JoeElectronics.com. This package also includes your Internet service provider (ISP) and an e-mail account. You need an ISP, like AT&T or AOL, to dial into the Internet. You need an e-mail account to converse with prospects and customers.

If you are selling consumer merchandise and want to offer items online, you can have a Web site on the Yahoo! Store shopping mall. This package is only $100 per month for up to 50 items. You can reach this site by going first to www.yahoo.com, then clicking on Yahoo! Store. If you are going to accept credit card transactions, Yahoo! can help you set up a *merchant account.* A merchant account handles the authorization of the credit card number and transfers the funds. You can receive your orders either by fax, e-mail, or have them downloaded to your software such as Microsoft Access. If you go this route, you handle order fulfillment yourself.

It is also relatively easy and inexpensive to set up your own site. Software to develop your site, display your merchandise, and process orders is readily available for $100 to $200, and you don't need computer programming skills. You can enlist a financial company to handle your credit card transaction for as little as $50 per month plus the cost of their software. If you are currently doing business offline, you already have order fulfillment resources. All you have to do is adapt to Internet sales. If not, and the arrangements are simple, you can do it yourself. If they are involved, you may want to outsource. For vendors, do a Web search using the keywords "Order fulfillment."

Other possibilities of outsourcing on the Internet are companies that handle the placement of your ads on other Web sites. Two of the best-known companies are DoubleClick (www.doubleclick.com), and Inter-AdNet (www.interadnet.com). Another Internet company of possible interest is DigitalWork.com (www.digitalwork.com). DigitalWork.com can help with many areas of online business. You can write a press release using their templates and they submit it to the appropriate publications. Costs are reasonable. For example, regional mailing of a press release is only $65. If you need help with other kinds of promotion, check the Internet for sources. Type in the keywords for the promotional category in a search engine's keyword box and you get a list of sources.

Following is a list of the items you will need to set up your own Web site.

1. **Web Page Design Software.** There are many good Web page design software packages on the market, one of which is Microsoft

Front Page. You will find a large selection in stores selling computer software. The software costs between $100 to $200. You do not have to be familiar with a programming language such as HTML to design your site and the instructions are easy to follow.

2. **A Computer Scanner.** To display merchandise on your site, you'll have to scan pictures of the merchandise. These scans are placed onto a page within your site. A scanner costs between $100 to $200. You can also take your pictures to Kinko's and use their scanner.

3. **Registration of Your Domain Name or URL.** Register your domain name or URL by contacting Network Solutions (www.networksolutions.com) and paying a $70 fee for a two-year period.

4. **Space on a Server to Host Your Web Site.** A *server* is a computer with extensive memory on which web sites reside. There are many companies offering web hosting, one of which is Net// works! (www.nwrks.net). They charge approximately $19.95 per month for this service. To obtain a list of others, search using the keywords "Web hosting." Most companies that host sites will also obtain a domain name for you.

5. **An E-Mail Address.** You will need at least one e-mail address to receive orders. You probably already have one. If not, the company hosting your site will usually supply one to you free of charge.

6. **Internet Service Provider (ISP).** An ISP is a company that connects you to the Internet, like AOL or AT&T. If you currently have an e-mail account, you already have an ISP. If not, select from one of the companies mentioned above or ask your contacts for recommendations.

7. **Electronic Transfer Software.** If your customers will be paying by credit card, you will need a company to approve the credit card and transfer the funds to your bank account. Icverify (www. icverify.com) and Cyber Cash (www.cybercash.com) have merged

and they are now the largest in the field. To obtain a list of others, search the Internet using the keywords "Electronic transaction software." This type of software costs between $500 to $1,000 plus a monthly fee up to approximately $50, depending on your volume.

You can put all of the above together without any programming knowledge. As you can see, the most expensive element is the electronic transfer software. If you are not going to accept credit cards, you will not need it. The remaining costs will probably be less than $300 plus a monthly fee of approximately $25 for your ISP. You can be up and running in a couple of weeks.

More elaborate Web hosting options are available, but they cost more money and you will need better computer skills. These options offer extensive links to accounting and other systems and contain a variety of sophisticated reporting and customer service features. The software prices start from $500 on up. If you want a custom design, want to own your own hardware, then you'll want to do in-house hosting. For example, IBM's Net-Commerce package is priced at $5,000 and includes hardware and software. You can find all the choices you need using the keywords "Web hosting."

Regardless of who designs your Web site, there are four items you want to keep in mind. Many of the Web sites already mentioned and some that follow are discussed in Jaclyn Easton's excellent book about the Internet, *Striking It Rich.com* (discussed in Chapter 2). If you want more information about the sites, pick it up. The four items are discussed below.

1. **Minimize your load time.** Stay away from extensive graphics, especially on your *home page*. Your home page is the first page of your site. A page with many graphics may take too long to load on computers with older and slower modems. A modem is a piece of hardware in your computer that connects you to the Internet and brings up the text and pictures. People surfing the

Internet have little patience. When they have to wait for information, they usually dump the site and return to the previous page. Test your site's load time on a computer that is a couple years old and hasn't had a recent modem upgrade. Take a look at Cassette House's site (www.tape.com) for its simplicity. Cassette House sells blank cassettes, DATs, and CD-ROMs.

2. **Make navigation easy.** Always execute the KISS strategy (keep it simple, stupid). Many business people are new to the Internet. Keep your front page short and simple and use a table of contents to connect it to all other pages. After a person clicks to another page, be sure it is easy to click back to the home page or on to the next appropriate page. Many sites, including those belonging to major corporations, offer no means to click back except for the back arrow on a browser or search engine masthead. The problem with this maneuver is that many people don't know how it works. If they do, it doesn't always work. Don't hide the click-back or click-forward in small type.

   If you are selling from your site, keep the total number of clicks to complete the buy to a minimum. Todd Mogren, Webmaster of Coastal Tool and Supply, restricts the number of clicks needed to buy to three. Check out his site at www.coastaltool.com.

3. **Engage and retain the viewer.** Surprisingly, most people don't realize that one of the primary promotional benefits of the Internet is to engage and retain the prospect. Very few other promotional devices let you do so. The Internet involves millions of people, but the best way to use it is one on one. For example, set up your site so it is easy for prospects and customers to e-mail you for more information. Maybe you can let them check the status of their shipments like Federal Express. You could run a contest or have a listing of upcoming events. KoreaLink (www.korealink.com) is a news site for Korean Americans that has public discussion boards, live chat, and personal ads for singles.

The main purpose of Saturn's site (www.Saturn.com) is to show off their cars and sell them. However, they don't stop there. They promote an annual homecoming where people come to their plant to view the new cars and enjoy a picnic. They also have car clubs wherein Saturn owners chat with each other over the Internet. *The Wall Street Journal* (www.wsj.com) lets viewers select fields of interest and then downloads appropriate articles to them. Amazon lets you select the type of books you enjoy and then e-mails you when new titles become available.

4. **Learn from the viewer.** If you interact with your prospects and customers, you can learn from them. Reading all the e-mail that is sent to your site is probably the best way to do so. Categorize the interests and suggestions from the mail, then revise your Web site accordingly. Be sure to answer each one with a personal message. Add the names to your database, then send periodic messages. You should monitor what they buy, and listen in on their chat on the appropriate usenet groups. Usenet groups comprise people with common interests who chat on the Internet. You can also put a counter on each page of your site to determine how many people click on each page. Your Web design software will tell you how to add this valuable tool.

How to Get Listed by Search Engines

The biggest challenge for successful Web sites is getting noticed. If you are going to use your site for customer support, then you can tell your customers about its location. If your objective is to sell merchandise or build an audience, you want to be listed by search engines and directories, as well as develop other strategies to build traffic.

First, let's consider how search engines search. When Internet users look for Web sites connected with their interests or things they need to buy, they type in related words in a box located on the home page of a search engine. The search engine shows the results as a list of sites with a ranking for each site. Major search engines pick up the keywords from Web sites with what are called spiders. Yahoo! analyzes sites manually. Ideally, you want to be listed within the top ten results. The top ten appear on the first page of a listing, all others are on subsequent pages. Surfers usually don't click beyond the first page, so if your site is on page two or beyond, you probably will not be seen.

Factors that determine whether you will be at the top of the list are: the name of your site, the headline on your home page, the first paragraph on your home page, and the title, description, and keywords entered in the source code. The source code does not appear on your Web pages. This information is only picked up by the search engines. Your site design software will show you how to enter it.

What makes it difficult to get near the top of the list is that the various search engines use different methods to catalog Web sites. For one search engine, it may be the name or headline or both. For a second, it could be the title, description, or keywords. For a third, it could be all four items. For a fourth, like Yahoo!, it could be none of the above, but rather an analysis of your whole site.

Most search engines will tell you what criteria they use to rank a Web site. You sometimes have to look around their site to find this information, but it is usually there. If it is not on the home page, keep clicking around. You will eventually find it. You can also get help from consulting firms. One of the best is Planet Ocean Communications (www. searchengine-news.com) They will send you about sixty pages defining what each search engine is looking for and e-mail you frequent updates. The cost is inexpensive. For help from others, use the keywords "Search engine searching."

Following is some advice on the factors the search engines will be looking for when ranking a site.

1. Select a site name (domain) that reflects your business and is easy to remember. Examples are www.askthebuilder.com, www. Korealink.com, and www.WebMD.com. WebMD supplies medi-

cal information to consumers and doctors. A descriptive name will make it more memorable to your customers and prospects.

2. Develop an appropriate headline and first paragraph for your home page. Like the name of your site, both the headline and the first paragraph of your home page should include words you believe prospects will use in their search. For example, Ask the Builder uses as a headline, "Welcome to Tim Carter's Home Improvement Center." His first paragraph reads, "I'll bet I have the information you need to solve your current home building or remodeling problem. Try me by typing a keyword(s) below."

   Coastal Tool and Supply uses the headline, "The Complete Web source for Power Tools." The first paragraph lists, "Bosk, Black & Decker, Dewalt, Makita, Delta, Milwaukee, Porter-Cable, Skil, Seno Drills, cordless drills, saws, routers, sanders, polishers, rotary hammers, demolition hammers, grinders, compressors, pneumatics, dust systems, vacuums, biscuit joiners." Anyone typing any of these brand names or a description of tools in a keyword box would be directed to this site.

   You want to insert all your keywords in the headline and first paragraph, but don't repeat the same ones several times because some search engines will not list your site. They will reject your site for what is termed *spamming*. Spamming is loading your text with the same words over and over. This is considered cheating to get listed. Pay special attention to your first paragraph, but keep returning to the subject throughout, because some search engines "spider," as they say, your complete site.

3. Insert a title, description of your merchandise, and the appropriate keywords that relate to what prospects will be looking for in their search into your source code.

   The source code is written using HTML, a computer language, but don't let that scare you. The Web software package will show you how to do it. This copy does not show up on your pages. It is only picked up by search engines. When you insert your "title" in HTML, it is usually the same as your headline, but it doesn't have to be. For example, Electrasports, (www.electrasports.com), an online store for women's exercise apparel, uses the headline: "The most comprehensive online collection of women's sports apparel." For a title they use, "Buy women's sports apparel, women's sports clothing, women's clothing, and fitness apparel."

Your "description" consists of one to two sentences describing what you are selling. For example, my description of the strategic marketing plan software I sell on the Web has this description in the source code, "Strategic marketing plan software. Great for asking what if. You answer the questions and the software plots your strategies."

The "keywords" you insert in your source code are the ones you hope prospects will use when they search for vendors within your market. However, as mentioned above, the search engines usually take into account more than just the words you list. The keywords I use: marketing plan software, strategic marketing plan software, marketing plan, strategic marketing plan, marketing plan interactive software, what if model.

4. Register your site with different search engines. After your Web site is completed, you download it to your server and it is now on the Internet. The last step is to register it with the various search engines, so when prospects search, hopefully you will be listed among the top ten sites. To register, go to the home page of each search engine and click on "register domain name or URL." There are companies that will register your Web site for you with a group of search engines, but they will charge you up to $50 for this service. Save the money. Do it yourself.

How to Promote Your Site

1. **Mention your site in all promotional material.** Add your Web address to your stationery letterhead and business card. It should

be featured prominently in all your ads, commercials, brochures, direct mail, and trade show exhibits. You may want to send out a direct mail promotional piece about your site.

2. **Consider using banner ads or other types of advertisements directing prospects to your site.** As mentioned earlier, banner ads are not effective for all sites and can carry a very high CPM. The banner ads that reside on specific pages are the most expensive and usually the most effective. These are the ads on special interest pages that contain a subject compatible with what you are selling. They are called *sponsorship banner ads* and you can get exclusivity. This means no competitor can appear on the same page. In comparison, other banner ads are referred to as being *ROP*, or *run of paper*, a term adapted from newspaper use. An ROP ad in a newspaper can run on any page chosen by the paper. Likewise, a Web host can run a ROP banner ad on any page of their site.

You can also negotiate a payment schedule based on the number of click-throughs to your site. Even better would be to pay for the number of sales resulting from the click-throughs, but most banner ad hosts will not accept this arrangement.

Another strategy is the one used by PENgroup.com (www.pengroup.com). This Web site matches professional consultants with companies looking for consulting services. Consulting firms pay as much as $4,000 to join the network. PENgroup.com bought keywords from various search engines so when someone types in "consulting," or other applicable derivations, the company's banner ad comes up at the top of the resulting page. The copy in their banner ad is persuasive. It reads, "Warning. Finding the right consulting firm can be extremely time-consuming. Click here and PENgroup.com will ensure that you will never waste time searching for the right consultant again."

What works for one site does not necessarily mean it will work for another. FragranceNet (www.fragrancenet.com), a site that sells fragrances, tried the same strategy and it didn't work. They bought the keywords "perfume," "cologne," and "fragrances." Their problem was the cost for the *sell-throughs* (cost of goods plus marketing costs) exceeded their profit margin for the shipments. Maybe the reason it worked for PENgroup.com is that they had such strong copy in their banner ad.

That is the beauty of the Internet. It is so easy to try different things and you can measure the results. When you get your Web site up and running, constantly try different strategies until you locate the ones that work the best for you.

You should also make periodic changes to your site to give it a fresh look. For example, iPrint (www.iPrint.com), which prints stationery, cards, and labels based on what you design on their Web site, offered a special for holiday cards and invitations. Along with a discounted price, they promoted softer typefaces and holly art borders. Motorcycle Online (www.motorcycle.com), a content site about motorcycles, monitors the number of readers for each of their articles. With this knowledge, they know which subjects draw the most interest and adjust their editorials accordingly.

3. **Try to network your site to as many others as possible.** A less expensive alternative to advertisements is to link to other sites that draw your prospects. For example, Electrasports promotes its site through a collective of similar Web sites. Member companies exchange free banner advertising on each other's sites. Since all members offer products and services for women, they can be certain that their advertisements are reaching potential customers.[1]

Many companies are interested in networking. Once your site is up, you will receive e-mail messages from others wanting to network. You should also e-mail other sites that seem compatible with your own to inquire about linking your sites. Put a "Link to us" icon on your site that brings up your e-mail page so interested parties can contact you. You might even want to share revenues with sites that bring you prospects that result in a sale. Yahoo! Store has a program that handles these types of monetary exchanges.

Ask the Builder has 300 other Web sites that link to its site and Cassette House has 500. This does not necessarily mean you have to link back to all that link to you. Ask the Builder only links back to ten and Cassette House, only thirty. The one that beats them all is Motorcycle Online. It has over 4,500 sites linked to it. Not surprisingly, the company states that the search engines provide less than 1 percent of their traffic.

4. **Extensive customer service can lead to favorable word-of-mouth.** FragranceNet gift wraps every package it sends. Personal message cards are free and, if it is not a gift, a thank you note to the buyer is included. In addition to favorable word-of-mouth advertising, these actions led to free editorial listings promoting their site on some of the search engines.

Taking Advantage of E-Mail, Your Customer List, and Other Forms of Prospect Contact

You should promote e-mail exchange and other forms of contact with prospects so you can insert their addresses, as well as those of customers, into a database. This information is priceless. Coastal Tool and Supply promotes e-mail exchange by offering "Free advice from the tool doctor." Ask the Builder suggests you call in your questions during his weekly radio and television shows. Electrasports uses contests such as, "Register to win the Royal Paisley Jersey by SheBeest." KoreaLink offers public message boards, live chat, and personal ads for singles. They have a successful fee-based membership that doesn't offer much more to the members than the nonjoiners. The company is not sure why they join, but concludes that they must think they should because they come to the site so often. With your resulting database, you can contact them all to promote your merchandise by e-mail, telephone, newsletters, or catalogs, which all of the above companies do.

It is interesting to note that there is a company mentioned in *Striking It Rich.com* that currently has a temporarily closed sign on its Web site. The company made no effort to stay in contact with its customers after the sale. The only e-mail a customer ever received was a confirmation of an order.

The Internet audience is bigger than that of radio, television, newspapers, and magazines combined, but don't forget that the best way to promote on the Web is one on one.

Note

1. Claire Tristram, "Happy Returns," *Small Business Computing & Communications*, May 1999.

___

Chapter Sixteen

Using a Sales Team to Close the Sale

Using a Sales Team

As the saying goes, "Nothing happens until you sell something." Other methods to sell a brand have been discussed, such as advertising, the Internet, direct mail, telemarketing, trade shows, merchandising, sales promotion, and publicity. Depending on the brand and the target audience, each one can be effective in closing the sale as well as being relatively inexpensive. For most brands however, using a sales team is the most effective sales tool in your bag. A possible problem is that the cost for making one-on-one presentations may exceed the resulting profit. For you to use a sales team, whether they are employees, distributors, or manufacturer representatives, the questions to ask are:

1. What is the average cost to make a sales call?

2. What is the conversion or *hit rate*?

3. What is the resulting profit before sales expense?

For example, assume for company A that the average cost to make a sales call is $75. Their conversion rate is 10 percent, which means that on the average they close once for every ten calls their salespeople make. Their average profit per sale before sales expense is $600. That means that the average profit per sales call is $60 ($600 multiplied by .10). Company A is losing an average of $15 ($75 less $60) on every call. If the sales team averaged ten calls a day, the net loss would be $150. You may say you would never continue to follow such a strategy, but amazingly many companies do. They fail to do this type of calculation and are not aware of the problem.

If you are faced with a similar losing proposition, but believe sales presentations are your best promotional strategy, you have several choices:

1. Do your calculations by market not product or service.

2. Concentrate on prospects with high potential.

3. Improve your closure rate.

As discussed in Chapter Three, do all your planning by market, because each market has prospects with different needs and wants. If you are selling your brand into more than one market, quite possibly your closure rate as well as your sales cost and profit before sales cost may vary. Some companies perform the above calculations by market rather than product or service and discover that they are losing money in some markets and making a profit in others. This was because in the profitable markets, either the closure rate was higher, the customers were closer, which resulted in lower sales costs, or they could sell at a higher price.

Regardless of how many markets you sell into, do not use your sales team as a marketing tool against all prospects. Concentrate on prospects with the highest potential. In most markets, the units, policies, or services that customers purchase vary considerably. Consider indexing your prospects and customers based on the amount of potential purchases. You can then do a cost analysis, comparing the possible profit versus the cost of a presentation(s). Some companies have found that they can only profitably call on those prospects and customers with an above average potential. Consequently, they use a less expensive marketing tool such as telemarketing to communicate with the others.

Probably the most important objective for a sales manager (or you) is to increase the closure rate for the sales team. The Reason: If the team is successful, almost all the results go to the bottom line. Usually, the only expense incurred is sales training, which is relatively inexpensive. For example, let's go back to the example given for company A. Assume the sales manager enrolls each salesperson in a special sales training seminar at the cost of $2,000 per individual. After the completion of the seminar, the sales force is able to increase its closure rate from 10 to 15 percent. The company is now averaging $15 in profit per sales call rather than losing $15 ($600 multiplied by .15 equals $90 less $75 in sales expense). Assuming each salesperson averages ten calls per day, the daily gain for each is $300. The training turned a daily loss of $150 into a daily gain of $150. The sales training costs are paid for in 3.5 days ($300 multiplied by 3.5 equals $1,050). Thereafter, the company makes a profit of $150 per salesperson per day. There are few factors, if any, that have more leverage in making a business profitable than increasing your sales closure rate.

Obtaining Sales Leads

How to obtain sales leads using other promotional methods has already been discussed in previous chapters. Following are some suggestions on how to do so by using your sales team, as well as yourself:

1. Networking

2. Speaking engagements

3. Writing for publication

4. Conducting seminars and conferences

5. Making cold calls

Just as you network your Web site to other sites, you should network with other businesspeople. If you need some tips on how to do so, follow the examples of the people selling life insurance. They are masters of this technique. For example, I recently moved to a new city and a short time thereafter met a man who sells life insurance. He also was a new resident. In the ensuing months, the insurance agent got involved in neighborhood poker games and Saturday golf. He is an active member of his church and is coaching kids' soccer. These activities are only the ones I am aware of. There are probably many more. Regardless, he is now probably networking with over 1,000 individuals.

Your business audience is probably more targeted, but the same strategy applies. Network with businesspeople who are in the market for your services as well as individuals who already know or will become acquainted with these people. Check the various clubs and associations in your city. See who are listed as members. Search your newspaper for listings of local meetings. Most likely you will find groups gathering for the purpose of networking. If you have a hobby, investigate what other businesspeople share the same interest.

You should know who is involved in the buying decision for your brand, or at least the names of the companies. If you run into a person involved in the buying decision at a social gathering, it is not considered unethical or in bad taste to ask if you can discuss business or make a presentation at a later date. Just don't do it the moment you meet or be too pushy. You may meet someone from one of your target companies who is not involved in the buying decision. If so, ask that person who is involved in buying and if an introduction could be set up. You may meet someone who is acquainted with people at one of your targeted companies. Your strategy should be to see if he can set up a meeting for you with someone in that particular company. It is not unusual for a salesperson to meet one person who networks the salesperson to another, who then networks the salesperson to another, and so on, until the salesperson gets the opportunity to meet his target. This is how networking works. Most businesspeople don't mind mixing business with pleasure as long as you don't discuss business while you are enjoying the pleasure of meeting each other.

One last thought about networking. If you are a male salesperson and have female competitors, be aware that many women do a better job of networking than men. Check the listing of networking meetings in your local newspaper. Most likely women's groups far outnumber those for men. This is just one sales management technique that women employ. Others will be discussed later in this chapter.

Try to position yourself as an expert on subjects relative to your market and the products or services you sell in all your activities. Two of the best ways are speaking engagements and writing for publication. Associations are constantly looking for speakers. You can address general audiences by contacting groups such as the Kiwanis or Rotary. If you are interested in reaching specific industries, an association for practically any type of business can be found in the Yellow Pages under Organizations and Business & Trade Organizations.

You don't make a sales presentation to these groups. Rather, you tell them about things such as market conditions in your industry, changes in technology, or how to use, repair, or improve various brands. For example, if you own a nursery, you could talk to general audiences about how to care for various plants. If you are a stockbroker, you could talk about your prognostications for the stock market. If you sell something that is used in only specific markets, skip the general audiences and concentrate on groups in the appropriate industries. Regardless of the type of audience, by speaking on a subject, you become the de facto expert. Someone interested in more information, or, hopefully, a purchase, will most likely seek you out. Consultants claim that practically every time they make a speech, they get at least one sales lead. Now you know how associations and other groups can always get a businessperson to drop everything to come and make a speech—free of charge.

If you can give a twenty- to thirty-minute speech in front of an association, there is no reason why you can't talk for one to two hours at a trade show or conference, or six hours at a seminar. I started out giving two-hour lectures. I was then asked to speak for one-half day. "No problem," said I. Next came the request for a full day. That panicked me. How could I talk and answer questions for six hours? I now conduct seminars that last up to five days. It scares you at first, but if you know your material, you can do it. You may think that someone in the audience will know more about the subject than you. But if you do your homework, it will never happen.

My suggestion is to start giving short speeches and then move up. Giving a speech at a trade show or conference attended by your prospects could be a gold mine for your company. If there are no appropriate trade shows or conferences, or even if there are these platforms, you may want to send out direct mail to your prospects announcing your own seminar.

Writing for publication is like giving speeches. You, the author, become the expert. As discussed in Chapter Fourteen, on public relations, the media have to fill pages and airtime. However, you are not contacting them about a product or service release for publicity. Your subject matter should be more general, but should still pertain to your market. Being more general usually makes an article more newsworthy and your chances of getting it placed are greater than for a publicity release. Taking it a step further, most authors of business books do not write to receive royalty income. They write to obtain sales leads. They make considerably more money from consulting fees because they are authors rather than from royalties on their book sales.

Most people do not like making cold calls, but this activity can be a good source for sales leads. To be successful you have to be persistent. If you give up after a few calls, a prospect will probably consider it a casual call. When you keep trying, the prospect knows you are serious. You have to be able to take rejection. You must really believe in what you are selling to the point that when people hang up, you conclude that it is their loss. They are the ones not smart enough to listen to your offer. Case study books are full of stories of companies that built their business on cold calls. You can, too.

Send a personal letter to a prospect before you call. It is easy to do using a word processing program. Put in just enough information to pique the prospect's curiosity. The only purpose of the letter is to persuade the recipient to take your call. Don't use any hard sell tactics. If you have a product or service that is new to the industry, describe briefly what it can do for the customer. Don't tell the whole story. Just insert enough to whet the recipient's appetite. When you don't have exciting news about your brand, consider referring to items of interest, such as market reports or independent research studies. Sell in your letter an acceptance of your subsequent phone call, not your merchandise.

You have a much better chance of reaching a prospect if you call early or late in the day. These are the times she is more apt to be in her office. If you reach her secretary, then you must add the secretary to your list of individuals in the buying decision. If you don't get through the gatekeeper, you won't have a chance to make your presentation. Treat the secretary like any other prospect. Get to know her. Call her by name. Show her respect.

If you reach an answering machine or voice mail, treat it as if you were talking to the person. Summarize why you believe a meeting would be beneficial. If possible, inject a reason for urgency in the request. Leave your number, but also say you will call back. If you are persistent, you will eventually get through to the individuals you want as customers. Keep the conversation short. You do not want to make your presentation over the phone. Try to give the prospect a choice of dates for the meeting so it will be either/or, rather than a no.

Making the Presentation

Maybe the term sales presentation should not be used because it implies that all a salesperson should do is make a sales presentation. This is not an effective way to sell. If a salesperson does all the talking, he will not know things such as whether the prospect can afford the merchandise or if the person understands what is being presented.

How does the salesperson know which benefits will appeal to the prospect and which won't? How does the salesperson know whether there are any objections and which ones they are? Maybe the nomenclature should be changed to *prospect meeting* to remind salespeople to get the prospect involved. If there is no meeting of the minds, there's no sale in sales presentation.

You want to get your prospect talking. It's the prospect's meeting, not yours. Ideally, before you begin the meeting, you should know all pertinent facts relative to the prospect—the who, what, where, why, and when. If it is impossible to obtain these facts before the meeting, questions about them is a good place to begin. It shows the prospect you are interested in her wants and needs rather than starting off trying to sell your product. Remember, everyone's favorite subject is his- or herself. If you do know the facts ahead of time, asking for elaboration shows the prospect you have done your homework. In addition, by inquiring, you can correct any erroneous information.

When you have sufficient background information, start presenting the benefits of your merchandise, supported by its features. Try to get agreement on each one as you go. Getting a person in the habit of saying yes to your questions will make it much easier to get a yes when you ask for the sale. Nicki Joy's book *Selling Is a Woman's Game* (New York: Avon, 1994) tells an interesting story about the effectiveness of this strategy. She went to a hypnotist to try to quit smoking. From the moment she walked into the doctor's office, he asked her questions that could only be answered by yes. After about ten such questions, the doctor said, "You are listening to the sound of my voice." Nicki answered, "Yes." Then the doctor said, "And your eyelids are getting heavy." At that point, Nicki started snoring.

The prospect will probably raise some objections during your presentation. Some people believe this is an act of rejection, but usually the opposite is true. If a prospect is not interested, she will say goodbye, rather than give you a chance to answer her objection by mentioning it.

Don't be afraid of objections. Capitalize on them the way most women salespersons do. Studies have documented that women are better listeners than men. They let a prospect talk and ask questions. Consequently, they make the prospect feel important while discovering what makes the prospect tick. They dig out the objections. An objection points to a problem in an area of interest or concern to the prospect. Knowing the parameters of the problem enables you to zero in on a solution. Always repeat the objection to the prospect before you answer it to be sure you understand what she means. Then present your reply. Don't disagree with, but rather, suggest a solution that more than compensates for the problem. This means you have to know the main benefits she is seeking, as discussed in Chapter Four on customer analysis.

Some sales experts recommend bringing up the anticipated objections yourself and then answering them. Others suggest not to, because they say the prospect may not think about them. You be the judge for determining your style. The key is to have the answers, whether the objections surface or not. When price becomes an issue, you may want to use a chart similar to the one discussed in Chapter Nine under the section titled Price Your Brand to Reflect Your Positioning. The benefits you present to a typical prospect have to be meaningful to him. If they are not, you are going after the wrong audience. That is why you should let the prospect do most of the talking. If the benefits of your brand are meaningful, he will pay a reasonable amount of money to obtain them. If he doesn't buy, then check your price. If your price is competitive relative to the benefits offered, the problem is in your sales technique.

Always Ask for a Debriefing

If a presentation is not successful, write the prospect a letter thanking her for her time and the opportunity to discuss your services with her. In the letter, mention that you would like to meet with her again to discuss why you didn't get the business. State that it will take only a few minutes. When you have this meeting, or debriefing, have an outline to follow. The outline should include reference to each of the benefits and features you presented, how you handled objections, and your company and its employees. There is no better way to improve your presentation.

Chapter Seventeen

Using Customer Service to Increase Repeat Sales

As mentioned in Chapter One, the customer service plan includes the activities of all employees not covered in the sales plan who interact with the customer, directly or indirectly. Examples are technical support, telephone operators, nurses, busboys, waiters, and flight attendants. This is one part of marketing where you can develop a major advantage over many other companies because overall service performance is so poor. A sad commentary on past performance is that many businesses avoid entering markets where customer service is relatively more important than in other markets because they know they will do a bad job.

Companies normally do not have a problem with the part of customer service that entails day-to-day servicing of clients' needs. Where they strike out is in the other areas of customer service—the handling of questions and problems. They neglect the opportunity to use it as a promotional tool. The reasons for this inadequate performance vary, but some of the most noteworthy are:

1. **Companies don't hire people with the right credentials.** Companies hire customer service staff based primarily on whether they have a pleasant attitude, which is adequate for routine duties. However, when questions or problems occur, just being polite to customers is not enough. You need individuals willing to take action—to find out what has to be done and then do it.

2. **It is often difficult to reach the right customer service person.** If a company offers several brands and the means of communication is the telephone, you invariably have to punch in several telephone keypad codes to reach a customer service employee. Then, as often as not, you are put on hold for several minutes. When you finally do make contact, you may be informed you have reached the wrong person and go back on hold.

3. **Company policies for the benefit of the company rather than the customer.** The result is ill will on the part of the customer toward the business, which results in less repeat business. Policies like: "We will not itemize your bill, except upon special request," "We will not honor a fax. You must mail it," and, "We will take back the merchandise, but only offer you a credit," do not create customer loyalty. Sometimes company employees admit the policy makes no sense, but are limited to saying, "I am sorry, but it is company policy."

4. **They treat all customers the same.** You don't have to be a marketing expert to realize that a customer who buys one hundred units a month should not be treated the same as one who only buys ten. When was the last time you received a free meal at the restaurant you frequent or free dry cleaning at the establishment you patronize weekly? Airlines and hotels have been an exception by establishing frequent flyer and frequent stay programs. Although some of these companies wish they had never executed

these strategies due to the financial drain, customers rank these features at or near the top in their list of reasons for selecting a business. Financial issues should not discourage you from favoring the heavy user. Just use better judgment in laying out your cost structure.

5. **There is poor communication between departments.** Many companies, in departmentalizing their business, stick customer service off by itself. They don't include it in the marketing function, which means customer service has no direct contact with the sales department or involvement with the development of the marketing plan. Consequently, there is no opportunity to use customer service as a promotional tool.

Each of these five common faults is discussed in greater detail in the remainder of this chapter. If you learn how to avoid them, you will have another promotional tool to use against competition.

Hire and Train the Right People

You need people in customer service who will take action rather than only offer sympathy when a customer has a predicament. For example, an employee at Midwest Express loaned one of his suits to a passenger who had lost his luggage. A sales clerk at Nordstrom refunded money to a customer dissatisfied with a tire she bought, even though the store doesn't sell tires. These two employees are doers. They listened to what the customer had to say and then did something about it. By their actions, they probably bonded these two customers to their companies for life.

Both Midwest Express and Nordstrom are known for their excellent customer service, so the action of these two employees is not surprising. You want to hire individuals, like these two, who excel in interpersonal skills such as listening and communicating. As in a sales presentation, a customer service employee should provide the customer with ample time to present the facts as he sees them and then clearly communicate a solution. An example of what normally happens in customer relations is when a town in North Carolina announced a ban on the watering of lawns. The town manager told residents the reason was low water reserves due to a problem in another city's water system that supplied some water to the town. As the ban continued the green grass in some yards turned brown and began to die. Communicating with town management was difficult. They were busy doing other things. Inquiries requesting alternate solutions were of no avail. Not until a resident presented his own solution for obtaining more water for the town did the problem subside. If this town was a company, it is doubtful that residents would continue to buy from it. In the future they may not have to—private industry is now selling water in other parts of the country.

In addition to hiring qualified individuals for customer service, you want to train them by communicating the types of solutions you expect them to execute. You can do this in writing. You can do it orally. Or, best of all, by your own actions. For example, there is a small-size department store in Connecticut that originated as a sporting goods store. It carries name brand merchandise, but its prices are higher than the major chains. Still, the store thrives. Additions are being added every couple of years. One day I was talking to the owner in his office when a salesclerk stepped in. She said to the owner that a customer wanted to return a pair of shoes. "What's the problem," asked the owner. The salesclerk told him, "She has owned them for more than a year." "So what?" said the owner. That's how the owner beats the chains. He has built a reputation for his store that guarantees the quality of its merchandise. If customers are not completely satisfied with it, they can return it anytime.

Try to run your business like the small-size department store. Hire a customer service person with good interpersonal skills who is willing to take action. Lay out a range of acceptable solutions, then let her act on her own. If she is good at what she does and you need to hire additional staff, involve her in the selection process. She'll know the kind of person you're looking for because these types of people seem to attract each other.

Provide Information Quickly

In years past most questions about brands or complaints were handled through the mail. You could contact customer service by phone, but usually you also had to put the inquiry in writing. Then the writing requirement began to disappear and many situations could be handled with a phone call. This was a period when customers ranked most companies satisfactory on customer service. These good times did not last because management, not being marketing oriented, decided they could cut costs by cutting back on the number of individuals answering the phones. They also reduced training costs by educating the phone personnel on only one brand or section of the company's business. In addition, they put frequently asked questions (FAQ) on the Web. You know the result. Punch a phone code and wait. Punch a phone code and wait. If you resort to the FAQ's, they are sometimes helpful, but most of the time they are too general.

Here's a guaranteed way to increase your sales. Provide your customers with a toll-free number and have it answered no later than the third ring by a qualified person who knows every part of your business. Notice I said the third ring. Try it. You will be amazed at the amount of favorable word-of-mouth your company will receive.

Policies Should Benefit the Customer

Review all your policies to determine whether their primary function is to benefit the customer or the company. Any policy that helps the company but hurts the customer should be altered or eliminated. The subject here is policies, not *terms*. There is nothing wrong with having various terms in favor of the company as long as they are reasonable. Terms refer to the payments from customers such as net thirty days or payment on delivery. Policies cover such items as size of order, warranties, customer support, hours of operation, refunds, alterations, and accounting practices.

You have probably experienced policies used by companies that alienated you as a customer. The question is: Are any businesses in your market doing the same? If they are, and you currently have matching policies, can you change yours to be more customer friendly, and by so doing, gain another advantage over competition? Most large-size companies cannot, or will not, process small orders. If you are a small-size company, you most likely can and should. Competition may offer one-year warranties. Can you offer two-year or three-year warranties? They may offer free customer support for ninety days. Can you offer it for one or two years—maybe for life? When a company is closed, it is closed. You can't get a peep out of anyone there. Can you and your employees take turns transferring your 800 number to your home phones at night and on the weekend? If the competition closes and you don't, at least some customers and prospects are going to conclude that your company cares more about their welfare. Go through your complete list of policies and determine where you can gain an edge.

Don't Treat All Customers the Same

Chapter Five discussed the importance of aiming your promotional efforts toward your target audience. As explained in that chapter, your target is the approximately 20 percent of the market that should account for approximately 80 percent of your profit. Use the same strategy in your customer service activities. This does not mean to abandon the 80 percent that account for 20 percent of your business. Treat them well. In fact, they may become members of the target audience in the future.

The key is the additional special services you offer your target audience. Should you install computers in their factories that track their inventory and automatically re-order your merchandise? Based on their volume, can you offer them special bonuses, ordering procedures, shipping time, or technical support? You want to convey the message that when they have a crisis, you will drop everything and service their needs. Accomplish that and no one can take that business away from you.

Take Advantage of After-Market Sales

B ecause most companies stick customer service off in a corner of their operations, the employees do not have extensive product or service knowledge. They may be familiar with the brand they are responsible for and probably only from a technical viewpoint. Therefore, they do not have the resources to sell additional merchandise to current customers when they call with a question or a complaint. It's a missed opportunity. You can easily train your customer service people in all aspects of your business, including your complete brand line. Then, when your customers call, your people are not only in a position to discuss all your services, but to also suggest the purchase of accessories or an upgrade.

For example, a computer user recently had a printer that no longer worked. He called customer service and the representative informed him that the printer had to be boxed for shipment—a difficult task for a fragile item like a printer—and sent to their repair center. The minimum cost for just checking the printer was $75. The user voiced his reservations, but added that he needed a printer immediately. The reply from the customer service representative was, "I am sorry, but that is our policy." Obviously, this customer was in need of a printer and was probably going to buy a new one the next day. If that customer called your company about the printer, you'd want to ensure that he kept doing business with you. He probably will be in the market for additional purchases of computer equipment in the future. What if you said you would ship him a new printer today and give him a discount due to his problem with the existing one? Maybe you could even upgrade him. The result is you sold another printer—albeit at a slight discount—and probably locked in a customer for good.

Look forward to every contact you have with your customers, even when there is a problem. What you want to do is to switch from a scenario of the company versus the customer to one of you and me versus the problem. Isolate the problem together with the customer and then take action. When a customer knows you are there to help, you are using the oldest and still the best marketing tool available—developing favorable word-of-mouth advertising. It sure beats saying, "I am sorry, but that is our policy."

FEEDBACK—USING CONTROLS AND MARKET RESEARCH TO COMPLETE THE LOOP

Chapter Eighteen

Feedback—Using Controls and Market

Research to Complete the Loop

Your Fact Book is the depository of the market facts needed to develop an effective marketing plan as well as for recording feedback on your performance during the plan year. The soundness of your current marketing plan, as well as any revisions, is based on the soundness of this supporting Fact Book. The soundness of your Fact Book is based on the soundness of your controls and market research. First, let's take a look at controls.

Using Controls for Feedback

By *controls*, I mean monitoring your measurable objectives. In Chapter One I pointed out the importance of assigning measurable objectives to each component of your marketing plan. Those are your controls. If you don't use measurable objectives for each component, how will you know whether that part of the plan is working. Don't forget: If a benefit can be observed, it can be counted, and if it can be counted, it can be measured. If you are spending marketing dollars to do something from which you receive no benefits, what is the justification for doing it? Conversely, if a strategy and accompanying tactics produce a benefit, that benefit can be measured.

Results from some components of a marketing plan are relatively easy to measure, such as your objectives for sales or revenue, sales closure rate, level of distribution, number of qualified leads from marketing communications activity and the Internet, coupon redemption, and the number of point-of-sale displays. A common mistake is that when the status of these types of objectives is measured during the plan year, nothing is done about discrepancies until the plan is rewritten at the end of the plan year. If you are off target on an objective, you have two choices. Either change the strategy or change the objective. If you believe the objective is valid, change the strategy. If you believe the strategy is valid, then change the objective. Don't wait until the end of the plan year to make this change. Do it as soon as your recognize a problem. Otherwise you have wasted the time between the date when you first recognized a problem and the end of the plan year.

Checking the results from other types of objectives can be more difficult. Don't let this fact serve as an excuse, because if you don't measure them you are asking for trouble. If you don't measure the effectiveness of your marketing communications, you could be wasting your entire budget. If you don't know the size of the total market in units and dollars, then you cannot verify your market share objective. You may be losing market share and not know it. If you keep losing share, you will eventually become out-financed by those competitors gaining share.

If you do not have adequate market research, your objectives may be doomed to failure. For example, you should know your competitors' reactions to your strategies. An objective that results in a doubling of your marketing expenditures may only result in an increase in costs if the competition matches it. If you don't know which individuals are important in the buying decision and what they want, you may be making mistakes like the four companies mentioned in Chapter Four. They were either spending their marketing dollars against the wrong target or they were sending out the wrong message. Don't forget to write and measure your objectives by market or you may be like the company mentioned in Chapter Three. They were losing money in one market and didn't know it, because they were pulling their profit and loss by product rather than by market.

If you are allocating $10,000 to an objective, it is better to spend $1,000 to $2,000 to check the effectiveness of the accompanying strategy rather than possibly squandering the complete amount. Let's move on to how you can obtain feedback through market research. Four types of research will be discussed. They are:

1. No-cost market research

2. Benchmark studies

3. Online research

4. Marketing communications research

No-Cost Market Research

Obviously, you want to obtain as much market data as you can from sources that don't cost any money. Five possible sources are market data from within the company, trade associations and magazines, the government, Internet search engines, and Web sites. You may be surprised to find out how much market data is lying around in various departments within your own company. When you notice valuable data on someone else's computer, and ask why you never saw it before, the usual answer is, "I didn't know you could use that stuff."

Another source of in-house data are the results of your marketing communications used on your Web site, your toll-free telephone number, inquiry cards, and coupons. You may need the assistance of your sales team to measure some of these the results. Be sure they understand the importance of this type of research. Always check with your sales force, technical support, customer service, and any other group of employees that has customer contact. Enlist these people to be your counterintelligence agents. Offer them a reward for valuable information. The reward doesn't have to be money—just something that will let them know you appreciate it when they provide you with helpful data.

Trade associations are an excellent source of no-cost market data, especially for industrial advertisers. Practically every industry has a trade group and one of their primary functions is to collect market data and disperse this information to their members. Trade magazines can also be helpful. Many of them conduct their own market research and publish the information for the benefit of their readers.

It has been said that the federal government has conducted more market research studies than all the market research companies combined. That may not be an accurate statement, but it is true that they have a vast collection of market data. It can be difficult to determine where to start looking for this information, so you'll want to begin your search by contacting your local office of the Department of Commerce. Online databases containing lists of market research studies conducted by the federal government by industry are available. You can obtain information about these online databases by contacting the librarian in the business department of your public library.

Obtaining market information from government studies is a two-way street. You can obtain data on competitors, but they in turn can obtain information about you. Therefore, especially in light of the freedom of information legislation, be extremely careful about the marketing information you provide the government. There have been instances when confidential information was given to a competitor. A pharmaceutical company's new product development information was obtained by the competition. The competitor was smart enough to petition a federal agency for a copy of the report that contained the data. The Federal Aviation Agency, after having been petitioned, gave all the engineering details of a company's new life raft design to a competitor. The competitor then used the information to build its own prototype. When bids were submitted to the first substantial customer, the competitor won the sales contract.

You can search the Web sites of newspapers and magazines to view their archives. Insert the names of your competitors, markets, and the job descriptions, demographics, and/or psychographics of individuals in the buying decision into the search box. I am sure you will be surprised by the number of articles that comes up in response to your queries. Definitely try the Web sites of *The New York Times*, *The Wall Street Journal*, *Fortune*, and *Forbes*. You can also search Yahoo! by first inserting the keyword and then clicking on the news section. Internet search engines can be used to find the names of your competitors and their corresponding Web sites. Check the sites out at least once a week to keep tabs on any changes.

Once you have exhausted the no-cost market research sources, make a list of any remaining questions you need answered to keep your Fact Book up-to-date. Seek the answers by using a benchmark study, an on-line study, marketing communications research, or a combination of these sources.

Benchmark Studies

You can obtain a reading of almost all facets of a market by using a benchmark study. A benchmark study's purpose is to provide you with a measurement of where you stand in a market. In a benchmark study, a sample of the participants within a market are interviewed, often by an independent research company. The sample size is normally between 200 and 1,000 individuals. You can project the results to your entire market as long as the sample reflects its composition.

There are basically three methods of conducting a benchmark study or survey: personal interviews, telephone interviews, and mailed questionnaires. Each one has advantages and disadvantages. The personal interview gives the research company the opportunity to ask the maximum number of questions; the interviewer can probe or ask follow-up questions; the product can be shown or visuals can be used; the interviewer can record his or her own observations; and there is a high completion rate of questions and interviews. The disadvantages are cost, time required, and interviewer bias. The advantages of the telephone survey are the short completion time, the lower cost compared to personal interviews, and the chance to call back if the respondent is busy. The disadvantages are that few questions can be asked; the person want may not come to the phone; and graphics cannot be used.

The advantages of the mailed questionnaire are that it provides anonymity; it allows respondents to answer the questions at their leisure; and is the least costly of the three methods. The disadvantages are the low rate of return of completed questionnaires; the possibility that the returned questionnaires may not be representative of the universe; the lack of opportunity to eliminate any confusion; and the time needed to get back completed questionnaires.

You could use your own employees to conduct any of these three types of benchmark surveys, but this presents two possible problems. One is that your employees are probably not trained in research methodology, which could result in their asking confusing or leading questions. The other is that the interviewees know who is paying for the research and may provide inaccurate answers. For example, interviewees may think your service is bad but are too nice to say so to your employees.

You can obtain a list of companies conducting benchmark studies by inserting "market research" in the keyword box of a search engine. It is difficult to get rough cost figures from these companies until they interview you and know exactly what information you need. However, to provide you with a handle on this subject, using the telephone to conduct a relatively simple survey with a relatively easy-to-reach sample will normally cost between $50 and $75 per completed interview. If your sample size is 300, your total costs would be between $15,000 and $22,500. That's a reasonable expenditure for feedback if you are spending three to four or more times that amount on your marketing program.

Online Studies

If you can reach the people you want to interview via the Internet, it will save you money and time. There are basically four methods you can use: e-mail, an online questionnaire, a questionnaire that respondents can download, and chat rooms. Using e-mail is the simplest and fastest method. Online surveys allow you to incorporate skip patterns (skipping questions based on previous answers) in the questionnaire and to add graphics and sound. You usually send e-mails to the target audience that directs them to the page on your Web site that contains the questionnaire. Downloadable surveys allow you to be more creative in your presentation because you can incorporate Windows-based controls and other fancy accoutrements.

Using chat rooms is an inexpensive way to conduct a focus group. Focus group surveys consist of ten to fifteen participants commenting on a questionnaire that, unlike a benchmark study, is not scripted. Therefore, focus group surveys are more free-wheeling than benchmark studies. Consequently, even if you conduct several focus groups, the results should not be projected to the entire market. However, a focus group can be helpful in obtaining general knowledge on various subjects and in the development of a questionnaire for a subsequent benchmark study. Focus groups are difficult to conduct, because, invariably, one or two persons will try to dominate the conversation. Using chat rooms for your focus groups presents an additional disadvantage in that you cannot read facial expressions. However, the price is right, so why not try them?

If you want more information on online market research, go to www.casro.org. This is the site for the Council of American Survey Research Organizations. You can type in "online market research" in the keyword box of Internet search engines to find other sources.

Marketing Communications Research

The purpose of communications research is to determine whether your communications activities (advertising, sales promotion, and public relations) are reaching their objectives. A major problem with marketing people is the tendency to judge communications activity, especially advertising, in light of their own preferences and idiosyncrasies, rather than the anticipated viewpoint of the target audience.

This is especially true for consumer advertisers. You have to remember that the target for mass consumer products and services is primarily the average man and woman. However, most of the marketing people who approve today's advertising campaigns represent the top 10 percent of the country in education and intelligence. They don't think or act like the public they are trying to reach with their brands. You have to learn to shift gears when you are preparing and critiquing your advertising. You must continually ask yourself: "How will the people in my target audience interpret this? Will they understand it? Is this the best possible way to present to them relative to their lifestyles, goals, and needs?"

Even the Federal Trade Commission, when determining whether advertising is misleading, thinks about how the men and women of middle America will react to a particular commercial. If the commission believes that they will interpret your message in a way that's misleading, you're in trouble. The FTC doesn't care what you thought the ad said. In fact, if your lawyer responsible for advertising clearance ever says, "This is what we intended," get yourself a new lawyer.

Industrial advertisers do not normally have such problems with misinterpretation of their messages. The FTC considers the industrial market more sophisticated than the consumer market, possessing a greater ability to discern fact from puffery. As a result, the FTC rarely reviews industrial advertising. This does not mean, however, that industrial advertisers don't miss the mark. The usual problem is that the advertising is too technical. It emphasizes features rather than benefits. A common situation involves an industrial advertiser who claims the advertising agency copywriter does not have the ability to write the technical body copy. "The writer just doesn't understand my product," is the complaint. Consequently, the client writes the copy, and the only people who can comprehend the message are the company's own technical staff.

If you write your own body copy, you're probably making a mistake. If you are a hotshot writer, then join an advertising agency. You'll probably make a lot more money. On the other hand, if you've given an agency ample opportunity to learn all the facts about your product and it still can't produce copy directed at the target, then fire the agency.

All the preceding commentary underscores the need for communications research. Most marketers cannot rely on sales records to determine whether their advertising is effective. You need research. This is not to imply that research is infallible. Research can be deceptive, but it is an invaluable marketing tool when properly conducted and interpreted. What follows is a discussion of advertising research, how to measure sales promotion results, and public relations research.

Advertising Research

There are basically three types of advertising research: *concept* or *copy testing*, *pretesting*, and *posttesting*. You should be able to isolate the benefits sought by the target audience for the products or services within your particular market from your benchmark study. You should now be in a position to select the primary benefit of the brand that you wish to promote. For example, let's say your product is a lemon-lime soft drink. You have written your creative strategy and your agency or in-house operation has come up with two concepts to display the benefit of the brand. (Normally, you should start with three to four concepts, but only two will be used.) One concept (A) positions the brand as the coolest refreshment of them all. It has a frosty, freezing taste. The second concept (B) positions the brand as an alternative to cola drinks. It claims a cool, clean taste that is preferred by older teens rather than the sweetness of colas, which should be left to younger teens. You believe that both concepts offer excellent opportunities. The problem is that you can go with only one, so you decide to subject them to concept testing to determine which one is the most effective.

Concept Testing

The ad agency prepares a brief series of graphics for each of the two concepts. These are not ads, but rather illustrations of ideas. There are no headlines or body copy on the concept illustration. However, you could separately test several different copy lines or phrases. When the art is completed, you set up your sample audience. This should be drawn from members of your target audience, not the universe at large. Many advertisers have failed to do this, and their data subsequently proved invalid.

The sample size can be modest. Usually you only need about one hundred people. The research should be done in person, unless you can mail the graphics to your sample, and then interview the respondents on the telephone. What you want to know is which concept has the greatest appeal. Factors you should consider measuring are interest, believability, meaningfulness, memorability, and the respondents' desire to buy. Ideally, you should have data from past concept testing to provide comparative scores. If this is your first concept test, you will not have your own data bank, but possibly your marketing research firm can supply this type of information.

For the purpose of this discussion, assume that concept A received a higher overall score than concept B. The next step would be to prepare the actual advertising (copy and layout for print, scripts for radio, and storyboards for television). Normally, two to four different campaigns would be prepared, each one an execution of the winning concept. We will discuss two campaigns here. The first campaign features young adults in various activities, such as playing pool and throwing a Frisbee on the beach. When they start drinking the brand, called Frigit, it starts to snow. The more they drink, the more it snows, and at the end of the commercial, it is a raging blizzard. The basic copy line is, "The frosty, freezing taste of Frigit. It's a blizzard."

The second campaign depicts the brand as so cool that when you pour it from the bottle, you don't need a glass. It forms the shape of a column, as if it were frozen. The commercial shows young adults in various activities, such as drinking Frigit with no glass and balancing it on their shoulders when they are water-skiing. The basic copy line is, "The coolest drink in town. It's a freeze!"

Now that the two campaigns have been developed, they can be tested against each other as well as against past research scores or norms, to determine which one is the most effective. This is called pretesting.

Pretesting

If you are using print media, representative ads of each campaign are prepared. They do not have to be completely finished. The ads can be tested several different ways. They can be pasted into a dummy magazine and research participants asked to read or glance through it. After they have completed this task, they are asked questions on several subjects, only some of which pertain to your ads. This keeps the reason for the questions a mystery to prevent bias. The sample does not have to be large. One hundred people seeing ad A and one hundred seeing ad B is sufficient, but be sure they all qualify as members of the target audience.

Another pretesting method for print is to show a set of six to ten ads, one of which is the ad you are testing, to the participants. The other ads can be competitors' ads or advertising for unrelated products or services. Ask the participants to rank the ads on such factors as interest, credibility, and their desire to try the product. Then you can ask them open-ended questions, such as, "What do you think this ad says? Does the illustration appeal to you? Why? What about the headline?" There are many other techniques that can be used for pretesting a print ad and you can get this information from your market research firm. The firm will also provide you with details on the type of questions that can be asked, sample size, and costs.

If you are using television, you may be able to pretest using rough commercials called animatics. Burke Marketing Research Inc., used to provide this service, but not any longer. If you are interested in this type of research, inquire about it when you talk to the various market research companies you locate on the Web.

Pretesting research should determine which execution of your ad is superior. You are now in a position to produce your campaign in final form and release it to the media you have selected. After your newspaper or magazine ads have run or your radio or television commercials have been aired, you can test them again, this time in their final form. This is called posttesting.

Posttesting

The least expensive type of posttesting research is readership or interest studies. Many researchers frown on using readership tests as a measurement of the effectiveness of advertising. It's true that testing the persuasiveness of an ad, or using awareness or recall techniques, comes closer to revealing whether advertising will influence sales. However, many advertisers simply cannot afford the cost of these more sophisticated types of research studies. Also, readership research can be very revealing if used the correct way. Roper Starch Worldwide Inc. (www.roper.com), is the leading proponent of readership research with its well-known Starch reports. The cost of these reports is inexpensive and should be a must if you use print advertising in magazines that they research.

In a Starch report, you receive four scores for your ad, as well as for all other ads in the magazine being researched. The first score is the percentage of people who can remember seeing your ad. This is your "Noted Score." The second score is the percentage of respondents who, in addition to remembering your ad, can also state the name of the advertiser. This is your "Associated Score." The third score is the percentage of the respondents who have read any part of the body copy. This is your "Read Some Score." The fourth score is the percentage of the respondents who read 50 percent or more of the body copy. This is your "Read Most Score."

When a Starch report is conducted on a particular magazine, the name of the advertiser in each ad is covered with tape. Interviewers call on one hundred people who subscribe to this particular magazine, go through each page with the respondent, and obtain the four scores. Because the sample is quite small, the standard deviation is quite large. This means that the only way to analyze Starch scores is to compare the big swings. Since you receive the scores for all the ads in the magazines, you have the opportunity to compare your own scores with your competitors'. If your ad receives a score of 30, you should not consider it superior to another ad that received a 28. But if you receive a 40 score on your ad and your competitor received only a 20, you can conclude that you are doing something right or your competitor is doing something wrong.

One of the major advantages of Starch tests is that they can weed out ineffective ads. It is true that an ad can have a high readership score and still not induce readers to try the brand, but you can never induce anyone to try your brand if people don't first read your ad. If your ad gets a high readership score, you at least know that it is being read. The remaining question is whether it helps sell your brand.

Market research companies do offer many other types of advertising research. For example, Starch offers database reports, creative analyses, basic campaign analysis, campaign tracking analysis, media analysis, on-line impressions studies, and Add+Impact. Their Add+Impact is an advertising evaluation test designed to measure attention levels, or intrusiveness of an ad, as well as levels of brand equity, message communication, and persuasion. The test answers such questions as:

1. Will the ad break through the clutter?

2. How do readers feel toward the ad—how does it impact their feeling toward the brand?

3. Will readers continue to see the ad in magazines or will it wear out after one exposure?

4. Which messages get through to the audience and are they relevant?

5. Are these messages accepted and do they enhance brand equity?

6. What needs to be done next?

There are also methods for posttesting newspaper advertising. However, there is not as great a demand for this type of ad research because most of these advertisers are retail merchants. They usually have the advantage of knowing whether their advertising is effective by counting the sales of the items featured. What they sometimes don't know, though, is how much more they could have sold if their ads had been more dramatic, eye-catching, persuasive, or unique.

Burke Marketing Research Inc., used to be the best known firm for posttesting television commercials, but their operation has been purchased by Ipsos-ASI (www.ipsosasi.com). Some of the methods they use are:

1. Consumers are recruited to evaluate a television program, but the real purpose is to evaluate the commercials.

2. Ads are embedded into a TV program as they would be on local prime time.

3. Consumers view the program (and advertising) on a videotape at home.

The measurements you receive from this kind of posttesting are *related recall, persuasion, brand equity*, and *communication and reaction diagnostics*. Related recall means whether the ad is remembered. Persuasion means the extent to which the ad is able to influence consumers' attitudes and behavior toward the brand. Brand equity is the measurement of differentiation and relevance of the message. By communications and reaction diagnostics, they mean understanding what consumers take away from the ad and whether this is on strategy.

Another method of testing television advertising is a unique format that attempts to determine the direct effect on the viewer's desire to buy the brand. Participants are invited into a theater for the ostensible purpose of critiquing a movie. Before the viewing, they are asked to fill out a questionnaire on their brand preferences. Next they see the movie, which contains a few commercials, and then are asked for comments. Finally, they are given between ten and twenty-five dollars to spend at the supermarket next door, and a record is made of brands selected. The effectiveness of the television commercials is judged on their ability to persuade the viewers to switch from their original preferences as stated on the questionnaire and buy the advertised brands in the store.

Not all advertisers need to subject their advertising to each step—concept testing, pretesting, and posttesting. However, when you examine the large range of research scores, you can see that it can be very beneficial. If research shows that one of your campaigns delivers a 20 percent recall and another 40 percent, then eliminating the first campaign and going with the second, in essence, doubles the effectiveness of your media budget. It should also be mentioned that advertisers that pretest receive higher posttest scores than companies that don't.

Evaluating Other Communications Activities

Measuring the effectiveness of a sales promotion activity is much easier than measuring the effectiveness of advertising because there are fewer variables. If your sales promotion involves coupons or premiums, you can count the number of each that are redeemed and compare the results with your original objectives. Trade allowances can be measured by how much merchandise you can load on the trade; contests and sweepstakes can be measured by the number of entrants; and price-offs by sales before and after the promotion. Once again, the most important aspect of sales promotion activity is to set an objective and to be sure that objective is going to be meaningful to the success of your brand. The key measurement should be whether or not your sales curve ends up at a higher level after the promotion is over and customers return to the market.

Concerning public relations, product publicity can be measured by the number of articles you get placed in magazines and newspapers, and by the amount of air time on broadcast media. Internal communications can be tracked by a series of in-house questionnaires, suggestion boxes, periodic question-and-answer meetings with employees, and the turnover within the company.

There are many excellent research companies throughout the country. You should contact two or three of them and discuss how they would propose measuring your communications activities. Some advertising agencies have excellent research departments. If you have no problem with having the same company that helps execute a plan to also measure the results, then enlist the services of your agency's research department. If you believe that one company should execute the plan and another test results, then use an independent research firm. What is most important is to subject your communications activities to some type of research. If you don't, you will have no idea whether your efforts are a success or a failure.

Conclusion

A s shown in the figure on the next page, which is a repeat of the first figure in Chapter One, your planning scenario starts with your Fact Book. The soundness of your plans depend on the soundness of your Fact Book. Your Fact Book contains all the information you can gather relative to the four components of a market—market economics, competition, your business, and customers. Today, with the advent of the Internet, this information is easier to obtain than ever before.

Based on the data in your Fact Book, begin your planning cycle with your strategic and/or business plan. The purpose is to select markets in which you will have the opportunity to make good money and in which you can get all your ducks in a row. In making this decision, be sure you look out the window. That includes a financial examination of the type of Web site that is best for you. If you are going to build your positioning statement around an entire business, then the decision on the type of positioning should also be included in these top-level plans. If you are going to have positioning statements by brand, then these decisions are made in your marketing plan. Your positioning statement should be

Components of planning.

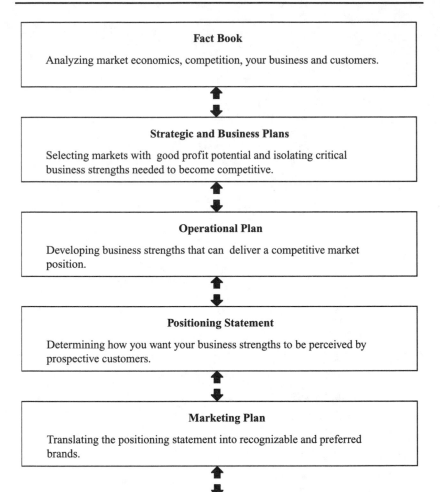

Fact Book

Analyzing market economics, competition, your business and customers.

Strategic and Business Plans

Selecting markets with good profit potential and isolating critical business strengths needed to become competitive.

Operational Plan

Developing business strengths that can deliver a competitive market position.

Positioning Statement

Determining how you want your business strengths to be perceived by prospective customers.

Marketing Plan

Translating the positioning statement into recognizable and preferred brands.

Action Plans

The detailed execution of one or more strategies.

Feedback

Using controls and market research to monitor existing and future conditions for inclusion in the Fact Book and subsequent plans.

unique, memorable, desirable, and believable, and all operational strategies should reinforce it.

Your strategic plan sets the parameters of your operational plans. These operational plans include the marketing plan. The purpose of these plans is to build business strengths to deliver competitive brands. For example, the purpose of the marketing plan is to translate the positioning statement(s) into recognizable and preferred brands.

This translation into recognizable and preferred brands determines your basic selling line and your target audience. These two factors determine the type of marketing tools you use. You want to use marketing tools that not only reinforce your positioning and drive home your selling message, but also reach the prospects in the buying decision. For example, if you are selling quality, you want to be like a Tiffany. If you want to be a Tiffany icon, then you need an elegant selling line and an upscale audience. That also means using marketing tools that reach those individuals and allow your message to be displayed dynamically.

You need marketing people that know marketing. Don't commission a person from another trade on a Friday to be a marketing executive on Monday. Use individuals experienced in marketing while you give others interested in the profession a chance to learn. Be sure to give them all, both experienced and the learners, a hockey stick.

The parameters of your marketing plan are taken from your strategic plan, and detailed in your product or service plan. This brand plan determines your pricing strategy and sets up the market variables, such as awareness, distribution, closure rate, and repeat sales, that you have to obtain to reach your revenue objectives. A what-if revenue model is an excellent tool to accomplish this task. After you determine the level of the market variables that have to be obtained to reach your revenue objective, calculate the execution costs and that becomes your marketing budget.

The purpose of the other five components of the marketing plan—marketing communications (advertising, sales promotion, and public relations), Internet, sales management, customer service, and market research—is to obtain the market variable levels set forth in the revenue model.

Use advertising to build awareness. Television is an excellent choice if your target is the masses and your story involves a demonstration or looks beautiful in living color. Remember, though, if you spend too little, you may waste every dollar. Radio allows you more market segmentation and is ideal if your message lends itself to the imagery of sound. Newspapers deliver a higher income group than the above and have fast closing dates. Magazines add dramatic color and both newspapers and magazines permit a longer or more complicated sales message than broadcast. Trade magazines are best for selling business-to-business. The CPM is high, but they provide a rifle approach to your target. Don't forget outdoor media, if your message is six words or less. It has the lowest CPM of all media.

Use direct mail to sell or produce leads. If you have, or can build a sound database—a must in today's marketing world—direct mail and telemarketing are excellent "rifle" tools. You can go after just who you want to, and consequently the total monetary outlay is relatively low. Your mailing should match your positioning. Don't send out the typical junk mail when you are a quality act.

Use trade shows to demonstrate what you are selling. When selling business-to-business, trade shows can deliver the key personnel in the buying decision. Shows are also ideal for brand demonstrations. If you can't sell off the floor, be sure to get the prospects' business cards. Remember to ask them what day and time is good to call.

Use merchandising and sales promotion for incremental sales. If you have access to the point-of-purchase for your product or service, be one of the marketers reinventing the art of merchandising. This is the most critical moment in the buying decision, so be sure to add some pizzazz to the surroundings. Sales promotion activity can move merchandise, but if it is a one-shot affair on the part of the purchaser, you are probably losing money in the long run. Develop events that zero-in on "loyal to competition" and "non-users" customer groups to push your sales curve to a continuing higher level.

Use public relations for free ads. The media has to fill their pages and air time. Take advantage of this situation by providing them with news about your business and brand. A press release that gets printed or aired is worth more than one ad. And the price is right.

Use the Internet. The question relative to e-commerce is not whether you should participate, but how. That does not necessarily mean you have to sell from your Web site. Review the five format options discussed in Chapter Two to determine which one fits into your overall plan. Then, by marketing trial and error—which is easy to do on the Internet—determine the best way to gain customer traffic.

Only use your sales team to close the sale. It's the most powerful marketing tool you have, but also the most expensive. Save it until the latter part of the phases customers go through when they are considering a purchase. Use less expensive tools, as mentioned above, to build awareness, preference, and leads. Then sock it to them—nicely—with your sales team.

Use customer service to increase repeat sales. Excellent customer service should be a given, but it is not. Hire people that first listen to a customer's problem and then do something about it. Make sure they are reachable and not encumbered with policies that make no sense to the customer. Do special things for special customers. Answer the phone on the third ring.

Use controls and market research to complete the loop. You only want to do things that offer a benefit, and anything that offers a benefit can be observed. If it can be observed, it can be counted, and if it can be counted, it can be measured. Be sure you have a measurable objective for each part of your marketing plan. Monitor your objectives and feed back the status into your Fact Book for use in possible revisions of your plans. Use market research to keep posted on any changes in market economics, competition, and your customers. The more you know, the better you will do.

Good luck!

APPENDIXES

Appendix A

A Marketing Plan Outline

To help you tie together all the material presented in this book, following is a suggested format for a marketing plan. The examples given of objectives and strategies, without timing and controls, were written by my marketing seminar participants. In these examples, the timing, or completion date, would be relegated to a time management chart and the controls, or costs, for each component included in the budget summary.

Section I: Strategic Position, Marketing Personnel, Fact Book Summary, and Major Marketing Objectives and Strategies
Section II: Product/Service Plan
Section III: Marketing Communications Plan
Section IV: Research Plan
Section V: Internet Plan
Section VI: Customer Service Plan
Section VII: Sales Management Plan
Section VIII: Budget, Timing, Plans, and Action Plans

Section I

Strategic Position, Marketing Personnel, Fact Book Summary, and Major Marketing Objectives and Strategies

A. Strategic Position

1. Relative profit potential of this market within the company.
2. Critique of company versus competition as to current status as well as ability to acquire the critical business strengths needed to become major player in this market.
3. Definition of strategic position (market share objective) and payout.

B. Marketing Personnel

1. State which components of the business are involved in the marketing function.
2. If you employ an advertising agency, state its role in the preparation of the plan.
3. State the name of the planning leader for the plan, the members of the planning team, the individual responsible for keeping the Fact Book up to date, and the individuals responsible for monitoring the various sections of the plan to be sure the strategies are executed correctly and the objectives are met.

C. Fact Book Summary

1. Statement on market economics.
2. Statement on marketing strength of competition.
3. Definition of target audience.
4. Delineation of company marketing strengths and weaknesses for competing in this market.

D. Major Marketing Objectives

1. Gross sales and market share objectives.
2. Distribution and depth of line objectives.
3. New product/service introduction objectives.

4. Awareness, preference, and sales closure rate objectives.

5. Repeat purchase rate and volume/profit per purchase objectives.

6. Marketing budget and timing.

E. Major Marketing Strategies

1. Positioning statement. Example: Position the brand as the only one with preprogrammed options, thus extending the use and value of the brand. The target is the numbers-oriented person (e.g., the engineer, aviator, accountant, or retailer).

2. Distribution strategy. Example: Position the brand among dealers as the most attractive service to the above-mentioned target, one that is not currently being reached by brands Able and Baker and thus not a duplication of inventory. Develop in-store merchandising units to demonstrate and allow consumer to "work" new model, thereby reinforcing brand difference at point-of-sale.

3. Communications strategy. Example: Thrust of marketing communications will be consumer "pull" rather than dealer "push." Build brand awareness and recognition of brand difference with target consumer, first through specialized media and later through mass media.

4. Internet strategy. Example: Use Web site as a promotional tool, rather than a transactional one, due to technicality of brand and possible damage to existing lines of distribution.

5. Pricing strategy. Example: Price competitively with major competition.

Section II

Product/Service Plan

A. Product/Service Plan Objectives

1. Set objectives for allocation of marketing dollars per brand, distribution, depth of line, packaging, pricing, awareness, preference, and repeat purchasing.
2. Examples
   a. Models 1040 and 1041 will receive 90 percent of marketing dollars due to higher profit margins.
   b. Increase the average price to $1,961 on models 1040 and 1041.
   c. Expand distribution among chains from 29 percent to 50 percent, among department stores from 50 percent to 75 percent, and among independents from 17 percent to 35 percent.
   d. Reduce packaging costs to $22.50 for chains, $20.25 for department stores, $15.50 for owned-and-operated (O/O), and $13.00 for independents.

B. Product/Service Plan Strategies

1. Set one or more strategies for each objective.
2. Examples
   a. All advertising and sales promotion will feature models 1040 and 1041. In addition, sales force will receive double bonus points on these two models.
   b. Prices will be raised for O/Os and independents to $2,100, coupled with the company's pledge for greater advertising support. Chain and department stores pricing will remain the same.
   c. Major expansion in distribution will be obtained through a 35 percent increase in the sales force and a 25 percent increase in the communications budget.
   d. The new technology of vacuum packaging developed last year by R&D will be used for all models within the next two years.

C. Product/Service Plans

  1. Develop at least one plan for each above strategy. The plan states how you plan to execute the strategy.

  2. Summarize the plan in the marketing plan and put the details in action plans. The action plan should include each step or task, who is responsible for each step or task, and the date by which each step or task has to be completed. If the strategy is to use trade shows to accomplish a certain objective, then the action plan should delineate each step necessary to execute the strategy, including selecting the shows, booking the space, designing the exhibit, and determining who will attend.

Section III

Marketing Communications Plan

A. Marketing Communications Plan Objectives

1. Include objectives on advertising, sales promotion, and public relations.

2. Advertising Plan Examples

 a. Increase awareness of Ryan minicomputer from 30 percent to 50 percent among senior data processing professionals in companies with sales over $20 million. Increase association with major selling point (more data storage per dollar) from 25 percent to 40 percent.

 b. Among dealers of small computer systems, increase awareness of brand from 25 percent to 45 percent and association with major selling point from 15 percent to 30 percent.

3. Sales Promotion Plan Examples

 a. Demonstrate high-impact resistance of new housing on energy monitors to 300 design engineers.

 b. Reduce sales time necessary to educate purchasing agents on specifications of thermocoupler line from an average of ninety minutes to thirty minutes.

 c. Generate $50,000 in direct sales of replacement parts.

 d. Reduce the number of unqualified leads sent to the sales force by 50 percent.

4. Public Relations Plan Examples

 a. Placement of two major articles in general business or weekly news magazines.

 b. Placement of major article on new Series 100 line in every data processing publication.

B. Marketing Communications Plan Strategies

1. Set one or more strategies for each above objective.

2. Advertising Plan Examples

    a. Creative Strategy

       (1) Major benefit: more data storage per dollar.

       (2) Copy points: Competitively priced; offers twice the number of circuits per chip; supports 30 percent more sectors per track versus competition.

    b. Media Strategy

       (1) Reach 65 percent of senior data processing professionals in companies with sales over $20 million with a frequency of eight over a twelve-month period.

       (2) Concentrate all media dollars in the leading trade vertical magazine, adding second magazine in the field only if necessary to reach required reach.

3. Sales Promotion Plan Examples

    a. To demonstrate impact resistance of new housing, take space in July WESPLEX show and design exhibit offering prize to anyone cracking housing with sledgehammer. Publicize exhibit and prize by direct mail to design engineers.

    b. Review brochures on thermocoupler line to incorporate complete specifications and clear explanation of differences between each item in the line.

    c. To build direct sales program for replacement parts, start with list of customers with models three to five years old. Set up system of twenty-four-hour handling of orders. Create approach to stress this fast service, resulting in less downtime for customer.

4. Public Relations Plan Examples

    a. Use the lure of an exclusive sneak preview of Series 100 line and/or set up exclusive interview with CEO for major business/newsweekly article.

    b. Fly in editors of all data processing publications for preview of Series 100 three months before introduction in order to secure major coverage in their May editions.

Section IV

Research Plan

A. Research Plan Objectives

1. Set objectives for methods you will use to measure: the effectiveness of your marketing plan; changes in the market; and new product/service development.
2. Examples
   a. Conduct a statistically projectable study of the target audience to obtain current levels on awareness, registration of selling message, preference, and intent to buy.
   b. Determine needs of the company's customers and the current ranking of the company's customer service department relative to competition.
   c. Determine two leading benefits of new model 707 to the aircraft instrumentation industry.

B. Research Plan Strategies

1. Set one or more strategies for each of your objectives
2. Examples:
   a. Conduct a benchmark study of 300 members of the target audience with a standard deviation of 2 and a precision of plus or minus 3 to obtain effectiveness levels of marketing communciations.
   b. Have an independent company conduct a free seminar on customer service for marketing personnel of current and potential customers; during the seminar, elicit from the customers their own needs and their current observations on performance of their suppliers, including our company.

   Conduct six focus group sessions among purchasing agents in aviation instrumentation companies as a guide to determining major benefits of model 707.

Section V

Internet Plan

A. Internet Plan Objectives

1. There are many marketing aspects of your Web site that should be addressed in your marketing plan. You can either address them here in the Internet plan or in one of the other appropriate sections of your plan. Probably the most important marketing aspect of your overall Internet plan is building traffic, using conventional marketing tools. This can be addressed here or in your marketing communications plan. However, there are other factors you should consider. If it is a promotional site that produces sales leads, then how these leads are handled should either be here in your Internet plan, or in your sales plan. If it is a customer service site, coordinate this activity with your offline operation in your customer service plan. If it is a transaction site, you should coordinate this means of distribution with your offline distributors, retailers, etc.

2. Examples
   a. Obtain an average of 2,000 "click-ons" per month by the end of the sixth month and 9,000 for the plan year.
   b. Maintain current offline distribution coverage of 60 percent.

B. Internet Plan Strategies

1. Set one or more for each objective.

2. Examples
   a. The Web site will be promoted in all ads and brochures.
   b. A three-part direct mail campaign will be sent to all listings in our database promoting the Web site. We will offer a red Jaguar convertible to the first customer who can decipher our new basic selling line from clues posted periodically on the site.
   c. Offline distributors will receive 10 percent of gross profit from all Internet sales made to customers in their distribution area.

Section VI

Customer Service Plan

A. Customer Service Plan Objectives

1. Set objectives for the performance of customer service (e.g., effectiveness ranking within the industry, management involvement, marketing involvement, knowledge of product/service line, number of telephone rings before response, cost of handling returns, and expertise of technical personnel).

2. Examples
    a. Company will be ranked number one in the industry in customer service effectiveness within two years.
    b. All phones will be answered by the third ring.
    c. Customer service personnel will be knowledgeable in all company brands by August.

B. Customer Service Plan Strategies

1. Set one or more strategies for each objective.
2. Examples
    a. All customer service personnel will be given a free weekend trip to either Disneyland or Disney World to permit them to observe the finest customer service organization in the world.
    b. An independent company will be commissioned to answer any customer service phone after three rings. The customer service department will be charged the complete cost, which will be deducted from customer service employees' bonuses.
    c. All customer service personnel responsible for brand knowledge will have access to a computer database that will allow them to punch in a few numbers to bring up on the computer monitor any type of information on any brand sold by the company.

Section VII

Sales Management Plan

A. Sales Management Plan Objectives

1. Set objectives on subjects such as sales goals per product/ service line, sales closure rate, cost per sales call, number of sales calls per day, and sales training.

2. Examples

   a. Maintain current field force of twenty people on service A and increase sales from $910,113 to $995,000.

   b. Increase average sales closure rate from current 22 percent to 28 percent.

   c. Average 20 percent of sales force calls by field force on service B to frequent travelers to speed up penetration of this market.

   d. Increase division profitability by increasing sales of service C from 30 percent to 35 percent.

B. Sales Management Plan Strategies

1. Set one or more strategies for each objective.

2. Examples

   a. Improve field sales force productivity on service A through a combination of efforts including: form home office unit with 1-800 telephone number lines to take over customer tracking and routine reorders and create a series of direct mail pieces to qualify inquiries before sending to field.

   b. To increase closure rate, a minimum of one-third of the entire sales force will be sent to a new one-week session on sales training that will incorporate a new concept of "town meeting" dialogue to improve each individual's ability to close.

   c. To increase penetration of service C, hire ten new salespeople to work as a task force rolling out service as each new region is targeted.

   d. To increase proportion of sales of service C, create bonus compensation plan based on points awarded according to margins on various services.

Section VIII

Budgets, Timing, Plans, and Action Plans

A. Budgets

All objectives should be measurable to enable you to determine whether you meet them. That means they usually require a goal, a control, and timing or date. In the preceding pages there are several examples of objectives with goals. You can put the control (usually the amount of money to be spent) or the budget, in each objective, or you can put the control for each objective in summary form at the end of the plan.

After you have approved goals and controls, monitor them each week to be sure you are on target. If you are off target sometime during the year, you have to change the goal or the control or alter the strategy.

B. Timing

Timing refers to the completion by which an objective must be achieved. Like controls, the timing can be inserted in each objective or can be summarized at the end of the plan. Like controls, timing has to be continuously monitored.

C. Plans or tactics

Plans or tactics are the execution of the strategies. They should be summarized in the marketing plan. After the complete marketing plan is approved, action plans should be written to provide the details. If you include all the details of executing a strategy in the marketing plan, you may be confronted with three possible problems:

1. You end up with a 50- to 200-page document that no one will read, and the plan just gathers dust on the shelf.
2. If the plan is not approved, you have wasted time developing all the details.
3. Using a separate action plan lets the people who will actually execute the plan decide for themselves how they should do it.

D. Action Plans

An action plan contains the detailed execution of one or more strategies and should include at least three factors:

1. Each necessary step or task
2. Who will be responsible for accomplishing each step or task
3. The required completion date of each step or task

For each marketing plan, you may have between five and twenty action plans. The sum of all your action plans is your *milestone calendar* or *PERT chart*. A milestone calendar keeps you on target relative to timing. A PERT chart determines which completion dates for certain steps or tasks are the most critical and have to be watched most closely. These critical steps or tasks are the ones that influence the beginning of another step or task.

Keep your action plans in separate binders. Your Fact Book should also be in a separate binder. This will enable you to have a short, concise, operational marketing plan that you can refer to each week. If your marketing plan is not operational, the preparation is nothing more than an exercise.

Thirty-Eight Market Characteristics That Can Influence Profit Potential

Figure B-1 lists 38 market characteristics that can have a major impact on whether a particular market offers profit potential to a company. A description of each follows. The key phrase here is "profit potential." These characteristics determine whether a market offers a business the potential to make good money. Even if a market scores favorably on this type of analysis, it doesn't necessarily mean a participating business will succeed. In order to do so, it will also need the business strengths required in this market to become a major player. The market characteristics discussed here are not meant to form a complete list, but they should give you an idea of the things you should consider when determining whether a market or segment can become profitable to your company.

The factors you select may not necessarily be the ones your competitors would use. For example, if the greatest strength, or basic thrust, of your corporation is manufacturing, the market characteristics you select

Figure B-1. Thirty-eight market characteristics that can influence profit potential.

1. Pricing sensitivity

2. Captive customers

3. Customer concentration

4. Economies of scale

5. Barriers to entry

6. Regulatory exposure

7. Ability to sell off the Internet

8. Ability to promote off the Internet

9. Ability to handle customer relations off the Internet

10. Ability to buy off the Internet

11. Foreign operations

12. Foreign investments

13 Opportunity to segment the market

14 Stage of the life cycle

15 Number of major competitors

16. Level of technology

17. Value added (% of sales)

18. Manufacturing costs (% of sales)

19. Investment intensity (% of sales)

20. Inventory (% of sales)

21. Promotion costs (% of sales)

22. Social attitudes

23. Environmental attitudes

24. Raw materials availability

25. Sales costs (% of sales)

26. Distribution costs

27. Customer relations costs

28. Service costs

29. Demand cyclicity

30. Demand seasonality

31. Potential for functional substitution

32. R&D costs (% of sales)

33. Gross margins

34. Growth rate

35. Size of industry/segment

36. Need for capital

37. Aggressiveness of competition

38. Trendiness

to critique a market would be different from those chosen by a company whose basic thrust is marketing. Because the potential profitability of each market in which you participate should be judged by the same set of criteria, the final decision on which factors to use should be made by top management.

None of these factors should be viewed separately. It is the sum of the profit potentiality positives and negatives that count. For example, a company could be in a market that is insensitive to price (usually a positive ingredient for profit potentiality), but one that also contains many aggressive competitors (a negative ingredient). Consequently, the company could have a rough time becoming profitable.

1. **Pricing Sensitivity.** A market may be very sensitive to price increases or decreases, very insensitive, or somewhere in between these two extremes. In a market that is very sensitive to price, a price increase of 10 percent would result in a decrease in volume greater than the 10 percent. Conversely, a price cut of 10 percent would result in an increase in volume exceeding 10 percent. Examples of highly price-sensitive markets are industrial and consumer paper products, metals, and industrial chemicals.

   A market is considered insensitive to price if, say, a 10-percent price cut results in a volume increase of less than 10 percent and, conversely, a 10-percent price increase causes a volume decrease of less than 10 percent. Examples of markets that are relatively insensitive to price are medical services and cigarettes. The question for you is which situation would be more profitable to your business. Usually companies would prefer to operate in markets that are insensitive to price, but if you are, or have the capability of becoming, the low-cost producer, then you may prefer a market where price sensitivity is high.

2. **Captive Customers.** Most companies would prefer to do business in a market where the customers are captive. That means that the customers don't have much choice other than to buy from you. Microsoft has enjoyed this situation for years. Their operating systems run over 90 percent of all personal computers in the world. However, their enviable captive customer position may change in the near future due to the current federal and state antitrust suits they are now fighting, and the recent growth in popularity of the Linux operating system. Some of the large

defense manufacturers also have a relatively captive customer in the United States government. If the federal government needs more nuclear submarines, aircraft carriers, or advanced aerospace technology, it has very few suppliers to choose from.

3. **Customer Concentration.** Customer concentration can be interpreted in many ways; two of them are geographical concentration and concentrated customer profile. When your customers are concentrated in a limited geographical area, it normally results in savings in activities such as distribution and selling expense. Customer-profile concentration can also lead to more efficient marketing. For example, Hewlett-Packard became a billion-dollar corporation by selling only to engineers. It was a case of engineers selling to engineers. Today, Hewlett-Packard has expanded into computers, printers, software, and hardware for e-commerce.

4. **Economies of Scale.** Economies of scale are applicable in some markets but not others. Where they are applicable, it means that as a company gets larger, its manufacturing, operations, and marketing costs per unit decrease. This concept was originally based on the learning curve, and in subsequent years on the experience curve. The premise behind the learning curve is that as employees keep doing a task over and over, they are able to do it more quickly. In addition, as volume increases, the individual tasks can become more specialized or limited in scope, which once again normally results in increased productivity.

The experience curve is a broader conceptualization than the learning curve, and takes into account more factors than just employee learning and specialization. If a 10-million-ton oil refinery would cost $10 million, then a 20-million-ton refinery would not incur a construction cost of $20 million, but most likely around $15 million. If it takes 5,000 employees to run a 10-million-ton refinery, it would not take 10,000 to run a

20-million-ton facility. Once again, it probably would require only a 50 percent increase, or 7,500 employees.

In addition, as companies get larger, they are able to hire better managers, not only because they can afford higher salaries, but also because they have a prestigious name. Which would you prefer, to be a manager at Dell or at some unknown computer hardware/software company? Larger companies usually are able to negotiate a better price from suppliers just through the sheer volume of their purchases. All these factors are components of the experience curve. The premise behind the experience curve is that every time you double your volume, you experience the same percentage savings in costs, measured in real dollars.

You can determine the *slope* of the experience curve or cost-savings percentage by plotting on logarithm/logarithm paper the historical relationships between costs (in real dollars) and quantity produced, from year one to the present. Some industries or markets, such as random-access computer chips, realize a very steep slope.

The question you have to ask yourself is whether or not your company can be profitable in a market where economies of scale or the experience curve is operative. Many Japanese manufacturing companies are masters at what is referred to as "pushing the experience curve." What they do is go for volume by pricing their product very low. Sometimes the price is even below their cost. By so doing, they push themselves down the experience curve, taking advantage of the cost savings each time they double their volume. They eventually get their cost down so low that they are then able to price their product at a level below competitors' costs, and still have sufficient margins to earn a respectable profit. In such a situation, competitors have no other choice but to close their doors. This is the way the Japanese have destroyed several American industries, including motorbikes, consumer electronics, and ball bearings.

5. **Barriers to Entry.** Companies with capital muscle usually prefer markets that have high barriers to entry. What that means is that it costs a lot of money to get into the market. If you are in a market that has high barriers to entry and you are doing well, it is more difficult for new competitors to enter. Conversely, companies with limited capital would prefer markets with low barriers to entry, although this does mean that if they are successful, it is much easier for competitors to enter.

   Exit barriers should also be taken into account. There is a strip-mining company that would like to close its doors because it is losing millions of dollars each year. However, the day it stops operations, it has to go back and refurbish the landscape as prescribed by federal regulations. It doesn't have enough capital to cover this expense, so it is stuck in a market it would prefer leaving.

   Industries such as steel, aluminum, and automobiles have high barriers to entry, whereas many of the service companies, such as real estate brokers, distributors, jobbers, manufacturers' representatives, and consulting firms, operate in markets with very low entrance barriers.

6. **Regulatory Exposure.** Most companies would prefer markets or industries with little or no regulatory exposure. Examples of markets that would receive a negative score on this factor are nuclear power, public utilities, shipping, and federal defense contractors.

7. **Ability to Sell off the Internet.** In markets where brand characteristics are viable for selling off the Internet, you can possibly extend your distribution at a relatively small cost. Where in the past, customers may have been required to either go to your store, contact a distributor or retailer, or negotiate with your sales force, now they could complete the sales transaction on the Web. However, to successfully use this vehicle, you have to be noticed on the Web, which can be difficult. Also, if you are

not up to speed in using Web technology, and your competitors are, this market trait could be a major negative for you.

8. **Ability to Promote off the Internet.** If you can promote your brand on the Internet, it could possibly reduce your overall marketing costs. For example, you could present your brochures and sales literature on your Web site, which would save printing costs. A Web site could also replace other marketing expenses such as advertising in trade magazines and on radio and television. Once again, however, you have to drive traffic to your Web site for it to be effective, and that may take more advertising expenditures than you are currently spending in nonInternet media.

9. **Ability to Handle Customer Relations off the Internet.** Handling customer service by telephone representatives has not worked well for many companies. The problem is that many times customers have to wait an extended period of time to be connected, and even after this occurs, they may be transferred several times to other representatives. Oftentimes in the end, no answer or solution to the customer's inquiry is reached. Therefore, in markets where customer service inquiries can be resolved on the Internet, this can result in improved customer relations and a substantial savings in customer service costs. For example, if in the past you used Federal Express for distributing your merchandise, you would have to call a toll-free number for tracking. Today, you just go to their Web site. It saves you time as well as saving Federal Express millions of dollars in lower customer service costs.

10. **Ability to Buy off the Internet.** In markets where you can purchase your supplies off the Internet you can engage suppliers from around the world.

11. **Foreign Operations.** Companies with international expertise would welcome markets that require foreign operations,

whereas smaller companies that currently have only domestic operations would view this as a negative. Also to be considered is the fact that many markets that are mature in the United States are growth industries overseas. Considering that growth markets are usually more profitable than mature markets, this could be an important factor. (See Factor 14.)

12. **Foreign Investments.** The distinction between foreign investments and foreign operations is that in foreign investments, the company has a nonoperating relationship with a foreign company. Examples would be selling your patent rights to companies offshore or purchasing part ownership in a foreign corporation that would assure you a supply of critical parts or services.

13. **Opportunity to Segment the Market.** Normally, the opportunity to segment is a positive market characteristic relative to profitability. In years past, Schlitz was the number-one selling beer and Anheuser-Busch's market share was only about 20 percent. Today, Anheuser-Busch's market share is approximately 48 percent, and Schlitz, where it is still sold, is only a price beer. (A price beer is one that is priced lower than major brands, and sells only due to its low price.) The major reason for the rise of one and the fall of the other is segmentation. Anheuser-Busch did and Schlitz did not. Anheuser-Busch segmented the market with such brands as Bud Light, Busch, Michelob, and LA. Conversely, if you are in a market where a nail is a nail is a nail— which means there is limited opportunity to introduce new models, sizes, shapes, brand names, and so on—then this would be considered a negative.

14. **Stage of the Life Cycle.** If they had their choice, most companies would prefer participating in markets that are in the growth stage of the industry life cycle. All industries go through four basic stages. When industries first come on the scene, they are said to be in the embryonic or introductory stage, such as ge-

nome therapeutics. The embryonic industries that are fortunate to be winners kick into what is referred to as the growth stage, such as cellular communications. This is the period of maximum annual growth—substantially higher than the growth in the Gross National Product (GNP). Eventually, all industries cool off and enter the mature stage, in which there is little or no growth. An example would be life insurance. Finally, industries inevitably are replaced by new technology and fall into decline, such as vacuum tube manufacturers.

Most companies would prefer operating in growth industries, because during the growth period you can increase your share of market without taking business directly away from competitors. Your competitors could be increasing their sales and feeling happy while, unknown to them, you are gaining market share because your sales are increasing at a faster rate. The embryonic or introductory stage normally is the second choice, especially if the company believes it will be a winner. The third choice usually is mature industries because products or services are less distinct between competitors. Essentially, they are commodities. In addition, the only way a company can increase its share of market is to take business directly away from competitors, which could mean a real dogfight. The fourth choice would be declining industries.

15. **Number of Major Competitors.** Most businesses would prefer an industry or market with relatively few competitors, because it is easier to estimate their reaction to your own business strategies. If you are in a market with just two or three competitors, and you are considering increasing your price, you should be in a relatively good position to ascertain which competitors will follow. The problem with doing business in a market with many competitors or in a fragmented market is that it is virtually impossible to read competitors' reactions to your plans and programs.

16. **Level of Technology.** There are three broad stages of technology: evolving, stable, and revolutionary. Most companies prefer an evolving technology because it permits new products and services, and the market is normally in a growth stage. Revolutionary technology can be a negative because by the time you get your product or service to market, it could be replaced or outdated by competitive brands. A stable technology is usually the middle choice between evolving and revolutionary. Computer software, telecommunications, and banking may represent evolving technology; biotechnology and the Internet represent revolutionary; and automobiles and insurance represent stable.

17. **Value Added (Percentage of Sales).** In most instances, high value added results in high profit. If a company pays $100 per unit for raw materials, fashions the components into a complex machine, and then sells it for $1,000, the value added is 90 percent of sales. Compare that with a distributor, who purchases the machine for $1,000 and sells it to a jobber, retailer, or end user for $1,200. The distributor is experiencing a value added equal to only 20 percent of sales. Everything else being equal, the manufacturer has a much greater opportunity than the distributor to obtain a large gross profit. (Gross profit is defined as the difference between the selling price and the cost of goods.)

18. **Manufacturing Costs (Percentage of Sales).** High manufacturing costs could be a positive indicator for profitability to some businesses, and a negative one to others. If a company's basic thrust is manufacturing, and it is or can become the low-cost producer through pushing the experience curve, or the effective use of automation, robotics, and the like, then high manufacturing costs could be an incentive for market entry. Conversely, undercapitalized businesses or those that have let their plant and equipment deteriorate would have a severe problem competing.

19. **Investment Intensity (Percentage of Sales).** High investment intensity drives down return on investment. Return on invest-

ment (ROI) is calculated by dividing the net profit of a business by the total investment in that activity. If a market demands large investments in plant and equipment, then the denominator will be very large and will necessitate a large numerator or profit to yield a decent ROI.

The main incentive for participating in markets that are investment-intensive is that productivity should also be high. Unlike investment intensity, the higher the productivity rate, the more profitable the operation. Therefore, high investment intensity is not necessarily a negative as long as you have high productivity. The businesses that get themselves in trouble are those that have a high investment with little or no increase in productivity.

20. **Inventory (Percentage of Sales).** The lower the inventory, as measured as a percentage of sales, the greater the profit. This is the reason for the development of "just in time" delivery, which was pioneered by the Japanese. Today, the winner is Dell Computer, which carries no inventory. Each computer is made to order by suppliers and then shipped to the customer.

Unlike distributors, jobbers and manufacturers' representatives do not take title to the manufacturers' merchandise they sell nor do they keep an inventory. Therefore, although they, like distributors, have a low value added (which is a negative profitability factor), they have little or no inventory costs, which has a positive effect on profitability.

To be successful in a market that demands extensive inventory, you have to be able to obtain high profit margins per unit, or turn over the inventory several times during the year. For example, a grocery supermarket has high inventory costs and low margins, but it can be profitable if it is able to turn over its inventory many times during the year. The petroleum industry has a different situation. In this market, inventory costs are excessive and turnover is slow. Therefore, to be successful, very high margins per unit are required.

21. **Promotion Costs (Percentage of Sales).** Because promotion costs are an expenditure, the higher the promotion costs, the lower the profit. However, as with so many of these market characteristics, what may be a negative for one company could be a positive for another. Procter & Gamble experiences high promotion costs in practically every market in which it competes. However, because it does such an excellent job in the creation of its commercials, it obtains much more customer impact per promotional dollar than the competition. The result has been good earnings year after year. Nevertheless, these earnings could be even greater if the company was in at least some markets where promotion costs were not so prohibitive. The market situation to be wary of is one that requires high investment intensity, high inventory, and high promotion costs. This leaves very few dollars for other expenditures and profit.

22. **Social Attitudes.** Everything else being equal, it would be easier to market solar energy than nuclear energy, health foods than cigarettes, and computers than guided missiles. Don't underestimate the power of social attitudes and their possible effect on taxation, tariffs, and employment desirability.

23. **Environmental Attitudes.** Environmental attitudes are similar to social attitudes. The bottom line of businesses in mining, chemicals, petroleum, forestry, automobiles, and many manufacturing activities is greatly affected by environmental attitudes. The automobile industry spent millions of dollars to develop and manufacture smaller cars in order to meet the federal requirements on miles per gallon of gasoline. Even so, it appears that they will suffer heavy fines in the years ahead because the American public is once again buying larger cars such as SUV's.

24. **Raw Materials Availability.** Guaranteeing raw materials availability sometimes necessitates vertical integration. That means that if you are a manufacturer, you may have to become your

own supplier or buy the companies that are currently providing the raw materials. IBM originally got into the computer chip business just to guarantee supplies for their computer hardware. It was a smart move. Not only did it guarantee supplies, but today they sell their chips to many other computer hardware companies at a profit. If you are in a similar situation, but undercapitalized, you could be at the mercy of your suppliers.

25. **Sales Costs (Percentage of Sales).** The average cost of a sales presentation today is somewhere between $400 and $600. That is an average, which means that some industries or markets have a much lower sales cost, and others have one that is much higher. Doing business in a market where you can sell by telemarketing or over the Internet has a strong advantage over operating in marketplaces where the sales force incurs airfare, hotel, and meal expenditures.

26. **Distribution Costs.** If you were a distributor, you probably would prefer markets that have high distribution costs, and if you were a manufacturer, you would opt for low distribution costs. Why manufacturers would prefer low distribution costs is readily apparent, but why most distributors should select markets with high distribution costs may be questioned. A distributor in New Jersey had always put emphasis on markets that had low distribution costs until I suggested that the company do just the opposite. The reasoning is simple: If distribution costs are low in a market, it usually means that the distributors do not provide many services or much value. Consequently, they can be easily replaced. Conversely, markets with high distribution costs reflect many distributor activities that greatly enhance the distributor's importance. In addition, there is more room for the distributor to cut his costs.

27. **Customer Relations Costs.** Markets with high customer relations costs are usually a negative for any business. High costs in this area usually mean that the brand is either not of the highest

quality, or is highly technical. In either case, the interface with the customer is performed by employees who normally lack the ability to satisfy the customer. Invariably it's a no win situation, unless you are a master like the staff at Disney theme parks.

28. **Service Costs.** High service costs, such as sending technicians out into the field to fix what you sell, is invariably a negative. Customers appreciate the service, but rarely appreciate the charge.

29. **Demand Cyclicity.** Demanding cyclicity is a negative. Automobiles, defense, metals, and construction are cyclical industries. Food, banking, medicine, and law are not. Simple logic tells you that if you have a few good years followed by a few bad years, you have to make considerably more during the good years to equal the profitability of a business that does not experience cyclicity. Some corporations look for counter-cycle markets to balance out their businesses in cyclical markets. For example, when the economy is sick, real estate and machine tools are down, and liquor, movies, and discount merchandising are up.

30. **Demand Seasonality.** Demanding seasonality is similar to demanding cyclicity, except that the demand fluctuates within a twelve-month period. Soft drinks, ice cream, skiing, and Christmas trees are seasonal. In the ski industry, if a ski resort operator doesn't have substantial ski lift sales volume during the two-week Christmas holiday and the one-week spring school break, the best she can do, even if there are great snow conditions the rest of the season, is break even. As with cyclicity, seasonality is considered a negative.

31. **Potential for Functional Substitution.** There is usually a greater opportunity for functional substitution in mature markets than in growth industries. Functional substitution is where a brand from another industry can be a substitute. For example, a snow shovel can be a substitute for a snow blower. This is another

reason growth industries are preferred over mature markets. However, you can have a brand in a mature market in which many people believe there is no substitute, such as Häagen-Dazs ice cream.

32. **R&D Costs (Percentage of Sales).** The fact that a market necessitates great R&D efforts is a negative in itself, because this is an expenditure. However, if your company thrives on R&D and you believe that you can do it better than the competition, as Boeing and Citibank did, then this could be a positive. When sales of new products/services account for a large percentage of total sales, it is a very strong positive factor in profitability, but developing this situation usually means high R&D expenditures, which is a negative.

33. **Gross Margins.** This one is self-explanatory. Markets with high gross margins are obviously preferable to markets with low margins. The only possible negative is that markets with high margins invite competition.

34. **Growth Rate.** As with gross margins, markets with a high growth rate are normally preferred to markets with low or negative growth experience. As previously stated, it's much easier to increase your share of market in a growth market than in a mature market. However, a high growth rate does not necessarily mean high current profits. Normally, during the growth stage, high expenditures are required to stay competitive, but a high share in a growth market should eventually lead to high profitability. Notwithstanding the preceding, you may want to put a cap on your preferred growth rate. For example, some companies do not want to participate in markets that are growing at a rate faster than, say, 10 percent because they simply can't handle it. They may also get beaten up by a competitor that is better capitalized, such as Microsoft.

35. **Size of Industry/Segment.** The ideal size of an industry or segment will vary from business to business. The ideal marketplace

for IBM would be many times larger than the ideal marketplace for a new computer manufacturer. You normally want to be in a market or a segment in which you can become a major player. Experience indicates that when a market or segment reaches maturity, only three businesses will remain profitable, and in order for the smallest of the three to be successful, its share of market has to be at least 25 percent of the market leader's share.

36. **Need for Capital.** If you have limited capital available, you do not want to fight your battles in a market where competitors are owned by huge conglomerates. Minnetonka Corporation in Minnetonka, Minnesota, had a very successful introduction of its new product, Soft Soap. The only problem was that it was too successful too fast. Procter & Gamble, the king of soaps, witnessed this rapid sales increase, and decided that it ought to get into the market. In a short period of time, it practically blew Minnetonka Corp.'s product out of the stores.

37. **Aggressiveness of Competition.** Even though Netscape had been aggressive in developing its Internet browser, the company could not compete with Microsoft. It is normally wise to stay away from markets that have competitors that act like Microsoft, General Electric, Citibank, and Procter & Gamble, because they may eventually eat your lunch.

38. **Trendiness.** Trendiness in a market is not a favorable attribute, because it is almost impossible to constantly predict the next trend. Many toy and clothing companies and restaurants have gone under due to this factor. Even Mattel is struggling. Of course, there are exceptions, like The Gap. But there are so many other common detriments to making money in a market, why pick one where your complete line of merchandise can go out of favor overnight?

Appendix C

Explanation of the What-If Sales Model

A marvelous tool for tying all your marketing factors or variables together is the "what-if" model. A what-if model allows you to calculate one or more major objectives, such as sales revenue and resulting
market share based on the performance of various market variables. The
objectives go at the end of the model, and all the market variables that
you believe will influence these objectives are inserted in front of them.
You then develop mathematical equations that indicate how the various
market factors interact with the objectives. If you structure the model
correctly, obtaining the market variables you use in your model should
deliver the resulting objectives.

The objectives used in this model for a hypothetical business are
sales volume and market share. Some examples of the market variables
used are size of market, awareness of your product or service, level of
distribution, sales closure rate, and the percentage of customers that
make repeat purchases.

You can keep making changes in the variables you control until you
obtain the desired volume and share figures. Then when you write your

marketing plan, you insert the level of the various variables and include marketing strategies and plans on how to reach them. If your strategies and plans work as predicted, you will obtain your volume and share numbers. However, if you subsequently believe you cannot reach the levels needed in the model, then you have to go back to the model and change the variables to levels you can reach.

Installing a what-if model on a computer enables you, by the use of simple formulas, to make changes in the variables, and then review the automatically calculated revisions in the objectives. See Figure C-1, which is the same as Figure 9-3 in Chapter Nine. Notice that the formulas are simple addition and multiplication. However, if you are not into computers, you can use a calculator or keep asking "what if" with a pencil and sheet of paper. You don't need models or other types of mathematical equations to develop an effective marketing plan, but as mentioned above, it can be very helpful. In addition, you should have some method to determine how a change in one market variable will influence others, and once again, a model could be beneficial. This will be illustrated below.

Two plans are used in the model to show the interplay of the variables. Only two relatively minor revisions have been made in Plan 2 versus Plan 1, but the results are significant. There is a 41 percent increase in sales. The two variables are the sales closure rate or conversion awareness to trial and percent triers customers repeating once. The sales closure rate is increased from 28 percent in Plan 1 to 33 percent in Plan

Figure C-1. Mathematics of a "what if" model for projecting market share.

Market	X	Awareness	X	Conversion	X
Distribution	=	Trial	+	Repeats	=
Purchases	X	Units/Price	=	Sales	/
Market	=	Market Share			

2, and the percent triers repeating once is increased from 40 percent in Plan 1 to 50 percent in Plan 2.

That is the beauty of a what-if model. You keep asking, "Can I do this, can I do that, and if I can, how does it affect my sales?" Putting the model together is quite simple, as will be shown, but if you are interested in purchasing the model ready for use, e-mail me at wml@wml-market ing.com.

The model consists of four sections or ranges as shown on charts that are titled Figures C-2 to C-5 for Plan 1 and C-2A to C-5A for Plan 2. The market variables are shown at the tops of the charts or as column headings. The other column headings refer to the calculations resulting from the interplay of the variables.

The four ranges are as follows:

FIGURE	RANGE	TITLE
C-2 & C-2A	One	Trial Transactions
C-3 & C-3A	Two	Repeat Purchases
C-4 & C-4A	Three	Unit & Dollar Volume
C-5 & C-5A	Four	Share of Market

Figures C-2 & C-2A—
Range One: Trial Transactions

There are four marketing variables involved. The first is "A. Total Number of Potential Buyers." This is shown at the top of the chart, and is the total number of potential buyers in your market for the type of brand you and your competitors sell. Fifty thousand is shown for both Plan 1 and 2. The second is "B. Conversion Awareness to Trial." This one is also at the top of the chart, and is the percentage of the potential buyers who become aware of your brand, and who you believe will subsequently purchase it. Twenty-eight percent is shown for Plan 1 and 33 percent for Plan 2. Variable three, "C. Potential Buyers Aware," is in column C. It is the percentage of potential buyers that you expect to become aware of your brand over a period of time. The anticipated levels for this variable show the awareness climbing to 61 percent by the end of the third year for both plans. Variable four is "F. Distribution," and is shown in column F. Distribution is the percentage of your market in which the potential customer can easily and conveniently buy what you sell. If your store or sales force covers 50 percent of the territory, you have a 50 percent distribution level. The distribution level shown here increases to 66 percent by the end of the third year for both plans.

To calculate the number of potential customers who become aware of the brand for Plan 1, you multiply variable "A. Total Number of Potential Buyers" by variable "C. Potential Buyers Aware." The answers are in column "D. Newly Aware." At the end of 36 months, 30,500 potential buyers have become aware of the brand, as shown in column "E. Cumulative Aware."

To calculate the number of buyers who will try the brand, you multiply column "D. Newly Aware" by variable "B. Conversion Awareness to Trial," and the resulting answer by variable "F. Distribution," as shown in column F. For example, during the first month in Plan 1, 1,500 potential customers become aware of the product (column D), of whom it is estimated that 28 percent (variable B) will try the brand. If the company had 100 percent distribution, that would mean that 420 customers would purchase (1,500 times 28 percent). However, the company has only 20 percent distribution at this time, so you have to multiply 420 by 20 percent, which gives you 84 buyers for the first month as shown in column "G. New Trial." For the 36-month period, 4,220 customers will purchase as shown in column "H. Cumulative Trial," which is 8.4 percent of the market as shown in Column "I. Potential Buyers Trying."

As mentioned, only one variable has been changed in Plan 2 as shown on Figure C-2A. The sales closure rate (B) has been increased from 28 percent in Plan 1 to 33 percent in Plan 2. This increases the total number of customer buying at the end of 36 months from 4,220 in Plan 1 to 4,973 in Plan 2. This is an 18 percent increase. In addition,

Figure C-2. "What if" model for projecting market share (trial transactions).

A. Total Number Potential Buyers: 50,000
B. Sales Closure Rate: 28%

	*********** Aware		***************	*****	Trial	***************	
	C. Potential Buyers Aware	D. Newly Aware	E. Cumulative Aware	F. Distribution	G. New Trial	H. Cumulative Trial	I. Potential Buyers Trying
Month	%			%			
0	0%	0	0	10%	0	0	0%
1	3%	1,500	1,500	20%	84	84	0%
2	6%	1,500	3,000	25%	105	189	0%
3	10%	2,000	5,000	29%	162	351	1%
4	13%	1,500	6,500	33%	139	490	1%
5	16%	1,500	8,000	36%	151	641	1%
6	19%	1,500	9,500	39%	164	805	2%
7	22%	1,500	11,000	42%	176	981	2%
8	25%	1,500	12,500	45%	189	1,170	2%
9	28%	1,500	14,000	48%	202	1,372	3%
10	31%	1,500	15,500	51%	214	1,586	3%
11	34%	1,500	17,000	54%	227	1,813	4%
12	37%	1,500	18,500	57%	239	2,052	4%
13	38%	500	19,000	58%	81	2,134	4%
14	39%	500	19,500	59%	83	2,216	4%
15	40%	500	20,000	60%	84	2,300	5%
16	41%	500	20,500	61%	85	2,386	5%
17	42%	500	21,000	62%	87	2,472	5%
18	43%	500	21,500	63%	88	2,561	5%
19	44%	500	22,000	64%	90	2,650	5%
20	45%	500	22,500	65%	91	2,741	5%
21	46%	500	23,000	66%	92	2,834	6%
22	47%	500	23,500	66%	92	2,926	6%
23	48%	500	24,000	66%	92	3,018	6%
24	49%	500	24,500	66%	92	3,111	6%
25	50%	500	25,000	66%	92	3,203	6%
26	51%	500	25,500	66%	92	3,296	7%
27	52%	500	26,000	66%	92	3,388	7%
28	53%	500	26,500	66%	92	3,480	7%
29	54%	500	27,000	66%	92	3,573	7%
30	55%	500	27,500	66%	92	3,665	7%
31	56%	500	28,000	66%	92	3,758	8%
32	57%	500	28,500	66%	92	3,850	8%
33	58%	500	29,000	66%	92	3,942	8%
34	59%	500	29,500	66%	92	4,035	8%
35	60%	500	30,000	66%	92	4,127	8%
36	61%	500	30,500	66%	92	4,220	8%

Figure C-2A. Plan 2: "What if" model for projecting market share (trial transactions).

| | | A. Total Number Potential Buyers: | | 50,000 | | | | |
| | | B. Sales Closure Rate: | | 33% | | | | |

	C.	D.	E.	F.	G.	H.	I.
	Potential	Newly	Cumulative	Distribution	New	Cumulative	Potential
	Buyers Aware	Aware	Aware		Trial	Trial	Buyers
Month	%			%			Trying
0	0%	0	0	10%	0	0	0%
1	3%	1,500	1,500	20%	99	99	0%
2	6%	1,500	3,000	25%	124	223	0%
3	10%	2,000	5,000	29%	191	414	1%
4	13%	1,500	6,500	33%	163	578	1%
5	16%	1,500	8,000	36%	178	756	2%
6	19%	1,500	9,500	39%	193	949	2%
7	22%	1,500	11,000	42%	208	1,157	2%
8	25%	1,500	12,500	45%	223	1,379	3%
9	28%	1,500	14,000	48%	238	1,617	3%
10	31%	1,500	15,500	51%	252	1,869	4%
11	34%	1,500	17,000	54%	267	2,137	4%
12	37%	1,500	18,500	57%	282	2,419	5%
13	38%	500	19,000	58%	96	2,515	5%
14	39%	500	19,500	59%	97	2,612	5%
15	40%	500	20,000	60%	99	2,711	5%
16	41%	500	20,500	61%	101	2,812	6%
17	42%	500	21,000	62%	102	2,914	6%
18	43%	500	21,500	63%	104	3,018	6%
19	44%	500	22,000	64%	106	3,123	6%
20	45%	500	22,500	65%	107	3,231	6%
21	46%	500	23,000	66%	109	3,340	7%
22	47%	500	23,500	66%	109	3,449	7%
23	48%	500	24,000	66%	109	3,557	7%
24	49%	500	24,500	66%	109	3,666	7%
25	50%	500	25,000	66%	109	3,775	8%
26	51%	500	25,500	66%	109	3,884	8%
27	52%	500	26,000	66%	109	3,993	8%
28	53%	500	26,500	66%	109	4,102	8%
29	54%	500	27,000	66%	109	4,211	8%
30	55%	500	27,500	66%	109	4,320	9%
31	56%	500	28,000	66%	109	4,429	9%
32	57%	500	28,500	66%	109	4,538	9%
33	58%	500	29,000	66%	109	4,646	9%
34	59%	500	29,500	66%	109	4,755	10%
35	60%	500	30,000	66%	109	4,864	10%
36	61%	500	30,500	66%	109	4,973	10%

when you increase the sales closure rate, almost all the dollars from the increased sales go right down to the bottom line. The major tool for increasing the sales closure rate is additional sales training, which is a relatively low expenditure.

Figures C-3 & C-3A—
Range Two: Repeat Purchases

If you have a brand that the buyer purchases only once, you would skip this part of the model. The first variable is "J. Average Repeat Purchase Cycle." This is the amount of time a buyer stays out of the market in between purchases. That could be a week for coffee, six months for a suit, or two years for a computer. Two months is the figure used in the model. The second variable is "K. Percentage Triers Repeat Once." This is the percentage of those buyers that tried the brand, and that you expect will make a second or repeat purchase. For Plan 1, 40 percent is used in the model. The third variable, "L. Percent Triers Repeat Twice," is the percentage that repeated once, and that you expect to repeat a second time. The fourth variable, "M. Percent Repeat Continuously," is the percentage that repeated twice, and that you expect to continue to repurchase. For Plan 1, 60 percent are expected to repeat twice, and 70 percent three and more times. Obviously, these repeat rates determine whether your brand will be a success or failure. Measuring repeat purchase rates not only provides you with a strong indication of the level of future sales, but also tells you whether or not your service or product lives up to the promise made in your promotional campaign.

Continuing with Plan 1, column N in this range is titled "N. New Triers," and the numbers shown are picked up from range one. Column O is titled "O. First Repeat," and the numbers shown are calculated by multiplying the number of new triers by the percentage indicated for variable "K. Percentage Triers Repeat Once." This rate of 40 percent is multiplied by the 84 new triers shown in column N for the first month.

(text continues on page 304)

Figure C–3. Plan 1: "What if" model for projecting market share (repeat purchases).

J.   Average Repeat Purchase Cycle (months):   2
K.   Percent Triers Repeat Once (%):   40.00%
L.   Percent Triers Repeat Twice (%):   60.00%
M.   Percent Repeat Continuously (%):   70.00%

Month	N. New Triers	O. First Repeat	P. Second Repeat	Q. Cumulative Second Repeat	R. Repeat Contin.	S. Total Repeat	T. Total Transactions	U. Repeat % Total
0	0			0		0	0	
1	84			0	0	0	84	
2	105	0		0	0	0	105	
3	162	34	0	0	0	34	196	
4	139	42	0	0	0	42	181	
5	151	65	20	20	0	85	236	
6	164	55	25	45	0	81	244	
7	176	60	39	84	14	114	290	
8	189	66	33	118	32	131	320	
9	202	71	36	154	59	166	367	
10	214	76	39	193	82	197	411	
11	227	81	42	236	108	231	457	
12	239	86	45	281	135	266	506	
13	81	91	48	329	165	304	385	
14	83	96	51	381	197	344	426	
15	84	32	54	435	230	317	401	
16	85	33	57	493	266	357	442	
17	87	34	19	512	305	358	444	
18	88	34	20	532	345	399	487	
19	90	35	20	552	358	413	503	
20	91	35	20	573	372	428	519	
21	92	36	21	593	386	443	536	
22	92	36	21	615	401	458	551	
23	92	37	22	636	415	474	566	
24	92	37	22	658	430	489	581	
25	92	37	22	680	445	504	597	
26	92	37	22	702	461	520	612	
27	92	37	22	724	476	535	628	
28	92	37	22	747	492	551	643	
29	92	37	22	769	507	566	659	
30	92	37	22	791	523	582	674	
31	92	37	22	813	538	597	690	
32	92	37	22	835	554	613	705	
33	92	37	22	857	569	628	721	
34	92	37	22	880	585	644	736	
35	92	37	22	902	600	659	752	
36	92	37	22	924	616	675	767	
Total	4,220	1,614	924		10,666	13,204	17,424	76%

Figure C-3A. Plan 2: "What if" model for projecting market share (repeat purchase).

J.	Average Repeat Purchase Cycle (months):	2
K.	Percent Triers Repeat Once (%):	50.00%
L.	Percent Triers Repeat Twice (%):	60.00%
M.	Percent Repeat Continuously (%):	70.00%

Month	N. New Triers	O. First Repeat	P. Second Repeat	Q. Cumulative Second Repeat	R. Repeat Continously	S. Total Repeat	T. Total Transactions	U. Repeat % Total
0	0			0		0	0	
1	99			0	0	0	99	
2	124	0		0	0	0	124	
3	191	50	0	0	0	50	241	
4	163	62	0	0	0	62	225	
5	178	96	30	30	0	125	304	
6	193	82	37	67	0	119	312	
7	208	89	57	124	21	167	375	
8	223	97	49	173	47	192	415	
9	238	104	53	227	87	244	482	
10	252	111	58	285	121	291	543	
11	267	119	62	347	159	340	607	
12	282	126	67	414	199	392	674	
13	96	134	71	485	243	448	544	
14	97	141	76	561	290	506	604	
15	99	48	80	641	340	468	567	
16	101	49	85	726	393	526	627	
17	102	50	29	754	449	527	629	
18	104	50	29	784	508	587	691	
19	106	51	30	813	528	609	715	
20	107	52	30	843	549	631	738	
21	109	53	31	874	569	653	762	
22	109	54	31	905	590	675	784	
23	109	54	32	937	612	698	807	
24	109	54	32	969	634	720	829	
25	109	54	33	1002	656	743	852	
26	109	54	33	1035	678	766	874	
27	109	54	33	1067	701	788	897	
28	109	54	33	1100	724	811	920	
29	109	54	33	1133	747	834	943	
30	109	54	33	1165	770	857	966	
31	109	54	33	1198	793	880	989	
32	109	54	33	1231	816	903	1,012	
33	109	54	33	1263	839	926	1,035	
34	109	54	33	1296	861	949	1,057	
35	109	54	33	1329	884	971	1,080	
36	109	54	33	1361	907	994	1,103	
Total	4,973	2,378	1,361		15,714	19,453	24,426	80%

The answer of 34 (84 times .40) is inserted in the third month of column O because the purchase cycle is two months. To calculate the second and third and more repeats, the rates for variables L and M are used. Total repeats during the first year are 13,204, as shown in column "S. Total Repeat." This figure is added to the 4,220 new triers to arrive at 17,424 total buyers or transactions as shown in column "T. Total Transactions."

Once again, just a slight increase in one of your variables can have a dramatic effect. In Plan 2 , the percentage of triers repeating once (variable K) has been increased from 40 percent in Plan 1 to 50 percent in Plan 2. A 50 percent repeat rate is not excitingly high, but combined with the minor improvement made in Plan 2 in range 1, total transactions increase from 17,424 in Plan 1 to 24,426 in Plan 2, as shown in column "T. Total Transactions" in Figure C-3A. That is a 40 percent increase.

If you have a brand that does not satisfy the customers' needs, then your repeat purchase rate is going to be low. But as previously mentioned, perception is what counts. Designer jeans don't wear as long as regular Levis, and Marlboro cigarettes (number one in the world) tastes the same as other cigarettes if you blindfold the smoker. In both these cases, high repeat sales is due to dynamic positioning.

Figures C-4 & C-4A—
Range Three: Unit & Dollar Volume

This range multiplies the number of transactions from range two by the number of units purchased and the price per unit, as shown in this range, to arrive at total sales in units and dollars. Three variables are used, and the same level is used for both plans. The first is "V. Average Number of Units Trial Transaction." The number 1.1 is used. This means that most buyers are expected to purchase only one unit, but a few will buy several, resulting in an average of 1.1. The second variable is "W. Average Number Units Repeat Transactions." The number 1.3 is shown. A higher number is used on repeat business on the theory that customers are now more familiar with the brand, and that some are likely to purchase higher quantities. The third assumption is "X. [Manufacturer's] Price per Unit." The price indicated is $.89.

To arrive at total units, the model multiplies the average number of units purchased as shown in the first two variables (V and W) by the number of transactions from range two. To calculate total dollars, the model multiplies total units by the price shown in the third variable (X). The previous minor improvements made in Plan 2 in ranges one and two result in a 41 percent increase in total estimated dollar volume. Total dollar volume for Plan 1 is $19,408, as shown in column "DD. Total" on C-4 and $27,375 for Plan 2, as shown in column "DD. Total" on C 4A.

Figures C-5 & C-5A—
Range Four: Share of Market

There are three variables. The first is "FF. Average Retail Selling Price." In the last range, the manufacturer's selling price to the trade of $.89 was used to calculate total revenues. When you calculate market share, you normally use the price to the end user; therefore, the price of $1.39 has been inserted into the model. This is the price the trade charges the end user. If your company sells directly to the end user, you would use the same price to calculate both revenues and share. The second variable is "GG. Total Market in Units," and the third is "HH. Total Market in Dollars." These two variables refer to the total expected monthly sales in units and dollars of the type of brand the company sells by the company, its competitors, and all potential buyers who have not yet made a purchase. In the model, the size in units is 10,000, and in dollars is $13,300.

To calculate monthly unit market share as shown in column "II. Unit Market Share," the model takes the monthly sales in units from column "AA. Units Total" in range three and divides it by monthly

(text continues on page 310)

Figure C–4. Plan 1: "What if" model for projecting market share (unit and dollar volume).

	V.	Average Number Units Trial Transaction:			1.10		
	W.	Average Number Units Repeat Transaction:			1.30		
	X.	Price Per Unit:			$ 0.89		
	Y.	Z.	AA.	BB.	CC.	DD.	EE.
	--------------- Units--------------------			------------ Dollars----------			Repeat
	Trial	Repeat	Total	Trial	Repeat	Total	%Total
Month							Dollars
0	0	0	0	$0	$0	$0	
1	92	0	92	$82	$0	$82	
2	116	0	116	$103	$0	$103	
3	179	44	222	$159	$39	$198	
4	152	55	207	$136	$49	$184	
5	166	111	277	$148	$98	$247	
6	180	105	285	$160	$93	$254	
7	194	148	342	$173	$131	$304	
8	208	170	378	$185	$151	$336	
9	222	216	437	$197	$192	$389	
10	236	256	492	$210	$228	$438	
11	249	300	549	$222	$267	$489	
12	263	346	610	$234	$308	$542	
13	89	395	484	$79	$352	$431	
14	91	447	538	$81	$398	$479	
15	92	413	505	$82	$367	$449	
16	94	464	558	$84	$413	$497	
17	95	465	560	$85	$414	$499	
18	97	518	615	$86	$461	$548	
19	99	537	636	$88	$478	$566	
20	100	557	657	$89	$495	$584	
21	102	576	678	$90	$513	$603	
22	102	596	697	$90	$530	$621	
23	102	616	718	$90	$548	$639	
24	102	636	737	$90	$566	$656	
25	102	656	757	$90	$584	$674	
26	102	676	777	$90	$601	$692	
27	102	696	797	$90	$619	$710	
28	102	716	818	$90	$637	$728	
29	102	736	838	$90	$655	$746	
30	102	756	858	$90	$673	$764	
31	102	776	878	$90	$691	$782	
32	102	797	898	$90	$709	$799	
33	102	817	918	$90	$727	$817	
34	102	837	939	$90	$745	$835	
35	102	857	959	$90	$763	$853	
36	102	877	979	$90	$781	$871	
Total	4,642	17,166	21,807	$4,131	$15,277	$19,408	79%

Figure C-4A. Plan 2: "What if" model for projecting market share (unit and dollar volume).

	V.	Average Number Units Trial Transaction:				1.10	
	W.	Average Number Units Repeat Transaction:				1.30	
	X.	Price Per Unit:				$ 0.89	
	Y.	Z.	AA.	BB.	CC.	DD.	EE.
	**********	Units ********		******* Dollars *********			Repeat
	Trial	Repeat	Total	Trial	Repeat	Total	% Total
Month							Dollars
0	0	0	0	$0	$0	$0	
1	109	0	109	$97	$0	$97	
2	136	0	136	$121	$0	$121	
3	211	64	275	$187	$57	$245	
4	180	80	260	$160	$72	$232	
5	196	163	359	$174	$145	$320	
6	212	154	367	$189	$137	$326	
7	229	218	446	$204	$194	$397	
8	245	250	495	$218	$222	$441	
9	261	318	579	$233	$283	$515	
10	278	378	655	$247	$336	$583	
11	294	442	736	$262	$393	$655	
12	310	510	820	$276	$454	$730	
13	105	582	687	$94	$518	$612	
14	107	658	766	$95	$586	$681	
15	109	608	717	$97	$541	$638	
16	111	684	794	$99	$608	$707	
17	113	685	798	$100	$610	$710	
18	114	764	878	$102	$680	$782	
19	116	792	908	$103	$705	$808	
20	118	820	938	$105	$730	$835	
21	120	849	968	$107	$755	$862	
22	120	878	998	$107	$781	$888	
23	120	907	1,027	$107	$808	$914	
24	120	936	1,056	$107	$833	$940	
25	120	966	1,086	$107	$860	$966	
26	120	995	1,115	$107	$886	$992	
27	120	1,025	1,145	$107	$912	$1,019	
28	120	1,055	1,174	$107	$939	$1,045	
29	120	1,084	1,204	$107	$965	$1,072	
30	120	1,114	1,234	$107	$992	$1,098	
31	120	1,144	1,264	$107	$1,018	$1,125	
32	120	1,174	1,293	$107	$1,045	$1,151	
33	120	1,203	1,323	$107	$1,071	$1,178	
34	120	1,233	1,353	$107	$1,097	$1,204	
35	120	1,263	1,383	$107	$1,124	$1,231	
36	120	1,293	1,412	$107	$1,150	$1,257	
Total	5,470	25,288	30,759	$4,869	$22,507	$27,375	82%

Figure C-5. Plan 1: "What if" model for projecting market share (share of market).

FF.	Average Market Selling Price:	$1.39
GG.	Total Market in Units:	10,000
HH.	Total Market in Dollars:	$13,300

Month	II. Unit Share Market	JJ. Dollar Share Market
0	0.00%	0.00%
1	0.92%	0.97%
2	1.16%	1.21%
3	2.22%	2.32%
4	2.07%	2.16%
5	2.77%	2.89%
6	2.85%	2.98%
7	3.42%	3.57%
8	3.78%	3.95%
9	4.37%	4.57%
10	4.92%	5.14%
11	5.49%	5.74%
12	6.10%	6.37%
13	4.84%	5.06%
14	5.38%	5.62%
15	5.05%	5.28%
16	5.58%	5.83%
17	5.60%	5.86%
18	6.15%	6.43%
19	6.36%	6.65%
20	6.57%	6.86%
21	6.78%	7.08%
22	6.97%	7.29%
23	7.18%	7.50%
24	7.37%	7.71%
25	7.57%	7.91%
26	7.77%	8.12%
27	7.97%	8.33%
28	8.18%	8.54%
29	8.38%	8.76%
30	8.58%	8.97%
31	8.78%	9.18%
32	8.98%	9.39%
33	9.18%	9.60%
34	9.39%	9.81%
35	9.59%	10.02%
36	9.79%	10.23%

Figure C-5A. Plan 2: "What if" model for projecting market share (share of market).

FF.	Average Market Selling Price:		$1.39
GG.	Total Market in Units:		10,000
HH.	Total Market in Dollars:		$13,300

Month	II. Unit Share Market	JJ. Dollar Share Market
0	0.00%	0.00%
1	1.09%	1.14%
2	1.36%	1.42%
3	2.75%	2.87%
4	2.60%	2.72%
5	3.59%	3.75%
6	3.67%	3.83%
7	4.46%	4.66%
8	4.95%	5.17%
9	5.79%	6.05%
10	6.55%	6.85%
11	7.36%	7.69%
12	8.20%	8.57%
13	6.87%	7.18%
14	7.66%	8.00%
15	7.17%	7.49%
16	7.94%	8.30%
17	7.98%	8.34%
18	8.78%	9.18%
19	9.08%	9.49%
20	9.38%	9.80%
21	9.68%	10.12%
22	9.98%	10.43%
23	10.27%	10.74%
24	10.56%	11.04%
25	10.86%	11.35%
26	11.15%	11.65%
27	11.45%	11.96%
28	11.74%	12.27%
29	12.04%	12.59%
30	12.34%	12.90%
31	12.64%	13.21%
32	12.93%	13.52%
33	13.23%	13.83%
34	13.53%	14.14%
35	13.83%	14.45%
36	14.12%	14.76%

market volume ("GG. Total Market in Units"). To obtain monthly dollar share, as shown in column JJ, the model takes monthly unit sales, also from column "AA. Units Total" in range three, multiplies it by the price shown in variable "FF. Average Market Selling Price," and divides the answer by total market monthly dollar volume ("HH. Total Market in Dollars").

The monthly market share for the hypothetical business used in the model in Plan 1 reaches a high of 9.79 percent in units, and 10.23 percent in dollars. For Plan 2, it's 14.12 percent in units, and 14.76 percent in dollars. The fact that this business has a higher share in dollars than in units means that its selling price is above the average for the market.

So there is an increase of about 4½ share points—about a 40 percent increase—just by adjusting two market variables. You should be using a what-if model like this one. It makes you, as Leo Burnett said, "reach for the stars."

Index